Additional Praise
Bread, Breaking Beats

"With intellectual rigor as beautifully detailed as Baroque counterpoint and the creative impulses of improvisational jazz, *Breaking Bread, Breaking Beats*, via interdisciplinary, dialogical, and communal analysis wedding town (faith and social communities and professional hip-hop artists) and gown (the academy), explores the intersections, juxtapositions, and reciprocal critique of the Black church and hip-hop. The Center for Engaged Research and Collaborative Learning (CERCL) Writing Collective wax eloquently and cogently as they explore socio-cultural contextual issues from historical, economic, and political matters to embodiment, gender, race, dress, sexuality, identity, oppression, resistance, globalization, ethics, and cipher. The authors brilliantly tell the story of the nonmonolithic Black church and the diverse realities of hip-hop from the late twentieth century to the present. *Breaking Bread, Breaking Beats* is a must read for those interested in social history, black church, and hip-hop."

Cheryl A. Kirk-Duggan
Shaw University Divinity School

"This is just the text I have been looking for! Pinn presents the results of an innovative teaching and learning experience to bring together the two guardians of revolutionary spirituality in the African American community: the Black Church and hip-hop. Too often these movements have been caricatured and thus prevented from engaging in the kind of conversation that can lead our people forward. This critical and constructive guide will be indispensable for anyone doing theology and ministry among African Americans today."

James H. Evans Jr.
Colgate Rochester Crozer Divinity School

Breaking Bread, Breaking Beats

Breaking Bread, Breaking Beats

Churches and Hip-Hop—A Basic Guide to Key Issues

The CERCL Writing Collective

Fortress Press
Minneapolis

BREAKING BREAD, BREAKING BEATS

Churches and Hip-Hop—A Basic Guide to Key Issues

Cover design: Tory Herman

Cover image: Segment of a colorful graffiti on urban wall © Luis Santos/iStock/ Thinkstock

Library of Congress Cataloging-in-Publication Data

Print ISBN: 978-0-8006-9926-0

eBook ISBN: 978-1-4514-8949-1

The paper used in this publication meets the minimum requirements of American National Standard for Information Sciences — Permanence of Paper for Printed Library Materials, ANSI Z329.48-1984.

Manufactured in the U.S.A.

This book was produced using PressBooks.com, and PDF rendering was done by PrinceXML.

Contents

Getting Started

This project grows out of a commitment to rethinking interactions between institutions of higher learning and the larger communities in which they find themselves. For the authors of this book, this rethinking centered on Rice University and the larger Houston community, and conversation concerning the challenges and benefits of such interaction took place within an experimental undergraduate course devoted to the topic of religion and hip-hop.

This class involved collaboration between the Religious Studies Department and the Center for Engaged Research and Collaborative Learning. CERCL (pronounced "Circle"), as the center is called, has as its core mission the development and enhancement of critical-thinking skills, effective communication strategies, and the promotion of rich information that can be used to transform communities. In short, the center is about the development of new forms of leadership that make use of a full range of resources to effect change. CERCL saw this course as a way of using an extremely important cultural development—hip-hop—to encourage critical thinking on religion and, by extension, moral frameworks and ethics.

While Anthony Pinn had been teaching courses related to religion and popular culture (including hip-hop) for a good number of years, Religion 157/311, Religion and Hip Hop Culture, offered in the spring of 2011, was the first time the topic had been addressed through a partnership between an academic and a highly regarded artist, Bernard "Bun B" Freeman. To our knowledge, this course led the way. True, hip-hop artists had given lectures and led workshops at other institutions; however, this collaboration was different because it involved Bernard Freeman and Anthony Pinn sharing all responsibilities for the course, from design to assessment tools. It was also unique in that the course, with funding from Rice, occurred off-campus at two sites in Houston, one at a church and the other at a nightclub. Houston citizens played a huge role in the conversations in those two locations, as we wrestled with the ethics of hip-hop and its role in religious life.

The reaction to the course was tremendous. MTV came to campus. There was a great deal of local attention, with people off-campus wanting to take the class. People in and outside the United States inquired about the course via e-mail. All those who expressed support and who touted the importance of the class got Dr. Pinn and the teaching assistants thinking. We wondered if there might be a way to think about and explore, in writing, the implications of the class. Taking up this challenge made perfect sense because of a recent trend: religious communities incorporating hip-hop (particularly rap music) into their ritual activities, ritual language, and general aesthetics of worship. How one might think about this move to incorporate hip-hop, and what might constitute the benefits, drawbacks, and consequences of this move kept coming up in our conversation. But it also became clear such concerns had to be addressed within the context of a general discussion of what hip-hop is for religion and religious communities, and what religion and religious communities are for hip-hop. And in this way, the Writing Collective contributes a bit more perspective and analysis to the growing literature on religion and hip-hop culture.

We decided the best format for this work would be a book, but not just an edited volume. We wanted to write a volume together, blending voices and collaborating on ideas in a way that would model an approach for exchange that might be useful to religious organizations and hip-hop as they continue their engagement in shared cultural worlds. Although each person was responsible for the initial draft of a given chapter, there was a process of conversation and exchange that widened the content beyond the thinking of any one person. Hence, the volume does not highlight one name over others, but instead first notes the CERCL Writing Collective as the author; only at the end of the volume do the contributing authors speak individually through the process of the cipher. Yet they are named only in the list of contributors: Jonathan Chism, Christopher Driscoll, Dr. Paul Easterling (one of Pinn's former students), Biko Mandela Gray, Dr. Margarita Simon Guillory (one of Pinn's former students), Darrius D. Hills, Jason O. Jeffries, Terri Laws, Aundrea Matthews, and Dr. Anthony Pinn.

This process of writing as a group is not meant to suggest that the members of this writing collective agree on the nature and importance of churches or hip-hop culture. Some of the writers are Christians; others hold to versions of humanism. However, all agree on the importance of hip-hop, and all recognize that the current religious-cultural landscape is marked by effort—often clumsy and misinformed—to develop bridges between churches and hip-hop culture. *Breaking Bread, Breaking Beats* is not the last word on black churches and hip-hop. To the contrary, this book is meant as a brief guide, a way of thinking about these two cultural developments as grounding for what is undoubtedly a long history of exchange and overlap between the two.

Breaking Bread, Breaking Beats is meant to offer a bit of food for thought on the topic of religion and hip-hop, in hopes that readers will then move on to more detailed discussions and readings. It is also important to mention that, while we are interested in hip-hop culture as a general phenomenon, we tend to give most of our attention to a particular dimension of it: rap music. We do not mean to create confusion or conceptual slippage by suggesting that rap music and hip-hop culture are the same. Clearly, rap music is only one component of a larger movement that speaks to dance, art, aesthetics, as well as the spoken rhythm of rap. However, we focus on rap music in particular instances because, of the various elements of hip-hop, it has received the most attention and therefore is the most easily misrepresented and misunderstood expression of hip-hop culture. Our approach, as the title makes clear, involves consideration of context—key themes, issues, and developments that mark out what we mean by churches *and/in* hip-hop.

The volume begins with an effort to unpack and contextualize key historical moments in the development of black churches and hip-hop as public realities. It is meant to give readers a sense of some of the overlapping public concerns that have shaped the language, conversation, and conduct of these two cultural phenomena. In this way, it establishes some of the groundwork for the following chapters. The next chapter gives attention to the ways in which the body—as biochemical reality and as a physical thing that is born, lives, and dies, as well as a discursive construction or a social reality—anchors the thinking and activities of both churches and hip-hop. It offers aesthetics in the form of clothing as a prime example of this shared concern.

Underscoring what physical bodies do in space and time gives way to the social issues that arise from what people "think" about bodies, in both good and bad ways. No discussion of black churches and hip-hop would be complete without consideration of the ways in which race and racism shape these two cultural worlds. We argue both black churches and hip-hop are formed in part as a response to the challenges of racism—but also as a positive pronouncement of personhood beyond the strictures of racial categories.

From discussion of race as a social marker, we move to an exploration of ways in which black churches and hip-hop culture both reject and reinforce U.S. economic strategies that privilege individualism over and against communal accountability and leave the structures of economic life that promote poverty unchallenged. A chapter addressing the ways in which gender plays out in hip-hop culture, particularly rap music, and black churches follows this discussion. Here we recognize and outline the often troubled and troubling notions of gender within the art form and within Black Church culture. Following this discussion of gender, we turn attention to the manner in which sex and sexuality are described and debated within hip-hop culture and Black Church culture. While both churches and hip-hop often fall short by reinforcing troubled representations of African Americans as hypersexual as well as assuming the correctness of heterosexual normativity, discussion of sex and sexuality within both is a necessary undertaking in that only through this type of discussion can advances be made that entail healthy ways of thinking about sex and sexuality. Attention to ethics within black churches and hip-hop culture is next, and in that discussion, we highlight the various strategies used within both contexts to determine and then apply proper action. Lastly, while most of this book is U.S. based, it is a mistake to believe black churches and hip-hop culture are restricted to North America. And so we include a chapter that outlines—through a case study of French hip-hop and black church missions—the global reach of both.

All the chapters up to this point provide a discussion of a particular theme as it plays out within black churches and then hip-hop (sometimes this is reversed). Readers are left to wrestle with ways in which synergies between the two might be fostered, and they are encouraged to reflect on the look of those connections within their own context. And while this attention to synergies between the two is important, the next chapter gives attention to barriers and challenges to collaboration between black churches and hip-hop culture. In this way, it seeks to provide a lens through which to view the similarities and differences addressed through the earlier chapters.

The book ends with a cipher, an effort on the part of the authors to contextualize the text. Each chapter concludes with study questions.

Readers will note that there are several blank pages between chapters; these are not a publishing oversight. They are intentional, and they are meant to encourage readers to take a moment to reflect on what they have read—to write notes concerning chapter content as well as information and ideas generated by the reading that might be useful in their own context. Further, readers should look at the appendix of this volume preferably before or while reading this book in order to experience the discography we recommend. The discography in the appendix is broken down by chapter with songs we thought best capture that particular section. What we present is meant to provide an interactive experience, one that allows one to read as well as hear what we are trying to say. In other words, one might gain a much richer experience by reading the text while listening to the songs that accompany each chapter.

The goal of this book is not to provide a complex and thick take on the topic, but rather to provide general ideas and thoughts that might be beneficial to prompt readers to investigate and explore. In other words, this is an introductory volume, meaning that this work is only the first step in what will hopefully be a long and fruitful discussion.

While the CERCL Writing Collective is alone responsible for the content of this volume, we must acknowledge the assistance of those who made this project possible and whose encouragement and support shaped our efforts. We must thank Bernard "Bun B" Freeman, legendary hip-hop artist, who co-taught with Anthony Pinn the course on religion and hip-hop. A word of gratitude is also owed to the many artists who gave of their time and wisdom by participating in the class. In the Rice classroom as well as the off-campus meetings, they made a contribution to our work that was invaluable. We are indebted to the students in that course, and we are grateful for the thoughtful dialogue and the strides that each student made to understand the relationship between religion and hip-hop. The myriad conversations that took place both during the class sessions via online discussion posts and in the off-campus panel discussions aided in the development of this project. We would also like to thank Rice University's academic administration for providing financial support and encouragement to think about the course in ways that pushed beyond the university campus and beyond traditional types of pedagogy.

The completion of this project would not have been possible without the steady support and well wishes of Maya Reine, Assistant Director at the Center for Engaged Research and Collaborative Learning (CERCL). We would also like to thank Anzel Jennings, Bun B's manager and course outreach adviser, who played an important role in helping us think about that course beyond the university campus. Lastly, but certainly not least, we would like to thank Ronda Prince, CFO and COO of Rap-A-Lot Records. Without her guidance and unwavering support, this venture would not have been possible. From the start, Ronda Prince has assisted us in ways too numerous to count. Her love for education, excellence, and success has been invaluable to this project.

We say a heartfelt thank you, thank you all.

1

Moments in the History of Black Churches and Hip-Hop

History is a story—a story of a people, a story of ideas, of events. History is *a narrative about an individual or a group of people's ways of thinking and being in the world*. Who a person or a people think they are is their sense of identity. In essence, identity is a statement that says, "This is who I am!," and it is expressed in any number of ways—through dress, language, body movements, and hair. Based on their identity, a people exercise their sense of **agency**.[1] That is, they take *actions to shape or construct their social, cultural, political, and economic world*. The intended and collective decisions that a group makes each day contribute to tomorrow's history. History is not merely a set of facts that occurred in the past to be forgotten, remembered, or celebrated. History serves many purposes. This book discusses some of the social issues that connect black churches with the hip-hop community, and these issues will take us in a variety of directions. What connects and grounds all of these issues are

---

1. Vivian L. Vignoles, Seth J. Schwartz, and Koen Luyckx, "Introduction: Toward an Integrative View of Identity," in *Handbook of Identity Theory and Research*, vol. 1, *Structures and Processes*, ed. Seth J. Schwartz, Koen Luyckx, and Vivian L. Vignoles (New York: Springer Science Business Media, 2011), 2.

the shared historical circumstances that gave rise to churches and hip-hop. When we look at religion and hip-hop through the lens of history, we begin to see how these two cultural expressions are interrelated in spite of how different they appear on the surface. Both of these culturally based creative forms come from and continue to respond to themes such as limited economic conditions, failing educational systems, oppressive political power structures, and societal ideas premised upon African American inferiority. Throughout their history, African Americans have responded to these concerns by expressing their identity on their own terms. All humans have a need to answer the question "Who am I?" through words and deeds. In the face of any number of negative circumstances and negative stereotypes, African Americans have continuously declared, "I am *somebody!*"[2]

Religion in Identity Formation and Social Agency

The history of **black religion** begins nearly as soon as enslaved Africans arrived on the soil of the British colonies and Spanish territories. It was, and remains, *the responses to the horrors of separation, torture, enslavement, and the good and bad circumstances that shape people's desire to ask the big questions of life—the who, what, when, where, and why of their and their community's existence.*[3] Entire books have been written on the various ways that black religion has been practiced

---

2. The phrase "I am somebody!" was popularized most recently by Rev. Jesse Jackson. Jackson had been present with Martin Luther King Jr. on the evening that King was murdered at the Lorraine Motel in Memphis, Tennessee. Jackson coordinated the Operation Breadbasket program within the Southern Christian Leadership Conference (SCLC) from 1966 until King's death in 1968. Jackson organized People United to Save Humanity (PUSH) in Chicago. The effort has continued to be his primary base for social justice activity since 1971. Rainbow PUSH Coalition, "Brief History," n.d., http://rainbowpush.org/pages/brief_history.

3. See Albert Raboteau, *Slave Religion: The "Invisible Institution" in the Antebellum South* (New York: Oxford University Press, 2004; orig. pub. 1978). See also Anthony B. Pinn, *Terror and Triumph: The Nature of Black Religion* (Minneapolis: Fortress Press, 2003).

in Christianity, Islam, Judaism, Vodun, and any number of other religious expressions. Today, many scholars agree that African American religion even includes nontraditional forms of life orientation, such as humanism and, for some, even hip-hop.

In the eyes of many, African American religion focuses on the **Black Church**, although it is not the only religious orientation in African American communities.[4] To a certain extent, this assumption is based on the fact that black churches have more members than other religious organizations, as the majority of African Americans consider themselves some brand of Christian. Writing in the late twentieth century, scholars C. Eric Lincoln and Lawrence Mamiya define the Black Church as *congregations in seven mainline denominations in which the leadership and membership is largely African American.*[5] These specifically include the African Methodist Episcopal Church, the African Methodist Episcopal Zion Church, the Christian Methodist Episcopal Church, the National Baptist Convention, U.S.A., Inc., the National Baptist Convention of America, the Progressive National Baptist Convention, and the Church of God in Christ. In these pages, we cannot cover the whole history of these denominations, much less the totality of African American religious expression; however, we do offer snapshots of the growth of black churches, the emergence of hip-hop, and certain moments where these stories collide. To do so requires that we discuss not simply the history of the Black Church or the history of hip-hop, but moments from within the history of African American religion, which is much more than any one church, tradition, or cultural expression.

---

4. See C. Eric Lincoln and Lawrence Mamiya, *The Black Church in the African American Experience* (Durham, NC: Duke University Press, 1990). See also Gayraud Wilmore, *Black Religion and Black Radicalism: An Interpretation of the Religious History of African Americans,* 3rd ed. (Maryknoll, NY: Orbis, 1998; orig. pub. 1973).
5. Lincoln and Mamiya, *The Black Church in the African American Experience*, 1.

Civil Rights History

We want to focus on a few of the key moments that easily demonstrate that African Americans influenced their social, political, and economic worlds through a demand for self-defined identity expressed as often inside of churches as outside. We show that African Americans first moved out from the locations they associated with hindering their ability to fully express their humanity. Then we show that religious identity through individuals, beliefs, and communities played a role in improving social, political, and economic conditions for African Americans. Moreover, for the sake of focusing our attention on more recent history, we begin the religious-history portion of this chapter in the same century that birthed hip-hop: the twentieth century.

As we write these words, those who were most active in the civil rights movement of the 1960s are starting to leave us. That is to say, the natural lives of the people who developed the ideas, walked the streets, and fought the courtroom battles of the movement are coming to an end. With their losses, we all might do well to reflect on the importance of their struggles and the impact of their efforts on us today, but to begin this history there is to fail to understand the social, political, and economic climate that set the stage for the possibility of those victories.

Historians have documented the impact of what is called the **Great Migration**. This massive people movement is believed to be the greatest in-country migration in U.S. history, and it shaped national and local social, economic, and political policies for the remainder of the twentieth century. In two waves between 1910–1940 and 1940–1970, African Americans moved from the rural South to cities in northern, midwestern, and to a lesser degree, western states. Black rural southerners also moved to urban areas in southern states.[6] Travel routes often followed railroad lines from Mississippi, Georgia, Alabama, and the Carolinas to cities such as Chicago, Detroit, Cleveland, Cincinnati, Indianapolis, St. Louis, Pittsburgh, and New York. Manufacturers and railroad companies sometimes offered free or discounted rail fares as part of the inducement for these valuable workers to leave their homes and relatives to labor in high-demand locales.[7] Scores of African American families left sharecropping, crop picking, ditch digging, and other manual-labor jobs to work in automobile assembly plants, steel mills, and slaughterhouses in the North.[8] Although the work in the North was largely unskilled, as it had been in the South, men could earn as much as three times the wages paid in the South; black women frequently worked as domestics and earned as much as double what they would have been paid in the South.[9]

African Americans who migrated north, west, and to the cities saw themselves as moving to a life with the promise of better economic opportunity. They believed themselves to be worth more than the conditions to which they had been consigned. They viewed themselves as moving away from the overt oppression of segregation and Jim Crow laws, along with their terroristic social practices and legal segregation in public places such as restaurants, movie theaters, and other entertainment facilities as well as in access to housing, hospitals, education, and employment. Life in the North, however, did not meet all of the hype of recruitment agents. As the migrants came to find out, new struggles awaited them in the urban centers of the North.

6. Laurie Lanzen Harris, *The Great Migration North, 1910–1970* (Detroit: Omnigraphics, 2012), 25.
7. Ibid., 32.
8. Ibid., 34.
9. Ibid., 34.

The swelling black population caused housing shortages.[10] Available housing was limited to the parts of town vacated by whites, leaving many African Americans to live in the crowded, run-down, older parts of town. In these housing patterns, segregation existed in the North, albeit not necessarily as reinforced in the legal codes as it had been in the South.[11] Rather, in the northern industrial cities, housing and school segregation was limited through social practices and people networks. For example, landlords might systematically rent only to people they knew, and if everyone they knew was of the same race (white), housing segregation formed and was reinforced along these sorts of racial patterns.[12] Schools were similarly segregated. Students might be assigned to attend schools near their homes in segregated neighborhoods. Whether black children were able to gain access to equal education hinged on facts such as the access to transportation (such as buses provided by school boards) and the quality and content of textbooks.[13] Resources for black students were minimal. Funding disparities widened as school boards often spent far less for black children than for white children in the same district.[14]

One of the children affected by segregated schools was eight-year-old Linda Brown, who lived in Topeka, Kansas.[15] Segregated housing

---

10. Ibid., 34.
11. Ibid., 34–36.
12. Ibid.
13. Peter Irons, *Jim Crow's Children: The Broken Promise of the Brown Decision* (New York: Viking, 2002), 54.
14. Examples of educational discrimination are well documented. One source is Richard Kluger, *Simple Justice: The History of Brown v. Board of Education and Black America's Struggle for Equality* (New York: Vintage, 2004), 163–65; orig. pub. Alfred A. Knopf, 1976). Charles Hamilton Houston, one of the attorneys and legal strategists for *Brown*, documents scenes he would want filmed if a documentary of school discrimination were being made. Houston's detailed notes describe no or minimal toilets and missing windows at a closed school where whites formerly had been taught. Still, use of the school was denied to black children whose school was in a worse condition. The black children attended a segregated school only one mile away, where there were cracks in the door, letting in cold air, and openings in the floorboards wide enough for dropped pencils to fall onto the ground. Source: Kluger, 163-65.

patterns did not cause Linda Brown's school to be segregated. Rather, the legal and social philosophy of "separate but equal" supported its existence. Linda's father was Rev. Oliver Leon Brown, a welder and part-time assistant pastor at St. John African Methodist Episcopal (AME) Church. Reverend Brown had attempted to enroll his daughter at the elementary school within walking distance from their home instead of at the school for black children, more than a thirty-minute bus ride away.[16]

Linda's journey started with her having to cross the railroad yard to the bus route. The bus system was unreliable. The bus that Linda needed was sometimes late and sometimes did not arrive at all, so she arose in order to catch an earlier bus, in case the one scheduled nearest to the school starting time had one of its routine scheduling mishaps. When the bus arrived as scheduled, Linda would be so early to school that during winter she waited in the cold for the doors to open.[17] Citing the dangers and inconvenience of the "separate but equal" doctrine causing Linda (and countless young people who looked like her) such problems, Brown allowed his grievance with the Topeka, Kansas Board of Education to become one of several test cases in an NAACP lawsuit that eventually made its way before the Supreme Court.

Central in the legal arguments of these cases was that maintaining racially separated schools made them inherently unequal and inferior to schools operated for white children; such practices, it was argued, were unconstitutional. The Supreme Court ruled in favor of Reverend Brown in Topeka and plaintiffs in several other states

15. Kluger, *Simple Justice*, 409–11.
16. Irons, *Jim Crow's Children*, 118–19.
17. Douglas Linder, "Meet the Browns: Esther Brown and the Oliver Brown Family," *Famous Trials: Brown v Board of Education of Topeka Trial 1951*, University of Missouri–Kansas City School of Law 2011, http://law2.umkc.edu/faculty/projects/ftrials/brownvboard/ meetthebrowns.html.

in 1954. Because the ruling was based on a constitutional issue, it applied across the nation. Due to the efforts of a small group of people and the sufferings of the entire African American community, legal segregation ended as a result of African Americans choosing to create their own opportunities and identities.

In addition to being a story about African Americans' fight for justice under the law, this famous story points out the subtle or indirect as well as foundational ways that religion was often interwoven into the lives of African Americans, especially through the shared connections of religious communities. Such communities served as locations for discussing political options, addressing individual spiritual or religious concerns, and soothing the wounds of the unjust social system. Desegregating schools was not the only place where religious communities attempted to contribute to the welfare of African Americans.

While one can debate the merit of religious organizations' involvement in the public life of the nation, it is the case that religious communities were among the institutions working to ease the transition from South to North. Migration patterns that followed the railroad lines facilitated the re-creation of similar cultural patterns among blacks from geographically proximate communities in the South. They formed churches and other types of networks of **mutual-aid societies** in which members and new comers volunteered to assist each other to meet various types of needs including food and clothing and sometimes finances.[18] Black churches did more than serve as culturally connected worship houses. They were also civic meeting centers that helped to anchor communities. In the cities of the North and the South, churches were places where African Americans could openly discuss ways to

---

18. Lincoln and Mamiya, *The Black Church in the African American Experience*, 242.

collectively confront their struggles against social, economic, and political injustice.

The Great Migration shifted much attention on black religious life to the North, where hip-hop would emerge in the 1970s, but the story of black religion in the South was still developing. It was there that many of the mid-century episodes that would become crucial to the civil rights movement would occur. The twenty-six-year-old Rev. Dr. Martin Luther King Jr. first came to prominence when he was a spokesperson for the Montgomery (Alabama) Improvement Association (MIA).[19] The MIA launched a yearlong boycott against city buses, sparked by Rosa Parks's decision to disobey a local ordinance. Montgomery city law limited blacks to the back of city buses. In fact, if there were insufficient seats for whites, blacks were required to give up their seats for white riders.[20] Blacks in Montgomery refused to use the city bus system until the transportation line made concessions to blacks' demands. After that year, African Americans were no longer required to pay their fares in the front of buses, exit, and reenter through the back door for their ride, and to give up their seats to white patrons who had paid the same fare.[21]

The success of the Montgomery bus boycott demonstrated the power of blacks' collective economic activity. It also demonstrated that the activities of religious people could be defined in very broad terms, in that many of the logistic hurdles of the boycott (ride sharing, vehicle coordination, etc.) were responded to through Black Church and Christian involvement. Moreover, it shows that the social, political, and economic strivings of African American equality

19. Taylor Branch, *Parting the Waters: America in the King Years, 1954–1963* (New York: Simon and Shuster, 1988), 137.
20. Douglas Brinkley, *Rosa Parks* (New York: Penguin, 2000), 105–108.
21. Ibid., 157–73.

have been shared by the religious and the nonreligious through activities that have been beyond traditionally religious undertakings.

Even so, the winds of social change through Christian organizations and other collective action were apparent, and a group of African American Baptist ministers wanted one of their prominent organizations to take a more significant and intentional role to break from its practice of promoting gradual change. Since 1895, the National Baptist Convention, U.S.A., Inc. (NBC USA) had been the largest black denomination in the nation. Rev. Martin Luther King Jr. was a member of the denomination and had attempted to persuade the denominational president, Rev. Joseph H. Jackson, that a more substantial role in the civil rights movement was part of demonstrating the relevance of the denomination and its care for improving daily life for African Americans.[22] King's appeal was to no avail, and Jackson's approach to the movement was in fact representative of a large number of black churches and their leaders. However, many black Christians were like King, in that they responded to the emerging movement in positive, progressive ways.[23]

Due to the failure of convention members to elect more progressive leadership, spurned members of the NBC USA began to discuss forming a new black denomination focused on a mission of social change. As a consequence of these meetings and conversations, the Progressive National Baptist Convention was formed in Cincinnati in 1961.[24] The mission of the PNBC embraced the social-justice aspects of ministry, and the leadership of this new convention lent support to such progressive efforts, in part, by encouraging their

22. Stephen Finley and Terri Laws, "Progressive National Baptist Convention," in *African American Religious Cultures*, vol. 1, ed. Anthony B. Pinn (Santa Barbara, CA: ABC-CLIO), 333.

23. There are many sources that describe the history of the conflict between Martin Luther King Jr. and Joseph H. Jackson. Peter Paris offers a scholarly comparison of their political and theological positions in *Black Leaders in Conflict* (Cleveland: Pilgrim, 1978).

24. Progressive National Baptist Convention, Inc., "History of the PNBC," http://www.pnbc.org/PNBC/History.html, accessed September 15, 2013.

congregants to participate in the civil rights movement in local and national protests. [25]

Increasingly, Christian clergy, interfaith leaders, and laity motivated by faith became involved in the social-change movements spreading across the nation. Septima Clark and Ella Baker are two of the most recognizable names from the civil rights movement. Ella Baker worked as the (unofficial) chief administrative officer of the Southern Christian Leadership Conference (SCLC) and as adviser-trainer to the Student Nonviolent Coordinating Committee (SNCC). Baker, a woman and not a preacher, like members of the official SCLC leadership, remained the acting executive director of SCLC for a number of years.[26] Septima Clark, a trained educator, taught in southern "citizenship schools," where students in citizenship courses learned information that would be instrumental in their earning voter registration. When her activities became known, she was summarily refused an employment contract in South Carolina schools in which she had taught for over thirty years; in addition, her pension was denied to her. Eventually, the SCLC ran several of the schools, and Clark administered the citizenship programs. Historian Rosetta Ross documents the religious biography of both women and how their religiosity expanded to mean more than their individual salvation, but rather was a means by which to address the day-to-day concerns of others.[27]

This sensibility of concern for others as religious obligation helped to create one of the most important episodes in black religious history: the Birmingham (Alabama) campaign of the civil rights movement. Freeman Hrabowski, now a mathematician and university president, recalled that as a twelve-year-old in

25. Ibid.
26. Rosetta E. Ross. *Witnessing and Testifying: Black Women, Religion, and Civil Rights* (Minneapolis: Fortress Press, 2003).
27. Ibid.

Birmingham in 1963, he argued with his parents to convince them that his turn to participate in history had arrived.[28] His parents knew the risk of both physical and social danger that such participation in protest involved. Young people left classrooms and filled jails when there were not enough adults able or willing to risk their employment. Yet the involvement of young people was crucial to the growing energy around civil rights—energy and determination with great impact in Birmingham.

By the time Martin Luther King was arrested on April 12, 1963 (incidentally, Good Friday of that year), the Birmingham campaign had already been under way for more than a week. King's arrest spurred him to pen a letter from the city jail that he specifically aimed at church leaders, mostly white, but some black as well. King's "Letter from the Birmingham City Jail" is one of his most famous and enduring writings.

King's letter was a response to a second open letter from white Birmingham clergy printed in local newspapers. In their first letter, the clergy had called on "their people," citizens and elected officials of Birmingham and Alabama, to comply with court rulings to desegregate collegiate admissions at public universities.[29] In that first letter, white Birmingham faith leaders were attempting to calm the potential for violence that white citizens might exact against blacks as the rhetoric heightened before the Birmingham campaign. After the campaign began, the white clergy wrote a second letter. This time they called on blacks to remain calm and to "refrain from involvement with 'outsiders' who, although they brought nonviolent

28. "Freeman Hrabowski Oral History Interview," Civil Rights History Project, *American History TV* (original air date May 4, 2013), 96 min., retrieved from C-SPAN at http://series.c-span.org/History/Events/Oral-Histories-Freeman-Hrabowski/10737439398/.

29. S. Jonathan Bass, *Blessed Are the Peacemakers: Martin Luther King, Jr., Eight White Religious Leaders, and the "Letter from Birmingham Jail"* (Baton Rouge, LA: Louisiana State University Press, 2001), 233.

resistive measures, were 'agitators' and 'extremists.'"[30] "They advised blacks to not 'incite' acts of violence."[31] King's response to the second letter "cited [St. Augustine's] conception of just and unjust laws and that, according to that formula, "an unjust law is no law at all."[32] Further, King argued against "structural sin [as the] societal sinfulness of injustice," the very injustice their movement was seeking to break.[33] King wrote from jail, and the street protests continued.[34] The continuous stream of bodies filling the Birmingham streets and jails drew national media attention. Dramatic news footage of public beatings by law enforcement officers, water hoses and dogs aimed at nonviolent protestors, and the masterful use of the media began to sway national public opinion.[35]

Now let us pause here to consider the history that has been recounted so far. From the vantage point of the twenty-first century, it is difficult to overstate the importance of 1963 in general and the Birmingham campaign in particular. In fact, Birmingham is a pivotal moment in the shaping of a "new" national black identity through the public work of citizens—religious people along with their secular counterparts. Women such as Rosa Parks, Septima Clark, and Ella Baker held religious affiliations, but as we have seen, they were also vital to civic organizations such as the NAACP and to **parachurch organizations** such as the SCLC. Parachurch organizations refer to

---

30. Bass, *Peacemakers*,235–36.

31. Ibid.

32. Martin Luther King Jr., "Letter from Birmingham City Jail," in *A Testament of Hope*, ed. James Melvin Washington, 289–302 (San Francisco: HarperSanFrancisco, 1986).

33. Ibid.

34. See Andrew Young's detailed memoir, including details of the Birmingham campaign, in *Easy the Burden: The Civil Rights Movement and the Transformation of America* (New York: HarperCollins, 1996).

35. Sasha Torres provides an account of the symbiotic relationship between the burgeoning television network system and the Civil Rights Movement in *Black, White and In Color: Television and Black Civil Rights* (Princeton, NJ: Princeton University Press, 2003). She argues that each made use of the other for their own promotional purposes.

faith-based organizations, including businesses and nonprofits, unconnected to specific denominational governance but often grounded in Christian principles to achieve specified social aims. In the twenty-first century, these organizations are often linked to evangelicalism.[36] This point not only helps to tell this piece of the history, but also should leave the reader thinking that church membership and its influences often extend far beyond church walls. But it is important to understand the full range of beliefs and opinions that informed activism; both religious figures and "nonreligious" figures played a vital—and at times overlapping—role in the push for civil rights. In the civil rights movement, religious and secular leaders and ideas, artists and entertainers and (extra)ordinary people came together to paint a piece of the tapestry of American history.

The year 1963 was only half over when President John F. Kennedy gave his June speech calling for civil rights legislation. The August March on Washington had yet to take place. That march brought an estimated 250,000 blacks and whites to the National Mall in support of civil and workers rights. Come September of that year, Klansmen murdered four little girls by bombing Birmingham's Sixteenth Street Baptist Church. By November, the popular young president, John F. Kennedy, would also have been assassinated. But Birmingham and later Selma gave his successor, Lyndon Johnson, the political agenda that would become a large part of his own legacy. President Johnson would push for congressional passage of the Civil Rights Act of 1964. This law made it illegal to discriminate based on race in the provision of public accommodations in places such restaurants, interstate travel, and libraries. The Voting Rights Act of 1965 provided access to the ballot box across the nation. It disrupted routine limitations placed on blacks' right to vote through the use of literacy and citizenship

36. Jerry E. White, *The Church and the Parachurch: An Uneasy Marriage* (Portland, OR: Multnomah, 1983).

tests and special fees known as poll taxes. It required that specified locations with an egregious history of voting discrimination get approval from the Department of Justice (a process called preclearance) before enacting changes that could affect voting. The convergence of events in 1963 and additional struggles in 1964 expanded the movement that had once been the efforts of a faithful few.[37]

Birmingham and 1963 were also pivotal for another reason: network television cameras. They broadcasted the striking difference in the behavior between the nonviolent marchers and that of racist white officials for the entire world to see. White police aimed vicious dogs at young protestors peaceably walking toward their target locations such as Birmingham City Hall. The cameras showed the white firemen assaulting them with the full force of fire hoses intended for putting out fires, not pushing around humans. Where the local press sometimes provided no coverage or stories buried in the interior pages of local southern newspapers, the national networks sent their pictures over the airwaves for the entire nation (and world) to see. Although local network affiliates might choose to black out coverage of special shows, the network coverage guaranteed people in the rest of the United States the opportunity to judge for themselves the arguments of the moral vision laid out by King and other leaders of the civil rights movement. Birmingham leaders strategically scheduled activities early enough in the day to ensure that the networks could get footage edited in time to air on the three national networks.[38] Not only were the shapers of black

---

37. It is worth noting that as we write these words, the Supreme Court recently determined that the federal oversight provision of the Voting Rights Act is unconstitutional, meaning there are now fewer checks and balances in place to ensure that voting discrimination does not occur. Adam Liptak, "Supreme Court Invalidates Key Provision of Voting Rights Act," *New York Times*, June 25, 2013, http://www.nytimes.com/2013/06/26/us/supreme-court-ruling.html?pagewanted=all&_r=0.

history making use of new technology to ensure that their positions and identities were made known, seen and heard, they set a precedent that continues within hip-hop today.

With time, cameras were shifted to other dimensions of the **black freedom struggle**, the long history of African Americans seeking recognition of their human rights to dignity, freedom and justice, such as the seemingly more threatening **Black Power** advocates who arose from outside groups such as the NAACP and the SCLC. The phrase *black power* was *a call for blacks "to unite, to recognize their heritage, to build a sense of community…to define their own goals, to lead their own organizations."*[39] In light of the history of hip-hop, the use of technology in the civil rights movement foreshadows evolving sentiments toward rap music decades later. The parallels between the 1960s and more recent times are expansive. In the late 1960s, increasing U.S. involvement in the Vietnam conflict took the networks and their cameras to locations 9,000 miles away, where the sons of Americans drafted to serve in the armed forces were

38. See Andrew Young's discussion of the Birmingham campaign's facilitation of media coverage in *Easy the Burden: The Civil Rights Movement and the Transformation of America.* (New York: HarperCollins, 1996), as well as Sasha Torres's intriguing and focused treatment of the simultaneous rise of the Civil Rights Movement and television network news in *Black, White and In Color.*

39. George Thomas Lloyd and Bennie Wayne Cook, "Black Power and the Military" (master's thesis, Naval Postgraduate School, 1974), 28–29. These authors are interpreting a quote from Stokely Carmichael. Theirs is one among various interpretations of the phrase "Black Power." Martin Luther King Jr. and the National Committee of Negro Churchmen also provided contemporaneous interpretations in response to the spreading popularity of the phrase after 1966. Lloyd and Cook state that first use of the phrase has been credited to then New York Congressional representative, Adam Clayton Powell. (28) Another source attributes the phrase as originating with Willie Ricks, a member of the Student Nonviolent Coordinating Committee (SNCC). However, popularization of the phrase is attributed to Stokely Carmichael who recently and contestably had become chairman of SNCC. Emerging from the Greenwood, Mississippi, jail and what he said was his twenty-seventh rights-related arrest Carmichael was reported as having questioned the effectiveness of the nonviolent strategy. He suggested that the "Freedom Now" phrase needed to be replaced with "Black Power." See Gene Roberts and Hank Klibanoff, *The Race Beat: The Press, the Civil Rights Struggle, and the Awakening of a Nation* (New York: Vintage Books, 2007), 398–400. Originally published Alfred A. Knopf, 2006.

beginning to die in a foreign war disconnected in many ways from black life in the United States. Meanwhile, in more recent times, as the War on Terror, the longest war in the history of the United States, is fought in part through what public intellectual Cornel West refers to as the "niggerization" of America.[40] That is to say, thanks to efforts at security undercutting liberty and freedom,[41] combined with constant and even increasing racism in the United States, more and more Americans across races are beginning to be treated with a disregard that echoes the oppression of African Americans. From the increasing fear of Arab and Middle Eastern peoples, to the perpetual political concern with "securing" the border between the United States and Mexico, people across racial and ethnic lines are facing many cultural, political, economic, and social struggles that are similar to those struggles of African Americans, and rappers have expressed this situation lyrically. For example, Talib Kweli discusses this situation in his song "Around My Way," when he tells us that African Americans didn't *really* become American until after the 9/11 attacks.[42] In many ways, the struggles of African Americans in the United States have strong parallels with those of people of other ethnic and racial identities.

The successes of black ministers included among civil rights leaders standing behind the southern-born president of the United States, Lyndon Johnson, as he signed major national legislation made it appear the civil rights movement had reached maturity and fulfilled its purposes to achieve equal rights for African Americans. Much as the young Martin Luther King's more brazen efforts had annoyed

40. Cornel West, "Niggerization," *The Atlantic*, November 2007, http://www.theatlantic.com/magazine/archive/2007/11/niggerization/306285/.
41. See, for instance, Timothy B. Lee, "Here's Everything We Know about PRISM to Date," Wonkblog, *Washington Post*, June 12, 2013, http://www.washingtonpost.com/blogs/wonkblog/wp/2013/06/12/heres-everything-we-know-about-prism-to-date/.
42. Talib Kweli Greene, "Around My Way," recorded on *Beautiful Struggle* (Rawkus/Geffen, 2004).

the court-based, test case strategies of the NAACP legal defense teams led by Thurgood Marshall, younger members of the freedom struggle garnered fascination and attention as the 1960s came to a close. Their more confrontational sense of black pride, including their clothing style and unapologetic, nonconformist Afro hairstyles, which pronounced loudly that "black is beautiful," drew attention from the church-based moral arguments, which seemed to have grown stale. Yet many black church leaders continued to call for justice. Leaders continued to rise out of religious communities to run for public office.

In the 1970s and 1980s, ministers such as William Gray of Pennsylvania and Floyd Flake of New York won seats in the U.S. House of Representatives. West Virginia native Rev. Leon Sullivan developed principles demanding that U.S. corporations be called to account for their investments and profits in apartheid South Africa. Black churches, despite a decline in membership following the end of the civil rights movement, retained some cultural significance. Today, many African Americans continue to identify Christianity as the grounding for their morality. Local churches continue to contribute to their communities by hosting public meeting spaces, polling stations, and support groups for persons living with HIV/AIDS, cancer, drug addiction, etc. Congregations provide aid through food pantries and benevolence funds. However, the *institution* of the Black Church as a moral force has not seen a return to the national prominence it once held during the civil rights movement.[43]

43. Anthony B. Pinn, *The Black Church in the Post–Civil Rights Era* (Maryknoll, NY: Orbis, 2002).

Hip-Hop History

Like African American history generally and the Black Church history so closely linked to it, hip-hop history is still being written. Yet the ascent of hip-hop began just as the Great Migration and the glory years of the civil rights movement and the Black Church were ending. Some key events have taken place within this history that help us understand just what hip-hop is and how it developed.

By **hip-hop**, we specifically mean *a multivocal, multiethnic cultural phenomenon and movement framed by and emerging from African American musical expression.* This movement is characterized by certain key features, including the DJ, breaking ("break dance"), the emcee, graffiti art, human beat-boxing, and individualistic expression of fashion. These features are built from creative appropriation of the cultural materials and social resources available to young people across the country during the post-civil-rights years. There is general agreement among scholars that hip-hop arose out of a distinct socioeconomic climate, appearing as a cultural creative force filling a variety of civic, social, and cultural voids left behind after all the dust had settled from the civil rights movement.[44] This has led some to even call the hip-hop generation the "post-civil-rights" generation.

Cultural critic Tricia Rose is the author of *Black Noise*, a comprehensive history and analysis of rap music and hip-hop culture. Rose is seen as an especially credible source not only because she earned a doctoral degree studying the history and culture of the United States, but also because she was a teenager who had grown up in NYC during the 1970s, when the creative process of hip-hop culture was taking shape, and she tapped into those experiences as well as extensive research to write the very first doctoral dissertation

44. Andy Bennett, "Hip-Hop am Main: Rappin' on the Tyne," in *That's the Joint: The Hip-Hop Studies Reader*, ed. Murray Forman and Mark Anthony Neal (New York: Routledge, 2004), 178.

exploring hip-hop culture in a systematic way. That dissertation was revised and published as *Black Noise*, and it helps to explain what hip-hop is all about.

Rose begins hip-hop history by taking readers back to 1970s New York City. The social and economic climate in this, the largest city in the United States, was on the leading edge of change soon to come to other large cities across the nation. Readers alive at that time may recall that New York City was about to declare bankruptcy and its mayor appealed to President Gerald Ford for a bailout. Famously, the headline on the front page of the *New York Daily News* gave Ford's (fictional yet representative) response to the city's request: "Drop Dead." The headline made news around the globe.[45] Although the city eventually did get funds to survive, the 1975 appeal exposed the extent of the city's financial problems. The city was no longer able to provide adequate services to its residents. The tax base was eroding as persons and businesses able to move out of the city did. Places like Times Square, as well as whole sections of the Bronx, Harlem, Brooklyn, and other parts of the five boroughs were so financially destitute they looked more akin to former war-torn cities in Eastern Europe than they did thriving metropolitan areas.[46] One could walk through sections of New York City and see burned-out vehicles and boarded-up tenement housing, making conditions hardly livable.[47] The financial crisis also had an effect on school systems and education, causing residents much grief and continued hardship.[48]

45. Tricia Rose, *Black Noise: Rap Music and Black Culture in Contemporary America* (Middletown, CT: Wesleyan University Press, 1994), 28.
46. Thomas Gibson III, *Letter to the President* (Image Entertainment, 2005).
47. Lance Freeman, *There Goes the Hood: Views of Gentrification from the Ground Up* (Philadelphia: Temple University Press, 2011), 27.
48. Marcus Reeves, *Somebody Scream! Rap Music's Rise to Prominence in the Aftershock of Black Power* (New York: Faber and Faber, Inc., 2009), 31–32.

Part of what made Ford's refusal so stunning was that although New York City was the largest city in the country and demonstrated the advanced nature of modernity, at the same time it appeared to be declining. Some of its primary industries—communications and financial services—connected the United States to the rest of the world. With the coming computer age, the ability to transact business quickly, even between nations, could occur more rapidly than ever before. Transatlantic communication no longer took months or weeks, as it had in centuries before. Now information could be shared in a matter of hours, and in the coming century, it would be minutes and seconds. Global trade could take more forms than the lifting and shipping of goods; now services too were within reach. This sort of work required different types of skills than had been demanded in the workplace previously. From the vantage point of the twenty-first century, it may be difficult to realize that these technological capacities have been available only a brief while, but in the pre-Internet mid- and late 1970s, New York's troubles represented the seismic global change to come. These extreme juxtapositions occurring in New York City mark the setting for the arrival of hip-hop, where intense poverty and limitation coalesced next to technological innovations opening up the possibility for new forms of interaction, commerce, and cultural exchange.

Recall that earlier in this chapter, the last bit of the Great Migration ended in 1970. Now by the middle of the same decade, manufacturing jobs were leaving the city for the suburbs and the South. Slow economic growth triggered a spike in unemployment. At nearly the same time, cities were tearing down and tearing through neighborhoods to make roadways that could carry workers to and from the various boroughs.[49] Quite simply, just as the last groups of African Americans were settling in these northern cities in an effort to find the American Dream, they found, to borrow an idea from the poet Langston Hughes, that "dream deferred" yet again.[50]

African Americans did not vote in large numbers in the 1980 presidential election, because they felt that neither Jimmy Carter nor Ronald Reagan would support a black political agenda.[51] Reagan's election ushered in a new conservative age in American politics. Several major political policies that were implemented during the 1980s dampened the social and economic climate of urban neighborhoods across the country. Marcus Reeves documents that after Reagan's election, the new president fired the U.S. Commission on Civil Rights chairman, Arthur S. Flemming, who was a supporter of affirmative action, voting rights legislation, and desegregation programs that bused inner-city youth to schools outside their neighborhoods. Also, the U.S. Department of Justice announced that it would not enforce affirmative-action programs. Further, the U.S. Department of Labor eased its antidiscrimination rules affecting federal job contracts. In addition to these policies, Reagan's administration cut student aid programs, so black college and university enrollment dropped significantly, and he cut the funding of social programs such as food stamps, jobs training, health care services, and antipoverty grants.[52]

As a result of the U.S. governmental policies during Reagan's presidency, many African Americans found themselves facing extreme levels of poverty and living in neighborhoods with high rates of crime and drug use. During the 1980s, the black unemployment rate rose to a stifling 22 percent.[53] As a result, the black poverty

49. Rose, *Black Noise*, 31.
50. Langston Hughes, "Harlem," in *The Norton Anthology of African American Literature*, ed. Henry Louis Gates Jr. and Nellie Y. McKay (New York: W. W. Norton, 1997), 1267.
51. Reeves, *Somebody Scream!* 27.
52. Ibid., 31–32.
53. Ibid, 32.

rate rose to 33 percent while the white poverty rate fell to 10.5 percent. Hundreds of thousands of families lost their benefits from social programs.[54] In addition to these economic disparities, crack cocaine was introduced to the urban black neighborhoods.

In the midst of *faltering social institutions, lack of jobs, and the growing urban poverty* that defined **postindustrial** communities in New York City, young people found ways to express their understanding of the world around them as well as to entertain themselves. For instance, sociologist Andy Bennett observes that Afrika Bambaataa was an ex-gang member who became an early and prominent figure in hip-hop. Bambaataa saw the need to help young people channel their energies from fighting to other activities that still allowed them to "represent" themselves, their talents, and their neighborhoods.[55] Bambaataa's story explains that many of these young people were actively choosing to find healthy outlets for their frustration and the social issues they faced, but the face of hip-hop is more general than stories of former gang members getting their lives in order. More basically, there were simply few social options for young black people in these urban centers. These young people combined technological innovations with available ways of socializing and expressing the content of their lives.[56]

In the study of religion, there is something we refer to as the *axis mundi*, literally translated as the center of the world.[57] Many of the myths that make up different religions start with some form of *axis mundi*. In Christianity, this is the Garden of Eden. If we imagine for a moment that hip-hop has its own religious story, then the *axis mundi* of hip-hop is 1520 Sedgewick Avenue, an apartment building in the

54. Ibid.
55. Bennett, "Hip-Hop am Main," 178.
56. Rose, *Black Noise.*
57. Oren Baruch Stier and J. Shawn Landres, *Religion, Violence, Memory, and Place* (Bloomington, IN: Indiana University Press, 2006), 18.

23

Morris Heights section of the Bronx in New York City. This was the home of a young, Jamaica-born immigrant named Clive Campbell, better known as DJ Kool Herc. From his native Kingston, DJ Kool Herc brought with him "reggae toasting."[58] As the disc jockey spun records for the party, he would add to the fun by talking to the audience to encourage them to interpret the song in dance. More than that, he used techniques such as stitching together "break beats," the brief rhythmic passages of songs, to keep the crowd moving.[59] This technique, called cutting and mixing, helped the DJ to keep the party alive, flowing with music and moving dancers.[60] While seeking to keep the crowd excited, the DJ would note that some parts of songs were more enjoyable than others, so he or she would play them more often; this is the beat breakdown or break beat. So much could take place during this time and in that space, made available through the skills of the DJ. Soon enough, as part of hip-hop's evolution, dancers and "emcees" would fill that space, called the break.

Young people with few material resources made use of what they did have: ability to create identities, over against social pressures, through their manipulation of sound, their voice, art, and dance style. There are ways in which hip-hop can be interpreted as having been ahead of its time by how it incorporated cultural elements from black America, the Caribbean, and Latin America, the cultural homes of its originators. Its various expressions—breaking or break-dancing, rapping, DJing, graffiti art, and clothing styles—have spread around the world. Those in the hip-hop scene in the late 1970s and early 1980s could not have known what it would become, but they would have had a sense that it was something new in the making.

---

58. David Toop, *The Rap Attack: African Jive to New York Hip Hop* (Boston: South End, 1984), 18.
59. Alan Light, ed. *The Vibe History of Hip Hop* (New York: Three Rivers Press, 1999), 16, 19–20.
60. Ibid., 16–17.

When hip-hop began to emerge, it seemed to many observers that it would be a passing fad contained within a few communities. Furthermore, people who were engaged in that scene were not writing about it. Writing about these cultural innovations would have been a way to inform people outside the immediate area. Yet this cultural development could not be ignored, so journalists, the guardians of instant history, began following the growing crowds and reporting on what they saw and heard.[61] Their work was welcomed in magazines, such as *Billboard* and *The Source*, that are dedicated to music and the industry that supports it.[62] Largely, it was an internal conversation being held among those who were involved, either directly or indirectly by knowing someone who knew someone. This changed in 1979.

With the 1979 release of "Rapper's Delight," the toasting tradition that became known as rapping hit the mainstream. Sylvia Robinson produced this song on her independent label, Sugar Hill Records.[63] The song was a rap over select portions of the very popular disco hit "Good Times" by the group whose tailored fashion sense was signified in their name, Chic. In "Rapper's Delight," a trio of emcees talk about their relationship with each other as friends in the same neighborhood, their aspirations for themselves as young men, their fantastical capabilities in sexual performance, and their skills as emcees. The song was humorous, even cartoonish, including a reference to a romantic rival who may be called "Super Man" but who is perceived (consistent with notions of masculinity at the time) as effeminate because he wears tights. In another cartoon-like description, one of the emcees invites audience members to think of a time when they might have needed to hastily leave a friend's

---

61. Murray Forman, introduction to *That's the Joint!*, 2.
62. Ibid., 9–10.
63. See Toop, *The Rap Attack*. See also Rose, *Black Noise*.

home, to the point of bursting through a closed door. What was the impetus for the quick exit? The horrible food the friend's mother made for dinner. He invites the audience to imagine that the food is so terrible it causes nausea and the need for an over-the-counter diarrhea solution. With no hard feelings, the friends reconcile within a few weeks.

Over the beats of "Good Times," the megahit displayed a fun-loving picture of young black life. It was well-received around the globe and in subsequent years appeared on lists of history-changing music.[64] It might appear that this fun is far removed from the nonviolent direct action that had taken so much attention during the civil rights movement, and there is some truth to it. However, on closer inspection, hip-hop says much more about young black people than their creativity and demand to have a good time. According to writer Dick Hebdige, rap provided a way for poor kids to create a sense of significance for themselves (their self-selected emcee handles) as well as for their neighborhood (Sugar Hill).[65] This quest for identity creation is one of the most important connections between what young people were doing in the 1960s and what they were doing through this new cultural movement. The emcees rapped about what is important to them and to their fans: respect, love, financial resources, and the like—which are many of the very issues we discuss throughout this book. Though a bit cheesy and inundated with a commercial appeal, "Rapper's Delight" set the stage for what would become ongoing themes in the genre: young people talking about everyday life, friendships, things that occur in the

64. Daryl Easlea, *Everybody Dance: Chic and The Politics of Disco* (London: Helter Skelter, 2004), xviii. See also Nelson George, "Sample This," in Forman and Neal, eds., *That's the Joint!*, 439. See also Michael Eric Dyson, "The Culture of Hip-Hop," in Forman and Neal, eds., *That's the Joint!*, 61.

65. Dick Hebdige, "Rap and Hip-Hop: The New York Connection," in Forman and Neal, eds., *That's the Joint!*, 223.

neighborhood, trying to earn a living (legally or otherwise) and heterosexual prowess.

This first national rap music hit fits into the continuing stream of African American history in which cultural expression signals self-determined identity as well as economic survival. David Toop sees Sylvia Robinson and other independent producers as entrepreneurs. In his account, some of them dabbled in the music business for years, sometimes producing or singing in doo-wop or other harmony groups, or they had grasped the value of music and dance shows and competitions.[66] They saw the same potential in the competitive street dance battles and musical competitions. These entrepreneurs managed the sales and distribution into the early 1980s, when corporate entertainment firms began signing rap artists to their record labels.

The early lyrical content and embedded competitive nature also signaled another trend present in many black churches that would continue in hip-hop: both often prevented women from full inclusion. Tricia Rose gives an insightful overview of factors that did not allow women to participate at the same levels as young men. Much of the exclusion of women is related to how young women were perceived as sexually available, leaving themselves open to possible assault, verbal or physical. There were also assumptions concerning the macho nature of the rap world. Rose notes, for example, that in the case of **tagging**, *the act of graffiti*, it was sufficiently dangerous for young men, and potentially more so for young women to sneak into a locked train yard to artistically mark subway trains during the middle of the night. Subway trains allowed the artist's vision to move around the city featuring his or her work in a number of neighborhoods. Early rap was also trying new things

66. Toop, *The Rap Attack*, 22–24.

to develop the art. The use of multiple turntables and **scratching**, *the inclusion of the sound of a vinyl record being scratched by the needle of the player as though it was another part of the rhythmic composition*, were techniques that young men perfected among themselves in private spaces such as at home on their own stereo systems before going public.[67] These private spaces were not conducive to the inclusion of women, where—as was true with break dancing and graffiti—the presence of young women could be interpreted as an indication of her sexual availability.[68] These gender-based exclusions were not unlike the rejections women faced in the restrictions from leadership in the faith-connected activity of the civil rights movement, as famously remembered by SNCC's Stokely Carmichael, who remarked that the proper position of women within the black freedom struggle was "prone."[69]

Economic strivings have been another significant niche relevant to hip-hop culture, and most often, an adoption of capitalism has been a general road map for such efforts. Earlier we identified the way early hip-hop featured the entrepreneurial pursuits of independent music producers, and the interconnection between capitalism, poverty, and hip-hop is the focus of chapter 4 in this volume. However, another entrepreneurial pursuit has also run concurrent with hip-hop history: the so-called crack epidemic. We are referring to it as "so-called" because research since the height of this epidemic suggests that media attention and public perception likely overstated some of the most frightening concerns about crack cocaine. Nevertheless, the effects of national and local public policy were real and devastating. In their 1994 research report to the Department of Justice, Bruce Johnson,

---

67. Rose, *Black Noise*, 57–58.

68. Ibid., 48–49.

69. David Barber, *A Hard Rain Fell: SDS and Why It Failed* (Jackson: University Press of Mississippi, 2010), 102.

Andrew Golub, and Jeffrey Fagan describe crack as a highly efficient means of delivering the high its users were seeking. Smaller quantities delivered the desired effects. The researchers also noted that though the abundant numbers of rich dealers is mythology, lucrative drug enterprises did exist. They were opportunistic employment schemes in communities with fewer and fewer avenues for legitimate employment.[70] This potential for economic boon also ushered in waves of violence in order to protect the dealers' turf. Early rap content, already replete with economic woes, now added references to the sinister presence of the drug trade, further neighborhood destruction, the violence that accompanied both, and increased police harassment and brutality. The refrain of one of the top hits of this era, Grandmaster Flash and the Furious Five's "The Message,"[71] expresses a sense of anger and frustration being felt in poor "minority" communities. In much the same way that gospel music has more than one form, rap music developed similarly. Sometimes gospel lyrics are rooted squarely in the hope of salvation from the New Testament. At other times, gospel takes its content from the pleadings of the Psalms. As an early example of political rap, "The Message" decries the neighborhood conditions, and its pointed lyrics note the need to stave off a sense of hopelessness.

This growing drug trade eventually coalesced into business ventures between those with drug money and artists looking for a break, leading to often blurred lines between drug dealing and rap music. An indicator of an assumed connection between rap and illicit activities involves increased police surveillance. For instance, the NYPD began to collect information in a binder on hip-hop artists.[72] This binder has taken on a mythic quality within hip-hop,

---

70. Bruce D. Johnson, Andrew Golub, and Jeffrey Fagan, "Careers in Crack, Drug Distribution, and Nondrug Criminality: Executive Summary of the Final Report to the National Institute on Drug Abuse" (Washington, DC: Department of Justice, 1994), iv, 14.
71. Forman and Neal, eds., *That's the Joint!*, 262.

but evidence suggests it is, in fact, very real and includes the names of some of hip-hop's most prominent artists, such as The Notorious B.I.G. and Jay-Z. Aside from marking a possible circumstantial connection between street money and rap money, the existence of hip-hop indicates a problematic aspect of the larger society's attempt to control and oppress black bodies. After all, J. Edgar Hoover had a running file on Rev. Dr. Martin Luther King Jr. as well.[73]

In addition to suggesting the economic perils facing people in urban centers, "The Message" demonstrates its rootedness in a particular space: New York City. But as rap music gained popularity, it moved from its base to other cities, and its content began to reflect the communities where it was emerging in new forms to speak to the similar issues and interests of its performers and its audiences. The next locale that emerged as a center for hip-hop was the West Coast. The community of Compton, California, in particular, had a pronounced impact on hip-hop, but more importantly, it had an even larger impact on public perceptions of rap and rappers. Rap content coming out of Compton responded to the ordeals of police brutality, continued economic hardship, and extreme violence that marked far too many black and brown neighborhoods across the country. From the perspective of local officials, aggressive policing was itself a response to the gang rivalry that threatened the peace and lives of innocent people who got caught in the crossfire. One group, N.W.A (Niggaz With Attitude), whose members included Eazy-E, Dr. Dre, Ice Cube, MC Ren, and DJ Yella, gained national attention when it recorded and released a song titled "Fuck tha Police." The straight-ahead confrontational style of the group and equally confrontational lyrics, along with the Ice-T release "Cop

72. Derrick Parker and Matt Diehl, *Notorious C.O.P.: The Inside Story of the Tupac, Biggie, and Jam Master Jay Investigations from NYPD's First "Hip-Hop Cop"* (New York: Macmillan, 2007), 239.
73. Nick Kotz, *Judgment Days: Lyndon Baines Johnson, Martin Luther King, Jr., and the Laws That Changed America* (New York: Houghton Mifflin Harcourt, 2006), 81.

Killer" just a few years later, led to an outcry from some within Congress and many within religious institutions, including many black church leaders.[74] Congressional hearings were called to draw attention to and give public voice to the content and impact of what some saw as a denigrating youth culture played out in rock and rap lyrics. At the same time, black religious and civic leaders were publicly vilifying what had come to be called "gangsta rap" as a scourge on the country, in particular black communities.

Rev. Calvin O. Butts, pastor of the Abyssinian Baptist Church in New York City, campaigned against rap music. He and activist C. Delores Tucker were among prominent African Americans who saw the music as having a negative effect on its young audience, largely due to its increasingly explicit sexually oriented lyrics and vapid morality.[75] Tricia Rose criticizes Butts for failing to generate thoughtful dialogue about the content of the lyrics. Lost in the fear and panic was any concern to stop and actually listen to the concerns of these young artists or to reflexively ask what the society was doing wrong to cause such rage-filled lyrics and sentiments. Instead, Butts and Tucker opted for public displays during which he oversaw the destruction of copies of the rap recordings, which Rose suggests was more akin to book burnings of the past than having a positive impact on communities. To her, both demonstrations amount to the same thing: censorship.[76] Rose's criticism of Butts is also a challenge to the church. Rap music and hip-hop culture are firmly established as a means through which the last two generations express the way that they see their world. As a result, even Rose's discussion of rap music is never too far removed from the social influences coming from

74. Ice-T, "Cop Killer," recorded on *Body Count* (Sire, 1992); N.W.A, "Fuck Tha Police," recorded on *Straight Outta Compton* (Ruthless, 1988).
75. Davarian L. Baldwin, "Black Empires, White Desires," in Forman and Neal, eds., *That's the Joint!*, 159–60.
76. Rose, *Black Noise,* 183–4.

churches, nor is it possible to treat hip-hop as if it has had no impact on churches.

Eventually, a system of parental warning labels was devised and placed on music so that only young people above a specified age could purchase it. Perhaps this warning label has proved helpful in certain respects, but to the rappers whose albums were forced to include such labels, the move looked eerily similar to "whites only" drinking-fountain signs in that, yet again, largely black voices were being overshadowed by a longstanding concern to protect America's largely white "innocent" young people—the same group who had swiftly become rap music's largest single consumer group.[77] Despite this tension, for the artists whose abrasive and pointed lyrics would cause their albums to include the warning, their lyrics represented social and political protest against the conditions that assaulted their humanity. To them, this chicken-and-egg problem began with aggressive policing, not with young men whose sense of identity might include membership in a particular gang.

Another interesting parallel between the civil rights movement and hip-hop arises regarding the large-scale buy-in of the white masses that led to the passage of the Civil Rights and Voting Rights Acts, on the one hand, and a similar type of white, suburban buying of rap music that would fundamentally alter the hip-hop landscape, on the other. If passage of the acts meant that the energy of the first movement was stalled in momentary celebration, the impending corporatization of hip-hop has consequences as significant for rap music and hip-hop. Those consequences have been positive and negative. Some of the positives include the immense impact of black voices present to the ears and eyes of a largely white (and growingly diverse) generation raised on MTV (Music Television) and

77. Tricia Rose, *The Hip Hop Wars: What We Talk about When We Talk about Hip Hop—and Why It Matters* (New York: Basic Civitas, 2008), 15.

progressively styled politics. The corporate world began to funnel immense sums of money in the direction of some artists, and those financial gains should be celebrated. But they have come at a cost. For instance, the entry of corporate entities not only expanded the reach of hip-hop but also heightened gangsta lyrical content. From the perspective of Tricia Rose and many others, as corporate executives finally caught on to the money-making potential of rap music due to its popularity among white suburbanites, creative decisions were made that perpetuated many of the stereotypes of black life as violent, overly sexual, ignorant, and criminal. Gangsta rap, aside from its benefits or shortcomings, became the prototypical face of hip-hop, as it seemed most easily marketable as an expression of stereotypes about black people already shaping public perceptions.[78]

The consequences were staggering, in that artists were often forced to choose between financial success and pure creative endeavor. Two of these artists, discussed variously throughout this volume, were Tupac Amaru Shakur and Christopher Wallace, better known as The Notorious B.I.G. The fine line between their creative brilliance and their marketed personas as violent black men with chips on their shoulders grew to reality. The violence their music espoused eventually led to both of them being murdered. Ironically, the albums of The Notorious B.I.G. (released while he was alive) were ominously titled *Ready to Die* and *Life After Death*. Though Shakur and Wallace stand near the top of gifted, young blacks within the hip-hop world, as their decisions (both good and bad) set a course for hip-hop still followed by many today, they also end up as part of the long list of young black men killed because the overall social issues and interests they faced were neither just nor fair nor fully livable.

78. Ibid., 87–88.

Today, some hip-hop artists see rap as having the potential to become a new religious movement. One such artist is KRS-One, a leader in the socially conscious hip-hop Stop the Violence movement in the late 1980s and early 1990s. Here, we do not want to evaluate KRS-One's line of thinking, but rather to demonstrate that for many, rap music gives meaning to its fans providing a meaningful experience that reaches out to their concerns in a way similar to the black church's historic role, providing meaning about this world and the next. Moreover, the last years of the 1990s and the first decade of the twenty-first century saw political movements emerge within hip-hop culture, such as the Rock the Vote campaign and others. In other words, whether hip-hop is a "religion" or not is less important than recognizing that by the turn of this century, hip-hop had begun to fill (for many) roles that had traditionally been defined and filled by the church and other organizations.

These alternative sets of meanings and activities do not have to be viewed as competitive. There has long been a blurred line with African American religiosity fuzzily on one side and secular entertainment on the other. For some generations, the entertainment part of the line was in juke joints. For others, it was in blues clubs or in harmonizing on street corners. For still others, it was in the disco clubs. In all cases, these cultural expressions were enjoyed *along with* or *in addition to* Sunday-morning choir singing and worship. Likewise, contemporary rap artists have a variety of religious identifications: some identify as Christians, some practice Sunni Islam, some adhere to the Nation of Islam or the Five Percent Nation. For those who profess a faith, their music is their profession and their lifestyle, but it is not their entire composition. In fact, some of rap music's early stars remain in the hip-hop scene even as they have become Christian faith leaders. For example, Reverend Run, as part of Run-D.M.C., blazed a trail other artists would follow.

Christian minister Kurtis Blow, another early rap superstar, is also a minister, using his appeal to hip-hoppers to preach the gospel of Jesus Christ.[79] Other artists such as Kirk Franklin have challenged the paradigm of religious leaders' dismissiveness by combining hip-hop sounds with Christian themes. His style demonstrates a willingness to unapologetically identify with Christianity and with hip-hop.

These examples demonstrate an evolving history of hip-hop's engagement with the world around it. As examples, the church and the hip-hop community can engage each other in considering ways to offer credible answers to the most difficult of life's questions. As Rose points out, and we wholeheartedly agree, the contentiousness between these two communities can evolve into dialogue.

Ongoing Considerations

Tricia Rose has raised a challenge over the manner in which C. Delores Tucker and Rev. Calvin Butts first engaged hip-hop. She suggests that their censorship perspective of rap music on moral grounds contributed to a historical contention between religion and hip-hop. African American studies scholar Davarian Baldwin has argued that the contention lies in authentic ways to be black and that African Americans have often been required to choose only an image that is extreme *or* one that is austere.[80] Examples of the extreme or, in Baldwin's terms, "excessive" lie in portrayals of black sexuality and violence, as well as the dichotomy of "keepin' it real" versus "keepin' it right."[81] Furthermore, extending Baldwin's argument, when those in hip-hop quarters express their extreme criticism of the tithe-raising

79. "Rapper Turned Minister, Kurtis Blow is 50," *All Things Considered*, August 9, 2009, http://www.npr.org/templates/story/story.php?storyId=111696980; "Reverend Run: From Rapper to Preacher," *Tell Me More*, December 19, 2012, http://www.npr.org/2012/12/19/167623728/reverend-run-from-rapper-to-preacher.
80. Baldwin, "Black Empires, White Desires," 160.
81. Chang, *Can't Stop, Won't Stop*, xiii.

"schemes" of the church, they fail to see how increasingly provocative rap lyrics can be less a description of oppressive social conditions and more a pursuit of profits. Likewise, when those in religious quarters express their extreme criticism of sex in hip-hop videos, they fail to acknowledge unchecked sexual exploitation of female (and sometimes male) congregational members by spiritual leadership. In any particular example, both religion and hip-hop can fall into either category—the extreme or the austere.

There is neither perfection nor poverty in a hip-hop approach or a so-called traditional approach to black identity and activism. That is the crux of this chapter: to show that the points of similarity between the black church and hip-hop set them to be much more closely connected than both sides usually admit. If one single point can be made in summary, it is what we set out with, that the history of the black church and the history of hip-hop are part of the history of African Americans—an *American* history actually, an ongoing effort to define one's identity on one's own terms, be it through believing in God, rapping over a beat, or creating a work of art.

Earlier in the chapter, we noted that the young Martin Luther King was chided by the established leadership of the National Baptist Convention, USA, for his confrontational rather than patient, gradual approach to civil rights activism.[82] As King grew older, younger members of the civil rights movement from SNCC challenged him to find a way to include their idea of Black Power. Throughout history, there are generational shifts in ideas and styles that in the course of history present themselves as branches of the same flowing stream. What we have written to this point is not the end, but simply an effort to explain that the Black Church and hip-hop might just flow down the same stream of complex life challenges and possibilities.

82. Paris, *Black Leaders in Conflict*, 1978.

In the chapters that follow, we encourage you to keep this "stream" of African American history in mind, remembering that both the Black Church and hip-hop continue together, unaware of what awaits them around the next bend. In the next chapter, we will explore embodiment and the various ways in which dress and style have helped African Americans define themselves in spite of oppressive conditions. Hip-hop and black churches make an effort to present black bodies in a way that disputes ideas of race, gender, poverty, and other forms of discrimination.

Study Questions

- Consider the relationship between the Black Church and the development of hip-hop culture. Identify ways that the history of each helps the other to remain relevant. Where do their stories interconnect? How do they diverge?

- How did black entrepreneurship foster the development of hip-hop culture?

- Consider that Tricia Rose was correct and that Reverend Butts missed an opportunity to start a dialogue. Since we cannot go back and revise that history, start from today. If you belong to any generation before the advent of hip-hop, how might you begin a dialogue with members of the hip-hop generation about how they see religion? If you were born during the hip-hop generation, how might you begin a dialogue with someone born before hip-hop about what he or she recalls about the start of hip-hop?

- How is the leadership and prominence of women helped and hindered in religion and in hip-hop?

- Black political activity was once grounded in churches. What are some ways that contemporary black political activity is linked to hip-hop culture and/or the hip-hop generation(s)?

2

Black Churches, Hip-Hop, and the Body

So far, we have discussed moments in the history of black Christian communities and hip-hop. We also suggested that black churches and hip-hop wrestle with issues of identity. In other words, black churches and hip-hop seek self-definition in the face of historical hardships and oppressive circumstances that play out in and through black bodies. Because of racism and other forms of discrimination, black bodies have been marked as dangerous, bad, and less than beautiful; hip-hop and black churches make an effort to present black bodies in more uplifting ways. For instance, African Americans have used clothes in churches and through hip-hop culture to counteract the negative depictions mentioned in this paragraph. In this chapter, we explore the ways black churches and those within hip-hop culture rethink black bodies through aesthetics—for example, through dress. Other considerations for discussion include managing the physical body through practices such as fasting, food codes, and exercise, as well as bodily forms of expression such as dancing. Both communities—church and hip-hop—wrestle with bodies, yet their responses are often at odds. We frame, or "clothe," our discussion of bodies by closely examining the dress and clothing choices made by members of black churches and those within hip-hop culture.

Embodiment

The **body** can be defined in two ways: *(1) as a biochemical reality—a physical, material substance that navigates the world and engages with other bodies; and (2) as a social or discursive body—the body as it is "created" and defined using language.*[1] We can understand these two definitions as two "perspectives" on the same body. In other words, the biochemical reality is always shaped by language, and vice versa. (Thus, when we use terms like *physical body*, we are highlighting the physical aspect of our bodies, and when we use terms like *social body* or *discursive body*, we are highlighting how language and other institutions are used to define and make sense of our physical bodies.) For example, even though we all share the same physiology, bodies are not considered equal because social group categories like race, gender, class, and other identity markers are used to value or devalue bodies.

The social system (complete with norms, language, socioeconomic, and political structures and substructures) helps in this process of valuing or devaluing bodies by determining patterns for the presentation and function of our physical bodies. This is often represented in religious experience as opposition and struggle. In other words, the social system tries to determine the ways in which the physical body is viewed and utilized within society.[2] That is to say, "The social systems restricted black bodies; during and after slavery, blacks were expected to dress and carry themselves

1. Anthony Pinn, *Embodiment and the New Shape of Black Theological Thought* (New York: New York University Press, 2010), 5.
2. Anthony Pinn, *Terror and Triumph: The Nature of Black Religion* (Minneapolis: Augsburg Fortress, 2003), 143.

in ways that represented their status. Whites expected to look at them and—through blacks' body language, their style and quality of their dress, and their overall comportment—feel confident that blacks understood and accepted their lot in life."[3] In other words, African Americans' dress, or **style,** can be *a process of cultural expression and a "sign of black humanity and pride.*"[4] African American style can be an important means to assert their own will in face of society's attempts to control them and view them as bodies made for labor. For instance, by dressing in their "Sunday's best," blacks were declaring that they were more than their physical work or their position in society, and that a sense of dignity and self-worth could survive and overcome even the most racist and hostile society. The clothes they wore during work, nondescript and uniform, tended to erase the black body, but their Sunday clothing enhanced and proclaimed it. African Americans defined themselves through dress[5] by using clothing to communicate their individuality, personality, group/familial associations, occupation, and status.[6]

Because of representations of blackness in the dominant culture, African Americans have been positioned outside of the social norm. Such depictions determine how members of the dominant culture will interact, relate, and respond to persons outside the status quo. The deeply ideological nature of imagery also determines how and what one thinks about the self. Those marginalized come to understand their bodies as political and central to their survival. African American communities, through dress, confront the values of

---

3. Ibid., 147.
4. Imani Perry, *Politics and Poetics in Hip Hop: Prophets of the Hood* (Durham, NC: Duke University Press, 2004), 196.
5. Ibid.
6. Patricia Anne Cunningham and Susan Voso Lab, *Dress and Popular Culture* (Bowling Green, OH: Popular, 1991), 2–3.

the dominant cultural aesthetics that devalue their bodies and their sense of self-worth.[7]

According to psychologist Richard Majors and sociologist Janet Billson, African Americans, especially black men, use clothing to attract attention and enhance self-image. Dress heightens visibility by creating a self-portrait in colorful, vivid ways that speak to importance.[8] Styling, especially flashy clothing and bright colors, signifies a need to be seen and heard. Hence, style of dress is used as a solution to invisibility and the silencing of the black body in American society, "a defense against multiple attacks on cultural and personal integrity."[9]

Black Christian communities have utilized dress to signal spiritual maturity, discipline, and dignity, and to counteract larger societal beliefs about the moral inferiority and deviancy of black bodies. For some black Christians, style of dress represents control of the body, a way to resist the secular struggles of everyday life. Dressing piously, for instance, is a response to American social beliefs about the sexuality and immorality of black bodies in society.[10]

African Americans made real efforts to distinguish their work clothes from their worship clothes. On Sunday, even if the clothes were made of the same material as their work clothes, they would make the color of the worship clothes different. For example, certain elders or matriarchs of the community would go into the woods, searching for indigo and sumac to make dye to color the clothing so that it would stand out for Sunday worship at the church. Even when clothes were no different in color, they were given extra care

7. Ibid., 130.
8. Richard Majors, *Cool Pose: The Dilemma of Black Manhood in America* (New York: Simon and Schuster, 1993), 80.
9. Ibid., 84.
10. Dwendolyn S. O'Neal, "The African American Church, Its Sacred Cosmos and Dress," in *Religion, Dress and the Body*, ed. Gabriella Lazaridis and Linda B. Arthur (Oxford; New York: Bloomsbury Academic, 1999), 125.

and attention to make them ready for Sunday. For instance, a former bondsman named Sid Jamison remembered how his mother would wash and carefully iron the clothes that he wore throughout the week in preparation for Sunday.[11]

In addition to addressing issues of black morality, clothing in black Christian communities is meant to fight the stigmas of race and class placed on black bodies in American society. African Americans, especially those born after World War II, speak of a common practice among black communities, whether northern or southern, that extended beyond social and economic status. That shared experience entails the way in which parents viewed spiritual behavior as tied to clothing.[12] Author Gwendolyn O'Neal recalls how black women, young, old, and in-between, made their way to church on Sunday mornings in New York City in their "Sunday's best" for a few hours of amnesty from the daily routine of tough and taxing physical labor. But this was not just a matter of playing dress up for God. On the contrary, O'Neal suggests elders believed dressing in their finest clothes, from the tip of their heads to the bottom of their feet, was the way people showed reverence and honor to God in God's house.[13]

Cheryl Townsend Gilkes argues that Sanctified Church women were encouraged to dress "holy" in order to contradict stereotypes used as rationale for abuse of black women's bodies. She states that one bishop in the Church of God in Christ (COGIC) was convinced that the sight of women in the denomination who were dressed according to the guidelines and regulations of the Women's Department would restrain even the most committed racists from inflicting harm on black women in those times.[14] Furthermore,

11. Ibid.
12. Ibid.
13. Ibid.
14. Cheryl Gilkes, *If It Wasn't for the Women: Black Women's Experience and Womanist Culture in Church and Community* (Maryknoll, NY: Orbis, 2001), 49.

historian Anthea Butler argues that COGIC women dressed in a particular way in order to communicate high morality to others. The clothing worn by church leaders such as Mother Lizzie Robinson provides a prime case of this thinking. She was usually dressed in a long-sleeved white blouse and tea-length black skirt that stopped near the ankles. Pants were unacceptable for women inside and outside of church. Robinson's entire outfit was pressed and heavily starched. Women were expected to wear ordinary hats without ribbons, bows, or feathers. And those able to sew were taught to make skirts out of pants and sew the seam in skirts so that they would not appear too revealing.[15] Their simple way of dressing and general modesty made COGIC women identifiable outside of the church. Their style allowed them to be "in the world, but not of it."[16]

In this COGIC world, women were considered most attractive with their natural beauty on display—without ornamentation. For COGIC women, it was unnecessary to wear makeup or treat their hair with chemicals.[17] This plain, modest appearance was encouraged in order to avoid appearing seductive to men, causing men to sin. On this point, Butler states:

> Women's buttocks, when visible, were sexually enticing, inevitably producing feelings of lust among COGIC men. . . . In Mother Robinson's view, the sight of the female physical body could only lead to covetousness and sin; in fact, Robinson taught that covetousness itself was a form of spiritual adultery: 'The word says, if a man looks on a woman to lust after her he has already committed adultery in his heart. So, if a man just looks at a woman, and would like to be with her, he sees her legs and sees how she looks; he has committed adultery without touching her. The women should keep their dresses down.' Choosing appropriate clothing, then, was not only about cleansing one's Spirit,

---

15. Anthea D. Butler, *Women in the Church of God in Christ: Making a Sanctified World* (Durham: University of North Carolina Press, 2012), 69.
16. Ibid., 69–70.
17. Ibid., 69.

it was about cleansing oneself and one's spiritual community of sexual desire. It was COGIC women's responsibility to control men's sexual behavior by controlling their own dress. This role was not unique to COGIC women but had been and continues to be the role of women in many Christian communities.[18]

This modest attitude toward beauty and dress was included in COGIC doctrine and beliefs as of the early 1920s. For example, Rule #4 for the Women's Department states, "All members and missionaries must not wear hats with flowers or feathers nor Short Dresses, Split Skirts or Short Sleeves." The fifth rule states, "All members and missionaries must dress in modest apparel as becometh holiness, professing Godliness with good work."[19]

COGIC was not the only denomination to establish a dress code. The National Baptist Women's Convention, for example, developed guidelines for women to consider when they dressed. Historian Evelyn Brooks Higginbotham argues that black Baptist women developed a "politics of respectability," which included ideals about the way they should dress and behave in order to influence the way whites perceived them. They believed they could win their fight for equality and please God by appearing and *being* respectable.[20]

In a way, dressing habits and practices reflect tension between the sacred and the secular. One dresses up to show reverence to God, but church on Sunday was one of the limited times blacks could demonstrate through appearance that racism and classism did not consume them.[21] In church spaces, not only do these clothes respond to the physical bodies given by the God Christians worship, but they also serve the double effect of responding to the negative images of social bodies denigrated by racism. As it will be shown,

18. Ibid., 80.
19. Ibid., 69–70.
20. Ibid., 77.
21. O'Neal, "The African American Church," 128.

this importance placed on dress does not stop with black Christian communities but extends to what we have come to call hip-hop culture.

Dressing the Hip-Hop Body

It is problematic to assume all hip-hop artists dress the same way. There are, in fact, various styles with national and international reach. Hip-hop personas such as Nelly, Sean "Diddy" Combs, Jay-Z, and 50 Cent have all created clothing lines that forced some fashion executives to change the way they do business.[22]

Some forms of hip-hop respond to social oppression through embracing capitalism as marked out by wearing expensive clothing that many in the black community can only hope to afford. Other forms of hip-hop respond to social oppression by valorizing African cultural heritage as represented by Afrocentric clothing. Therefore, to associate hip-hop attire only with sagging pants, baseball caps, do-rags, or white Ts (plain white T-shirts) is a limited understanding of the diverse nature of hip-hop dress and embodiment. In fact, multiple dress codes in hip-hop can be linked to various types of rap: (1) status rap; (2) gangsta rap; and (3) progressive, or "conscious," rap. These categories overlap with each other often.[23] Rappers may display characteristics of more than one category on a particular album or during the course of their career.

Status Rap and Hip-Hop Dress

Status rap is *a form of rap music concerned with social standing within the hip-hop world and the larger society.*[24] It consists of the rapper

---

22. "'A Salute to Hip-Hop Clothing': The Third Revolution in Fashion" (NAAAS & Affiliates Conference Monographs. 2010), 292.
23. Anthony B. Pinn, *Why, Lord? Suffering and Evil in Black Theology* (New York: Continuum, 1999), 125.

bragging about his or her sexual prowess and possession of money and other material status symbols such as high-valued cars, jewelry, and so on. Some examples of status rappers include Kurtis Blow, Run-D.M.C., Jay-Z, Lil Wayne, and Missy Elliott.[25] The political or social component of their music may be hard to see initially. It is usually limited to asserting the self in the face of a society that deems the black body as invisible or flawed. Without directly challenging the existing political order, this form of rap music is still political in nature. In other words, it argues that African Americans desire to enjoy American society and will find a way to enjoy life regardless of economic and social circumstances or consequences.

The way status rappers express the best of life within the American capitalist system can be best described by Richard Majors's "cool cat," as outlined in his book, *Cool Pose: The Dilemma of Black Manhood in America*. According to Majors, the cool cat is an exceptional artist of expressiveness and flamboyant style. She or he artfully utilizes dress and other forms of bodily adornment to create her or his identity. The cool cat is set apart from the ordinary because of his or her creative color and style combinations.[26] The legendary rap duo Run-D.M.C. exemplifies the cool-cat style in early hip-hop. These rappers provided the first noticeable "look" in hip-hop, rocking shell-toe Adidas sneakers without shoestrings, Adidas sweat suits, and black godfather hats.[27] Their style exuded confidence. In the creation of a unique self, status rappers engage in consumerism, displaying and bragging about their possessions.[28]

24. Ibid., 125–26.
25. Kurtis Blow, "If I Ruled the World"; Run-D.M.C., "My Adidas"; Jay-Z, "Money Ain't a Thang"; Missy Elliott, "Funky Fresh Dressed"; Lil Wayne, "Bling, Bling."
26. Richard Majors, *Cool Pose: The Dilemma of Black Manhood in America* (New York: Simon and Schuster, 1993), 79.
27. Marcus Reeves, *Somebody Scream! Rap Music's Rise to Prominence in the Aftershock of Black Power* (New York:Faber and Faber, Inc., 2009), 41.

Gangsta Rap and Hip-Hop Dress

The remaining categories of hip-hop, gangsta rap and progressive rap, use clothing to speak against socioeconomic circumstances through the use of anti-fashion. **Anti-fashion** involves *dressing the body in a manner that rejects current fashion trends.*[29] In anti-fashion, dressing the body in a way that is most likely seen as inappropriate, offensive, or rude by the larger society can be viewed as a means of making a political statement. Anti-fashion can also send a message to a larger portion of society about the group that embraces this style. It often reflects beliefs, attitudes, and ideas outside of societal norms. According to Patricia Anne Cunningham and Susan Voso Lab, anti-fashion styles of dress "function as a sign of rejection of the norm and hence the status quo, as well as an adherence to thought and ideas of the fringe of society."[30] Some may view anti-fashion as rebellious or antisocial in nature; however, it provides the possibility of alternate social space for some advocates of hip-hop culture.

Gangsta rap is *a form of rap that provides a critique of society by highlighting (through an embrace of it) the damage that has been done by capitalist greed and oppression.* This form of rap, which emerged during the late 1980s and reached its peak during the 1990s, points out the way in which the system operates on principles that victimize black urban youth. Although gangsta rap has been associated with violence, even death among young black males,[31] we cannot directly attribute gang violence to the use of gangsta dress in hip-hop culture.[32] It is important that we distinguish the use of a gang culture aesthetic

---

28. Elena Romero, *Free Stylin': How Hip Hop Changed the Fashion Industry* (Santa Barbara, CA: ABC-CLIO, 2012), 10.
29. Cunningham and Lab, *Dress and Popular Culture*, 14.
30. Ibid.
31. Majors, *Cool Pose*, 81.
32. Pinn, *Why, Lord?*, 127.

to make a political statement through anti-fashion from the harsh realities of gang activity.

During the late '80s, the gangsta style of dress was made popular by one of the earliest and most influential gangsta rap groups, N.W.A. The group dressed in mostly black, adorning itself with the black hats and jackets of two of Los Angeles's professional sports teams, the Raiders and the Kings.[33] N.W.A rose to popularity based on its gritty tales about the crime-ridden streets of Los Angeles in the '80s, in the post–Black Power era, when unemployment in the black community was out of control. Lack of jobs led many to turn to the underground economy, hustling and crime, in order to make ends meet. The spike in crime throughout the Los Angeles area, police enforcement in the war on drugs (with its mandatory sentencing standards), and the collapse of the manufacturing sector forced youth to turn to gang activity as a legitimate way of making a living.[34] N.W.A aspired to tell the stories of the lived experience of blacks residing in L.A., exposing the tragic nature of street life and police harassment and brutality.

In light of these social and political conditions, their dress does double symbolic duty and speaks out against oppressive circumstances of Compton and South Central Los Angeles. Their mostly black attire expresses rebellion against the oppressive forces in their community. Their use of black clothing may remind some of the black leather jackets, gloves, and berets of the Black Panthers, who in the late 1960s and 1970s wore black and expressed rebellion against the police and racist laws. The black displayed by N.W.A may also be an attempt to express a sense of mourning—symbolic of

33. "NWA: 'Our Raps Are Documentary. We Don't Take Sides,'" *The Guardian*, August 7, 2013, http://www.theguardian.com/music/2013/aug/07/nwa-1989-classic-interview.
34. Reeves, *Somebody Scream!*, 101–106.

the deaths that occur in the neighborhoods or a sense of hopelessness with American society.

Another trend that is disturbing to the larger society is sagging pants, which is letting one's pants hang low enough to expose the underwear. This style of dress is controversial and has resulted in local ordinances imposing bans on the practice.[35] Many believe the practice of sagging pants has roots in prison. However, this practice can be seen as a non-prison-related form of rebellion. According to Chike Jeffers, even if the prison origin story is true, "sagging is much more clearly associated with a musical culture—Hip-Hop—than with incarceration." For Jeffers, sagging ultimately communicates an "unruly sense of freedom and the refusal of black cool to be kept tightly bound."[36] In the end, sagging communicates a political position of anti-assimilation.

Progressive Rap and Hip-Hop Dress

Similar to gangsta rap, progressive rap utilizes anti-fashion, but in a more constructive manner. **Progressive (or "conscious") rap** is *the form of hip-hop that interprets the cycle of poverty and dehumanization producing limited life options and despair.*[37] In contrast to the documentary nature of gangsta rap, it "provides an interpretation of American society and a constructive agenda for the uplift" of black communities. [38] Ultimately, it seeks to change the system by educating blacks about their history and culture, by pointing out the intrinsic value of black life, and by increasing the black community's political awareness and engagement. Examples of progressive rap

35. Chike Jeffers, "Should Black Kids Avoid Wearing Hoodies?," in *Pursuing Trayvon Martin: Historical Contexts and Contemporary Manifestations of Racial Dynamics*, ed. George Yancy and Janine Jones (Lanham, MD: Rowman & Littlefield, 2012), 135.
36. Ibid., 136.
37. Pinn, *Why, Lord?*, 130–31.
38. Ibid., 130.

include KRS-One, Public Enemy, Afrika Bambaataa, and the group Black Star (including Talib Kweli and Yasiin Bey, the artist formerly known as Mos Def).

The dress style of the early progressive rappers attempted to foster African Americans' connection to Africa. In others words, African American history did not begin during transatlantic slavery, but rather it is rooted in Africa.[39] Therefore, early progressive rappers and groups, such as Afrika Bambaataa and X-Clan, attempted to change African Americans' understanding of themselves as Africans, who come from a long history of advanced culture and civilization. They used colors they associated with Africa (red, black, and green) and employed African-style hats, canes, kente cloth, African symbols, and other references to Africa on their clothing and accessories. Progressive rap groups like Public Enemy—specifically, Professor Griff, the "Minister of Information," and the Security of the First World (S1W)—sought to reinvigorate black political involvement by dressing in military-style attire and wearing berets, as did the Black Panther Party of previous decades.[40]

Ongoing Considerations

One of the most difficult issues for the church to overcome with regard to the hip-hop community is the way hip-hop loyalists dress. In an essay entitled "Isn't Loving God Enough?," Cassandra Thornton expresses the general tenor of many black Christian churches concerned about the ways hip-hop youth dress. Criticizing both men and women in hip-hop for their dress, she argues that many church pastors believe the style presented in hip-hop is the result of spiritual immaturity.[41] From the perspective of the church

---

39. Albert Raboteau, "Death of the Gods," in *African American Religious Thought: An Anthology*, ed. Cornel West and Eddie S. Glaude Jr., 239–84 (Louisville: Westminster John Knox Press, 2003).
40. Reeves, *Somebody Scream!*, 64.

and its leaders, the general belief is that as one's spiritual relationship with God deepens, one dresses in a different, more church-like manner. That is to say, God's Spirit will teach one how to dress.

This offers us a moment to note the significance of what many refer to as "holy hip-hop," a brand of hip-hop "created specifically to glorify Jesus Christ and bring the good news of Jesus Christ to those who are living in and influenced by Hip-Hop culture."[42] Holy hip-hop attempts to connect the two seemingly different communities but comes at the expense of watering down elements of each. Nonetheless, on the issue of dress, some holy hip-hop artists prove helpful in expressing the tension of black church members regarding how hip-hop members dress in the church. Holy hip-hop artist Lecrae pushes against this tendency among many in churches to judge people according to their dress. Lecrae explores the conflict between the church and hip-hop youth in his controversial song entitled "Church Clothes." In the song, Lecrae expresses his frustration with the criticism handed to him by the church based on the way he dresses his body. He also discusses the lack of moral commitment of seasoned church leaders and members to Christian living, and responds to this lack of moral commitment by working out his own Christian spirituality outside the restrictions of more traditional church rules concerning dress. Opposing Thornton's suggestion that many members of black churches see hip-hop dress as a sign of spiritual immaturity, Lecrae points out the lack of piety within the church among some pastors, choir members, and others who are traditionally seen as the most dedicated and seasoned members of the church. For Lecrae, dress is not a reliable marker of spiritual maturity. He holds that black Christians should not dismiss

41. Emmett G. Price III, *The Black Church and Hip Hop Culture: Toward Bridging the Generational Divide* (Lanham, MD: Scarecrow, 2011), 123–24.
42. Efrem Smith and Phil Jackson, *The Hip-Hop Church: Connecting with the Movement Shaping Our Culture* (Downers Grove, IL: InterVarsity, 2012), 131.

him and other Christian youth because of their hip-hop style. He feels it is possible to be both Christian and hip-hop at the same time.

Hip-hop culture is effectively changing the rules of dress and style in American culture and the church. While it is possible to be both Christian and hip-hop, where does one draw the line?[43] In an attempt to resolve the conflict between the Black Church and hip-hop regarding the importance of dressing black bodies, this chapter surveyed the issue of embodiment within both hip-hop and Christianity, arguing that recognition of and struggle to safeguard human bodies, both male and female, have been vital to the development of both cultural forms. We argue that the practice of dress in both hip-hop and Christianity is a significant way in which African Americans have been able to reclaim, at least in part, their bodies from the prevailing social, economic, and political circumstances they encounter, including issues of race, class, and gender. When dressing their bodies, blacks have aspired to create an identity or deliver a message to society that refutes the derogatory discourse about black bodies. The importance of the body can easily be seen in how members of both cultures, hip-hop and black churches, dress.

43. Jeffers, "Should Black Kids Avoid Wearing Hoodies?," 135–36.

Study Questions

- What has been the significance of dress in both African American Christianity and hip-hop?

- Compare and contrast the similarities and differences in at least two types of hip-hop. What do these styles say about black bodies in light of social and political environments?

- How does "Sanctified" dress differ from "respectability" dress?

- Consider your style of dress. How has your style of dress been influenced by black Christianity and/or hip-hop? What message does it communicate about your body?

- What can both hip-hop and Christian communities do to resolve the conflict over appropriate dress and the presentation of black bodies in society?

3

Black Churches, Hip-Hop, Race, and Ethnicity

In the previous chapter, we discussed how certain societal categories came to bear on the bodies of African Americans, and how members of black churches and hip-hop communities responded to these categories through how they dress. In this chapter, we focus our attention on one of those categories: **race**. Race, by definition, is *a social construct focused on the color of one's skin that has no biological or genetic basis.*[1] We are as many colors as we can imagine, but those colors do not actually offer any biological reason or means of distinguishing between different groups of people. In short, race is not biological but is a very real social issue and "is a product of history, not nature."[2] Over time, humans have made race significant. In fact, calling it a social construct refers to the idea of race being "constructed" in and through human communities. Our cells and our

1. What we mean when we say black, white, brown, yellow, etc. definitely matters, but it doesn't apparently matter to our DNA. David R. Roediger, *Towards the Abolition of Whiteness: Essays on Race, Politics, and Working Class History* (New York: Verso, 1994), 2.
2. Morgan Kousser and James M. McPherson, eds., *Region, Race, and Reconstruction: Essays in Honor of C. Vann Woodward* (New York: Oxford University Press, 1982), 143–77.

DNA do not care about race, but history tells a very different story about the significance of race in the United States.

Historically, race has been used to categorize people into groups based on a variety of "traits" and markers that, in turn, have shaped the life options and opportunities of generations of people. These include skin color, hair texture, speech patterns, and a host of other visual and nonvisual markers (e.g., touch, taste, hearing, and smell) that are given meaning by society.[3] We argue that race and racism inform and influence black churches and hip-hop communities and that both communities have used creative strategies to alter racist ideas and practices to challenge institutionalized racism. By **racism**, we mean *the belief that certain races are inferior or superior to other races.* Racism is usually supported by institutional structures that shape the law, economics, politics, education, religion, and aesthetics of a given society.

In this chapter, our aim is to describe certain trends regarding how black churches and hip-hop communities have responded to race and racism. We turn first to a brief discussion of the emergence of the concept of race in the West. We then explore black-church responses to racism by offering a typology that is useful in exploring race as it has played out. We then explore ways the hip-hop community has responded to racism by attending to hip-hop as an aesthetic form of resistance to racism that refused to assimilate into the dominant culture.

The Emergence of Race as Social Construct in the West

According to philosopher and public intellectual Cornel West, the principal factor affecting African Americans in the West has been

---

3. Mark M. Smith, *How Race Is Made: Slavery, Segregation, and the Senses* (Chapel Hill: University of North Carolina Press, 2006), 2–3.

racism.[4] Racism is based on a system of white supremacy, which deemed white, European values and aesthetics as superior to nonwhite and non-European values, aesthetics, and cultural practices.[5]

The idea of grouping people by skin color was first employed by François Bernier in 1684. He divided humankind into four races: Europeans, Africans, Orientals, and Lapps.[6] By the eighteenth century, Carl Linnaeus and Georges-Louis Leclerc de Buffon acknowledged that hybridization of the species occurs, and they viewed races as chance variations, with the white race as the "real and natural color of man [and woman]." In other words, they thought white was right and that there was something biologically wrong with non-Europeans. According to Johann Friedrich Blumenbach, one of the founders of modern anthropology, all human beings belong to the same species, and the more moderate the climate, the more beautiful the face.[7] Thus, since African peoples (and their descendants) live in hot climates, Blumenbach would rate them inferior in beauty to Europeans.

"Scientific" proclamations based on observable characteristics of racial classifications gave rise to what we now refer to as the pseudo-sciences—i.e., sciences that are "fake"—of phrenology (the reading of skulls) and physiognomy (the reading of faces).[8] These pseudo-sciences, which worked to validate and justify racism, opened a platform for the spread of white supremacy based on classical aesthetics and cultural ideas of European civilization. Phrenology, for example, was premised upon faulty interpretations and comparisons

4. Cornel West, *Prophesy Deliverance: An Afro-American Revolutionary Christianity* (Louisville: Westminster John Knox, 2002), 47.
5. Ibid.
6. Ibid., 55.
7. Ibid., 57.
8. Ibid., 57–58.

of cranial and facial measurements of the heads of human bodies from various racial, ethnic, and geographic locations. Phrenology justified the belief that human character and behavior could be determined by the head shape and structure. Basically, facial features and head measurements that resembled the ancient Greeks were considered classically ideal, and those of blacks were said to resemble the "measurements of apes and dogs [in contrast to] human beings."[9] By implication, these pseudo-sciences did much to perpetuate the centrality of white supremacy. Therefore, they were not harmless, apolitical exercises solely meant to expand scientific knowledge. Instead they are evidence of institutional racism so deeply rooted in society that many scientists sought to use these "disciplines" to explain, in "scientific" terms, the perceived inferiority of persons of African descent in line with social customs.

Beyond "rational" interpretations of black inferiority as a topic of intellectual curiosity, this scientific racism also served to take away the humanity of Africans as they were transformed into objects of exotic fancy for scientists and museumgoers. For example, consider the tragic case of Saartjie Baartman, described by Karen Teel as "a nineteenth-century African woman who was displayed as a curiosity all over Europe and whose genitals, brain, and skeleton were preserved after her death at age twenty-five. Baartman's body remained on museum display in this manner until the 1970s, and only in 2002 did France return her remains to South Africa for burial."[10] Many years after Baartman, scientists within the U.S. government still registered black bodies as objects. Also consider the case of the infamous Tuskegee experiment that lasted from 1932 to 1972. In this scientific "study," black men, unaware of their syphilitic condition, were left untreated, despite the availability of a cure, in order to pique

9. Ibid., 58.
10. Karen Teel, *Racism and the Image of God* (New York: Palgrave Macmillan, 2010), 146.

the medical community's interest regarding the disease's effect on human bodies. As with Baartman, white scientists wanted to *study* black bodies, not *comfort* them.

Such experimentation on black bodies is not surprising, given the context of the pseudo-scientific racism, which further influenced the beliefs that white doctors and scientists had about black people. Historian Edward Beardsley notes, "Until the early twentieth century most white doctors believed . . . that blacks were biologically inferior and subject to a different pathology from that governing whites. Further, they regarded blacks as psychologically unfit for freedom and for the most part uneducable in the ways of better hygiene. Among many white doctors, the thinking was that it was futile to even try to rescue black health."[11]

Owing to these instances where race and racism were argued to be biological or natural, the idea that black people are actual human agents is still a relatively new concept in the modern/postmodern world.[12] The race-based theoretical underpinnings mentioned here have served as the ideological precursor for several forms of negative treatment and social stigmatizing of black communities. Such include the racialized findings in Richard Herrnstein and Charles Murray's study of intelligence within *The Bell Curve* (1996).[13] Herrnstein and Murray find that the average intelligence of different ethnic groups can be assessed. For example, black people are biologically inferior to whites; the working class tends toward poverty because they are genetically inferior; and differences between blacks and whites, as well as men and women, have nothing to do with discrimination,

---

11. Edward Beardsley, *A History of Neglect: Health Care for Blacks and Mill Workers in the Twentieth-Century South* (Knoxville: University of Tennessee Press, 1987), 12.
12. West, *Prophesy Deliverance*, 44.
13. For a well-known refutation of *The Bell Curve*, see Stephen Jay Gould, *The Mismeasure of Man* (New York: Norton, 1996).

historical, and/or structural disadvantages, but rather stem from genetic differences between the groups.

Black communities have found avenues to create structures of community and solidarity to offset the isolation and dehumanization that emerged from race science claims. These responses continue today; unfortunately, so does racist thinking and the institutional racism arising from the thinking we have described here. African Americans have responded to racism in a variety of ways—ways that play out, for instance, in and through both black churches and the hip-hop community.

Black Churches and Race

For African Americans, racial discrimination continually raised concerns and questions about injustice and suffering. Black churches struggled with these agonizing dilemmas in a variety of ways. For example, black preachers addressed these issues in sermons, speeches, and public ceremonial activities.[14] Some black ministers preached that slavery and racism were part of God's plan, what has been called a "redemptive suffering" approach to race and racism.[15] Famously, even Dr. Martin Luther King Jr. once noted that "unearned suffering is redemptive,"[16] not a valorization of enslavement, but a justification for human suffering as a result of God's plan. In this perspective, race and racism were usually registered as problems, but "God's plan" was appealed to as a means of addressing it or finding some teachable lesson from it.[17] At other times and places, black church

---

14. James H. Cone, *God of the Oppressed* (Maryknoll, NY: Orbis, 1997), 17, 22.
15. Anthony B. Pinn, *Why Lord? Suffering and Evil in Black Theology* (New York: Continuum, 1999). In particular, see Pinn's discussion in the chapter "Nineteenth Century Black Thought on Black Suffering."
16. Michael Eric Dyson, *I May Not Get There with You: The True Martin Luther King, Jr.* (New York: Simon and Schuster, 2000), 183.
17. Pinn, *Why Lord?*, 55.

leaders suggested that racism created a false and hypocritical version of Christianity and made a mockery of democracy.[18]

In the spirit of liberation, black church leadership insisted that African Americans devote themselves to educating and improving their communities. As a result, independent black churches took on a variety of crucial roles in black community life—as sources of economic cooperation, meeting places for political action, houses of refuge, promoters of education, and centers for recreation. Black churches' responses to race and racism often overlap. Mindful of this, our objective is to offer multiple ways black churches engage race and racism, and since our earlier focus on history explained much of the impact of racism on black churches, here we describe how black churches have responded ideologically and theologically.

Biological Blackness, Black Supremacy

The first type of race response seen in black churches is a reversal, of sorts, of white supremacy discussed in the beginning of this chapter. This we refer to as **biological blackness** or **black supremacy**, which, according to Rev. Albert Cleage, refers to *the idea that the history of Christianity has African and nonwhite origins.* God's chosen people, the Israelites, were black or have African ancestry.[19] For Cleage and many like him, these black origins are not metaphoric. Responding to the idea of black inferiority, this response by religious communities has included the claim that both God and Jesus Christ are biologically black and culturally African.

Cleage (who in the 1970s changed his name to Jaramogi Abebe Agyeman), the founder of the Shrine of the Black Madonna, asserted that the historical Jesus of the Bible was ethnically black.[20] He based

---

18. Andrew Michael Manis, *Southern Civil Religions in Conflict: Civil Rights and the Culture Wars* (Macon, GA: Mercer University Press, 2002), 77.

19. Albert Cleage Jr., *The Black Messiah* (Mission, KS: Sheed and Ward, 1968), 38–40.

his claims about Jesus' blackness on the genealogy offered by one of the Synoptic Gospels[21], which traces Jesus's ancestry through his mother, Mary. Cleage argued that Mary was a member of the Israelite tribe of Judah, which was a group of nonwhite, that is, black, people from various countries in Northern Africa and the region now referred to as the "Middle East."[22] He explained that Israelites were "nonwhite" because they were a mixture of Chaldeans, Egyptians, Midianites, Ethiopians, Kushites, Babylonians, and other dark people who also mixed and intermarried with black people of Central Africa.[23] Based on this understanding of Jesus' biological ancestry, Cleage concluded, "Jesus was a Black Messiah born to the Black woman."[24] Identifying God and Christ with biological blackness helped boost the self-esteem of many African Americans by allowing them to worship a God who looks like them.[25]

Christ's black identity was not the only benefit of biological blackness. Cleage put his theology in practice when he founded the Shrine of the Black Madonna on March 26, 1967, in Detroit, Michigan. On that Easter Sunday, Albert Cleage revealed a painting of a black Madonna holding a black baby and changed the name of the church from Central Congregational Church. The painting is eighteen feet tall and displayed a dark-skinned, barefoot black mother of Jesus, wearing a flowing blue robe with a white head covering, and holding a dark-complexioned baby boy.[26] The pair stood on rocky, gray ground in front of a blue sky. Glanton Dowdell, the portrait's artist, contends that the painting symbolized the connection

---

20. Kelly Brown Douglas, *The Black Christ* (Maryknoll, NY: Orbis, 1994), 55.
21. Albert Cleage, Jr, The Black Messiah (Mission, KS: Sheed and Ward, 1968), 3–4.
22. Ibid.
23. Ibid.
24. Ibid.
25. Ibid., 30.
26. Juan Williams, *This Far by Faith: Stories from the African American Religious Experience*, 1st Amista ed. (New York: William Morrow Paperbacks, 2003), 278.

between the Madonna and any black mother whose child encountered difficulty.[27] The painting itself was a visual symbol of Cleage's theological position that Jesus, the biblical Messiah, was born of a black woman, Mary, and came to save the black nation.[28]

The officers and members of the Shrine of the Black Madonna believed that the black church could become relevant to the Black Revolution. Based on this belief, they aimed to create a "Black Nation" within a nation, following the teachings of the Black Messiah, Jesus of Nazareth, and reinterpreting or reclaiming Christian theology to be relevant to the black social reality in the United States. They were black separatists, convinced that African Americans did not have to live in poverty and oppression imposed by white society. Instead of viewing separation as negative, the leadership and members of the Shrine of the Black Madonna thought that separation was the foundation for political and economic self-determination.[29] As a religious institution, they committed to free the minds of black people from psychological identification with white society, arguing that integration was an extension of slavery. That is, integration forced blacks to accept notions of black inferiority by embracing white cultural values in favor of black values.[30]

Cleage's usage of biological blackness referred to more than Jesus' dark-skinned complexion. Cleage was saying that African Americans and Jesus were black in the same way, suggesting that Jesus had "an ancestral relationship to Black Americans,"[31] and that such a relationship had a powerful social and political message refuting racism and white supremacy. This biological connection was helpful

27. Angela Denise Dillard, *Faith in the City: Preaching Radical Social Change in Detroit* (Ann Arbor: University of Michigan Press, 2007), 288.
28. Ibid.
29. Albert B. Cleage, *Black Christian Nationalism: New Directions for the Black Church*, ed. George Bell (Detroit: Luxor Publishers of the Pan-African Orthodox, 1987), 45.
30. Ibid., 44.
31. Ibid., 55–56.

in responding to white supremacy but retained some of the very features of white supremacy by simply inverting who was at the top and who was on the bottom of the ranking. But many within black churches have retained the idea of Christ's blackness without reinforcing that the historical Christ was biologically black.

Ontological Blackness

The next black-church response to racism is referred to as ontological blackness. Ontology, in science and philosophy, refers to questions of being, such as "What does it mean to be?" or Hamlet's famous question, "To be or not to be?" **Ontological blackness** refers to *the idea that race, even if not biologically grounded, is real in a different sense. Race is real based on a shared experience of dealing with its social construction.*[32] Discussed in many parts of this book, and for good reason, theologian James Cone's statement that "God is black" was actually held by African Americans at least as far back as 1895, when African Methodist Episcopal Bishop Henry McNeal Turner claimed, "God was a negro."[33] Statements like Turner's and Cone's represent the "ontologically black" position. For Cone, this shared experience is the experience of suffering.[34] God, for many in black churches, is black because God empathizes with the oppressed.

In developing his argument for Christ's blackness, Cone borrowed from twentieth-century theologian Paul Tillich's definition of ontological symbols. Tillich recognized that humans, finite beings, cannot adequately express or capture in words the divine, who is an infinite being. In this respect, ontological symbols have at least

---

32. Angie Pears, *Doing Contextual Theology* (New York: Routledge, 2009), 117.

33. Anne H. Pinn and Anthony B. Pinn, *Fortress Introduction to Black Church History* (Minneapolis: Fortress Press, 2002), 38.

34. James H. Cone, *A Black Theology of Liberation*, 40th anniv. ed. (Maryknoll, NY: Orbis, 2012), 66–70.

four characteristics: (1) they point beyond themselves to the divine; (2) they participate in that to which they point; (3) they "unlock" aspects of the divine reality that otherwise might be closed to humans; and (4) they open up "hidden depths" of human reality.[35] As an ontological symbol, "black" points to the essence of the black experience in "twentieth-century America" and to the contemporary identity of Jesus as Christ. Cone defined the black experience as a constant struggle to survive and become free from white racism. He argued that discrimination against blacks was primarily connected to the color of their skin, proclaiming that "the Christological importance of Jesus Christ must be found in his blackness."[36]

James Cone's version of Christ's blackness is symbolic and does not refer to Jesus' ethnic characteristics. It was a representation of Jesus's existential commitments, not a statement regarding his physical body or his genealogy. In this regard, blackness was not incidental to who Christ was, but was an essential aspect of Christ's nature.[37] Furthermore, and in a connected fashion, Cone claims that there is a theme of survival and liberation in the Bible. It reveals that God will liberate the weak—in this case, black people—from their oppressors. In Old Testament scripture, it was the children of Israel; however, Cone sees a link, a common experience shared by the children of Israel and African Americans: both communities faced suffering based on who they are, and God works to end injustice for those of faith and commitment to the will of God in both contexts. In other words, God is on the side of the oppressed. For Cone, the Old Testament story of Exodus demonstrates that God is interested in the protection of the poor and that God is the one who established the rights of the oppressed.[38]

35. Douglas, *The Black Christ*, 58.
36. Ibid., 59.
37. Ibid., 58.
38. Cone, *God of the Oppressed*, 58–66.

Black people's oppression was not the only decisive factor in Cone's claim that Christ is "Black"; there was also the sense that Jesus identified with the oppressed during his own time. Based on his reading of the New Testament, Cone argues that God reveals a plan of salvation through Jesus Christ. Christ shows through his teachings, actions, and ministry that Jesus had a special calling from God and that his mission was the liberation of the oppressed. Jesus, then, is seen as the liberator of oppressed humanity and therefore black.[39] Reflective of slave Christianity, Cone argued that Jesus' commitment to the oppressed characterized what it meant for him to *be* Christ.[40]

For Cone, then, and for many black churches influenced by his (and many other black theologians') efforts, Christ's blackness was informed by Jesus' historical identification with the oppressed and by the fact that in a white racist society, black people are the oppressed ones. Cone explained, "Christ is black, therefore, not because of some cultural or psychological need of black people, but because and only because God *really* enters into the world where the poor, the despised and the oppressed are."[41] Such a perspective represents ontological blackness and has been a powerful response to white supremacy. However, some have suggested that ontological blackness falls short of the needs of the entire African American community.[42] Churches influenced by this theological depiction of Jesus the Christ express a commitment not only to avoiding negative depictions of blackness, such as the negative impact of using only depictions of a white Christ, but also to preaching and rituals that highlight the connection between God's justice work in the biblical world and God's demand for justice in our contemporary context. These churches do so by

39. Ibid., 71–74.
40. Douglas, *The Black Christ*, 59.
41. Ibid.
42. See, for instance, Victor Anderson, *Beyond Ontological Blackness: An Essay on African American Religious and Cultural Criticism* (New York: Continuum, 1999).

highlighting the value and beauty of African Americans and by working to safeguard this value and beauty through programming, community projects, and so on.

Relational Blackness

Others in black churches have not been so sure of ontological blackness or completely convinced by biological blackness. In fact, some sought to move to something we might call relational blackness. **Relational blackness** refers to *a moral attitude toward the world and human life beyond one's preoccupation with his or her own group.*[43]

Here, race may be understood as a deep symbol rather than a biological reality based on genealogy or an ontological reality based on being or experience.[44] **Deep symbols** are *words or ideas that "constrain and guide"*[45] *us as we navigate the social world today.* This becomes a bit complicated, but in short, these words and ideas function as deeply rooted categories of social meaning.[46] Deep symbols have four characteristics: (1) they are ideals that regulate the way we act in the world; (2) they keep society open to mystery; (3) they can and do change as history unfolds and new knowledge is obtained; and (4) "they are located in a master narrative that reflexively identifies and defines social action in human communities."[47]According to ethicist Victor Anderson, deep symbols "arise within and express the historical determinacy of a community."[48] Deep symbols arise within communities in the social

43. Victor Anderson, *Creative Exchange: A Constructive Theology of African American Religious Experience* (Minneapolis: Fortress Press, 2008), 50.
44. Ibid., 30.
45. Ibid.
46. Ibid.
47. Ibid.
48. Ibid.

and cultural images of those communities, and they offer those communities a means of making sense of the present based on the sum total of the historical past.[49] As we noted in the first chapter, the historical record is a record of people making sense of who and what they are, and one of the symbols guiding this process, according to Anderson, is the symbol of race. As a deep symbol, race guides human relations and can be manipulated to unite people on various levels.

On another note, and in response to Cone in particular ways, theologian J. Deotis Roberts's version of the black Christ is an example of relational blackness because his version of Christ extends beyond the concerns of black peoples for liberation and works to incorporate the well-being of all through attention to reconciliation. Roberts's understanding of Christ begins with the incarnation.[50] By becoming Christ (the God/human), God identified with the concerns and needs of all of humanity, not just one particular ethnicity or social group. Hence, Christ's significance is found in Christ's universal relationship with all people.[51] In Roberts's understanding, this deep symbol, the universal Christ, became known to all people in their particular social and political context, so all people have the right to define Christ through their own experience and to imag(in)e Christ in their own likeness.[52] For Roberts, Christ's blackness is an aspect of what it meant for God to become incarnate. God could also be imagined by any other race or ethnic group, as the "Black Messiah is also the universal word made flesh."[53] To this extent, black churches that adopt such a position, or individuals within black churches, are able to connect their racial concerns to their own experiences and then to the experiences of others.

49. Ibid., 50.
50. Douglas, *The Black Christ*, 61.
51. Ibid.
52. Ibid.
53. Ibid., 63.

Up to this point, we have sought to explore how various types of responses have played out in black churches and black religious thought. However, as should be evident but is worth stating, there is no one response to racism within these churches, just as there is no "one" black church, and the benefits or drawbacks to any of the many options are nearly as varied as the people who hold to them. However, the examples of church responses to racism presented here offer a window into how black churches have understood and addressed issues of race and racism as a religious or theological problem. With that done, we turn to hip-hop's understanding of race and responses to racism.

Hip-Hop and Race

As with black churches, hip-hop communities have exhibited consciousness of racial oppression and have done so at times by drawing, as did churches, on an ontological or experiential likeness between black people and the divine. This begins with an expression of the pain and suffering often associated with the social ramifications of blackness in the United States. One instance of this type of commentary is offered by Dead Prez (a hip-hop duo of M-1 and stic.man), whose lyrics express a sense of being fed up with the way white supremacy and racism have served to limit the legal and political freedoms of African Americans. In their most popular song, "It's Bigger than Hip Hop," they discuss anger and frustration at white politicians, whose lawmaking and governing has made it increasingly difficult for many African Americans to create better lives for themselves.[54]

Beyond this example, questions of race have long been a part of hip-hop, and there is no shortage of musical or artistic examples of

54. Dead Prez, "It's Bigger than Hip-Hop," recorded on *Let's Get Free* (Relativity, 2000).

race and the experiences of racism operating as an influence on this form of cultural expression. By narrating the life stories of urban black youth and the challenges they experience as underprivileged minorities, on the question of race, hip-hop speaks to (and for) generations of young black, brown, and yellow people. Often, commentary from the civil rights generation argues that things were harder in years past, yet those within the hip-hop or post-civil-rights generation experience things like racial profiling and a race-based lack of life opportunities. Here, we turn to some of the principal means by which those within hip-hop communities have responded to these challenges, in an ever-present quest to "keep it real" and to resist racialized oppression through creativity.

Hip-Hop as a Creative Form of Resistance

Many outside the hip-hop community may be tempted to see rap music from a superficial vantage point, but here we want to push for alternative interpretations that acknowledge hip-hop is not merely entertainment. In a sense, hip-hop can be thought to emerge as a creative response to black racial oppression. One early way hip-hop accomplished such resistance involved the creation of a certain "look"—an artistic presentation that was meant to signal creativity, freshness, and the status of being cool. Michael Jeffries comments on the representatives of this liberating aesthetic in *Thug Life*: "As 1970s deindustrialization and new trends in urban planning destroyed impoverished black and latino/a neighborhoods, residents in New York and other American cities took to the streets, b-boying (also known as break dancing), Djing, and rapping in the face of economic neglect and injustice."[55] DJs, B-boys and B-girls, and emcees not only took messages about their social experiences to a broader public,

55. Michael P. Jeffries, *Thug Life: Race, Gender, and the Meaning of Hip-Hop* (Chicago: University of Chicago Press, 2011), 1.

but did so with a certain attitude—a defiant display of individual expression that contradicted the often negative representations of young blacks offered by the larger society. Their clothing, record scratching, acrobatic dance moves, and tenacious rhymes entailed a look and feel that demonstrated their "somebodiness."

Hip-hop culture provided a useful tool to resist the racial and economic hardships that befell marginalized communities. The rhymes and rhythms of those musical cadences, according to hip-hop legend KRS-One, provided an avenue that stimulated the creative energies of a community of persons who sought a way out of their oppressive circumstances.[56] Embracing hip-hop, both as an art form and as a mode of visual expression, allowed them self-expression on their own terms, through a style and framework of their own making. In doing so, they were able to affirm themselves and their cultural productions without the undue influence of those they believed meant them harm and sought to denigrate their racial identity.

The explosion of hip-hop culture, to be sure, did not go unnoticed by the dominant culture, and it came as no surprise when producers and other business magnates sought to capitalize on the growing popularity of rap music as well as the other dimensions of hip-hop culture. This process of commercialization and capital investment created a new set of challenges for hip-hop artists and their fan base. What happens when those with no voice are suddenly recognized by the very persons who sought to deny them that voice? How could or would hip-hop artists respond to the rising tide of commercial interest in their cultural production?

Hip-hop artists have endeavored to resist racial oppression through musical creativity. As we saw with Albert Cleage and James Cone,

56. KRS-One, *Rumination,* 24.

who asserted the blackness of Christ in part to uplift the self-image and validate the humanity of black people in a racist society, hip-hop culture has afforded members of black communities a means to assert their worth and dignity as human beings. Hip-hop artists have aspired to tell the stories of black urban life in creative ways. In those hip-hop spaces, whether under the lights of the club or on the pavement of the neighborhood streets, black bodies (male and female) took on an added significance beyond that of the designations levied by racist society.

"Keepin' It Real"

Besides noting that hip-hop emerged as a creative form of resistance to racial oppression during the post-civil-rights period, it is also worth pointing out that the hip-hop generation understands race and black-white racial dynamics differently than many persons who came of age during the civil rights era. Todd Boyd, scholar of race and popular culture, marks three generational shifts that have taken place during the twentieth century within black culture: the "Race Man [Woman]," the "New Black Aesthetic," and "the Nigga." The race man or woman grew up in the context of the civil rights movement and experienced legalized segregation, such as laws mandating that blacks and whites should dine at separate restaurants and drink from separate water fountains.[57] The race man or woman cannot erase this experience from his or her memory, and this historical reality "forever informs" his or her worldview although the era of legal segregation is gone.[58] The New Black Aesthetic generation came of age immediately after legal segregation ended. This generation, referred to as "soul babies" by Mark Anthony Neal (professor of

---

57. Todd Boyd, *The New H.N.I.C. (Head Niggas in Charge): The Death of Civil Rights and the Reign of Hip Hop* (New York: New York University Press, 2002), 5.
58. Ibid.

African and African American studies) was "born between the 1963 March on Washington ...,, came to maturity in the age of Reaganomics and experienced the change from urban industrialism to deindustrialism, from segregation to desegregation, from essential notions of blackness to metanarrative on blackness, without any nostalgic allegiance to the past."[59] The New Black Aesthetic generation benefited from the gains of the civil rights movement and was given the opportunity to live the American Dream and achieve a "middle-class lifestyle."[60] Boyd characterizes the hip-hop generation as "the Nigga" to highlight that this generation is bent on breaking the rules and pushing the boundaries of acceptability. For example, the N-word is a controversial term that many blacks deem should not be employed at all due to its negative association with the derogatory racial slur *nigger*. Yet the hip-hop generation and hip-hop artists have appropriated the controversial racial term *nigga* nonetheless.[61] For example, the rapper DMX "reclaims" the term as an expression of "endearment" in his song "My Niggas." Here, DMX employs the word as a synonym for "brothers" or "friends" and as a symbolic expression of deep loyalty and solidarity.[62] By redefining language through employing controversial words such as *nigga*, the hip-hop generation seeks to move away from the civil rights generation's understanding of race and racism.[63]

The civil rights generation and the hip-hop generation have fashioned different understandings of blackness because the generations grew up in different historical contexts. For many persons from the civil rights generation, especially black leaders such as Martin Luther King Jr., who pushed for black integration into

59. Ibid.
60. Ibid., 8.
61. Ibid., 38.
62. Ibid.
63. Ibid., 42.

mainstream society, black identity was often strongly linked to the experience of being excluded from white society. Because blacks struggled against forces of segregation and discrimination that prevented them from accessing their rights as American citizens, many blacks from the civil rights generation adopted a politics of respectability and held that blacks should dress and carry themselves in a certain manner (see our discussion in chapter two). Seeking to be accepted by whites, many blacks did not want to "offend the tastes of dominant White society"[64] and aspired to accommodate themselves to dominant white cultural norms and standards.[65] In contrast, blacks in the post-civil-rights hip-hop generation do not associate their understanding of blackness with the same experiences of discrimination and segregation. Due in large part to the struggles of persons from the civil rights generation, blacks from the hip-hop generation did not experience sitting at the back of the bus or being legally barred from entering into white spaces with the same force of law.

For blacks in the hip-hop generation, the experience of legalized segregation typically does not have a strong influence on their worldview. Subsequently, their understanding of race and racism takes on different forms. Rather than being preoccupied with obtaining entrance into the dominant culture, the hip-hop generation is concerned with being **real**, defined by Todd Boyd as *"honoring the truth of one's own convictions, while refusing to bend over to accommodate the dictates of the masses."*[66] Hip-hop does not care about the opinions or "approval" of whites or middle-class blacks and ultimately views "compromise as false, fake, and bogus."[67] In this vein, the hip-hop generation's conception of race stands as a category

64. Ibid., 10.
65. Ibid., 11.
66. Ibid.
67. Ibid.

of its own and is different than biological blackness, ontological blackness, or relational blackness. For the hip-hop generation, being black is being real or simply having the courage and the audacity to be oneself.

The civil rights and hip-hop generations' different understandings of blackness have often led to contention between the two generations. For example, the renowned civil rights activist Rosa Parks and her legal team filed a lawsuit against Outkast (Andre 3000 and Big Boi), a hip-hop duo based in Atlanta. Parks, who is known for refusing to surrender her seat on the bus to a white man and for helping to spark the Montgomery bus boycott after her arrest, accused the rap group of defaming her name by using it in their song entitled "Rosa Parks" without her permission.[68] The two rappers in Outkast were not seeking to denigrate Parks's name but were using the back-of-the-bus imagery to show their superiority over other rappers, as well as to demonstrate their ability to entertain.[69] According to one cultural critic, Outkast was "instructing their competitors to get out of the way . . . to 'hush that fuss,' shut up and move, for they, Outkast, are the type of people who 'make the club get crunk,' in other words, make you get up and jam."[70] Outkast changed the meaning of the bus imagery, manipulating it to be more relevant to the group's particular moment and place in hip-hop. The legal battle that ensued represents the generational differences, conflicts, and misunderstandings that exist between blacks from the civil rights generation and from the hip-hop generation.

68. Ibid., 6–7.
69. Ibid.
70. Ibid.

Hip-Hop and Racial Transcendence

As hip-hop has spread throughout the United States over the course of the past few decades, it has connected with multiracial and multicultural audiences. Some argue the group most easily credited with introducing hip-hop to the mainstream of rock and pop culture was Run-D.M.C. For example, when the song "Sucker M.C.'s" came out in the 1980s, it promptly took over the airwaves. Run-D.M.C. pioneered the rock/rap crossover in the '80s with the songs "King of Rock," "Rock the Box," and "Walk This Way," featuring the popular rock group Aerosmith. The "King of Rock" video gave hip-hop access to MTV, and soon Run-D.M.C. were well on their way to becoming the first superstars of rap. The record was more than a commercial triumph. According to hip-hop mogul Rick Rubin, "I think it was important in that it brought it to the mainstream and it was 'music,' and if people had a wall up, here was a familiar reference that they could use. It allowed Hip Hop into homes where it had never been before."[71] The success of Run-D.M.C. brought an introduction to the idea that hip-hop could appeal to mainstream white audiences.

As mainstream audiences embraced the music that reflected New York's burgeoning hip-hop vibe, the Beastie Boys hit the rap scene in 1986. Their debut album, "Licensed to Ill," became the biggest-selling rap album since 1981. The Beastie Boys' whiteness created controversy and at the same time broadened hip-hop's appeal. The Beastie Boys' breakthrough song, "Fight for Your Right to Party," had major crossover success, going to number seven on *Billboard*'s top 100,[72] and together with the presence of Run-D.M.C., they

71. Upshal A. Ogg, The *Hip Hop Years: A History of Rap* (New York: Fromm International, 2001), 84.
72. "Artists: Beastie Boys," Chart History, *Billboard*, http://www.billboard.com/artist/280828/beastie boys/chart?f=379, accessed November 22, 2013.

forged the path that gave hip-hop mainstream appeal. The music, lyrics, and currency carved out hip-hop's own niche in the world of entertainment and in the record industry.

In addition to the Beastie Boys, white rap artists like Vanilla Ice, 3rd Base, and Eminem also embraced hip-hop. Vanilla Ice was considered rap's first Elvis because of the sensation he created with his song "Ice Ice Baby." His first album, *To the Extreme*, became one of rap's best-selling albums and turned him into the white face of hip-hop. Yet he paled in comparison to other rappers, as some hip-hop artists did not view his style as being original and "fresh." His popularity within hip-hop was short-lived.

Meeting with greater recognition for having "skills," 3rd Bass, now defunct, gained some notoriety. Composed of two white Brooklyn kids (MC Search and Prime Minister Pete Nice) who staked a claim to the black urban male style, 3rd Bass was accepted as "real."[73] Through verbal play, the group demonstrated that white rappers could express the richness and flavor of African American culture.

In addition to 3rd Bass, one of the most gifted white emcees that emerged in the '90s was Eminem. Nurtured and shaped by hip-hop's underground institutions, Eminem released *Slim Shady EP* in 1999. His debut album rose to number two on national charts and within a month achieved gold status. By the time Aftermath, Dr. Dre's record label, released Eminem's album, white fans of hip-hop embraced a rapper who could speak to the experience, fantasies, and rage articulated against the machine by white youths in America. Enthralled by hip-hop's beats and fascinated by the "me against the world" attitude of black rappers, white youth embraced Eminem. Proficient at rapping, Eminem was able to connect to a population of young folks as the voice of America's poor white population.

73. Ogg, *The Hip Hop Years*, 36.

His ability to freestyle allowed him to unleash his inner thoughts and to portray an image of a crazy white dude with real-life issues. As a product of an "All-American" environment, Eminem revealed that white youth were also in some sense experiencing "ontological blackness" and were dissatisfied with being at the bottom of America's socioeconomic status. His popularity grew among whites and blacks because he mastered the art of conveying the attitude, bravado, and style of hip-hop in a unique and "real" way.[74] For example, in his song "Rock Bottom," Eminem laments living a life where malnourishment, unemployment, and despair are everyday realities. As a white man, Eminem used hip-hop to display the underside of poor white existence. Through his music, he sought to show another side of white America, one where life options are limited and opportunities are few, and he did this by telling his own life story and sharing his own personal struggles.

In being transparent about his own hardships and struggles, Eminem showed that hip-hop culture, for all intents and purposes, transcends the boundaries of culture, race, and history. The move to mainstream forced America to redefine and acknowledge the poor and dispossessed among all races, as well as another side of the rage and frustration of America's youth that echoes black voices and perspectives. Although black youth played a role in the genesis of hip-hop culture, hip-hop culture is larger than black cultural expression.

As hip-hop has transcended blackness and become mainstream, the "realness" of hip-hop has been brought into question, as becoming mainstream comes at the price of assimilating into the dominant culture. According to sociologist Michael Jeffries, "Hip hop emergence drew the attention of people outside the urban

74. Marcus Reeves, *Somebody Scream! Rap Music's Rise to Prominence in the Aftershock of Black Power* (New York: Faber and Faber, 2008), 253.

neighborhoods where it arose, and during the 1980s and 1990s the recording industry turned hip-hop into big business."[75]

Ongoing Considerations

Throughout this chapter, we have examined different ways black churches and hip-hop communities have responded to race and racism. Black Christians have resisted racism through their sermons, and hip-hop artists have raised awareness about the pernicious effects of racism through their lyrics. Black churches dream that one day, people of faith will take action to liberate all of humanity from all forms of oppression. Hip-hop has a dream that every day the voice of a powerless generation will be heard and the people will be empowered to live another day. Yet as demonstrated, there are generational differences between many members of black churches and hip-hop communities. The critique of hip-hop by some members of black churches is that "unfortunately, many of our young people don't understand how many their parents, grandparents, and ancestors had to suffer just because they were black. Therefore, they don't know how significant God was and still is for it was God who brought us this far by faith."[76] The critique of black churches by hip-hop communities is that times have changed and that the civil rights era has passed.

During the era of Barack Obama, the first African American president of the United States, race and the existence of racism have been brought into question. Do we live in a post-racial society? Despite advancements made since the civil rights movement, especially the election of our first African American president, we hold that racism continues to exist. The economic and political

---

75. Jeffries, *Thug Life*, 1.
76. Emmett G. Price III, *The Black Church and Hip Hop Culture: Toward Bridging The Generational Divide* (Lanham, MD: Scarecrow, 2011), 86.

fortune of most blacks has not advanced over the decades since civil rights legislation. Study after study points to discrepancies in wealth, education, life expectancy, and so on that mark the difference between black and white in the United States.[77] And recently, the Trayvon Martin case provided a graphic example of this continuing dilemma, indicating that race is still a relevant social concern—one that can result in death.

Study Questions

- What are some ways black churches and the hip-hop communities have historically responded to racial oppression?

- Is racism still "just a black thing" in the twenty-first century, during the era of our first African American president?

- How can hip-hop and black churches combine their efforts to eliminate racial and ethnic oppression for all persons and to promote human rights?

- How have hip-hop culture and black churches contributed to the dialogue about race and race relations in the United States and throughout the world?

---

77. See, for example, Pew Research Center, "King's Dream Remains an Elusive Goal; Many Americans See Racial Disparities," Social and Demographic Trends, August 22, 2013, http://www.pewsocialtrends.org.

4

Black Churches, Hip-Hop, and Poverty

Some black Christians have demonstrated a limited understanding of the diverse ways in which members of the hip-hop community have addressed poverty in the United States. Such narrow thinking includes the rhetoric of figures such as G. Craige Lewis, who castigated hip-hop music for promoting materialism and self-indulgence.[1] Furthermore, some black ministers have blamed the hip-hop community for influencing (and enhancing) the cycle of poverty within minority communities. Meanwhile, Christian rappers like Shai Linne blast many church leaders for speaking on or boasting about their material wealth. And "secular" artists have not held back either. For example, in his rap songs, the late Pimp C from UGK derided preachers for primarily being involved in ministry to make money and exploit people rather than to serve the downtrodden in their communities. Here we explore parallels between economic thinking embedded in hip-hop and the economic opinions espoused

---

1. G. Craige Lewis argues that God revealed to him that hip-hop music was demonic and one of the "rising money making schemes" that has numerous youth entangled in spiritual captivity. G. Craige Lewis, "Vision Page," *Ex Ministries.com,* retrieved from http://www.exministries.com/vision/.

in black churches. Furthermore, and in a more focused manner, we discuss both communities' responses to poverty. In short, hip-hop and black Christian communities have exhibited responses to poverty that are **materialistic** (meaning they *refer to a preoccupation with acquiring material things*) and **socially conscious** or progressive (meaning they *demonstrate an awareness and emphasis on social structures and systems*). Hence, rather than merely blaming each other for the poverty that exists in black communities, or suggesting that one has done more than the other to respond to poverty, we suggest that these communities have employed strategies and tactics for responding to poverty in ways that can prompt reflection on how these communities might collaborate and cooperate regarding issues of poverty within their overlapping constituencies. By way of definition, **poverty** is *an economic condition in which a person or group of people lack essential material goods and resources and are incapable of meeting their basic human needs for items such as food, clothing, and shelter*.[2] Although we regard poverty to be an economic reality, we also view poverty broadly as a material and social justice issue.

The chapter consists of three sections. In the first section, we analyze the materialistic and progressive orientations within the Black Church. We concentrate on the prosperity gospel and social gospel, and we indicate ways adherents of both forms of the gospel have opposed poverty. The second section examines materialistic and progressive (or "conscious") orientations within hip-hop culture. We discuss some hip-hop artists' ostensible infatuation with obtaining luxuries and their accommodation to American **capitalism**, *an economic system that promotes ownership of private property and seeks to maximize profits through controlling the means of production and*

2. U.S. Census Bureau, "Poverty," People and Households, http://www.census.gov/hhes/www/poverty/methods/definitions.html#poverty thresholds.

maximizing the sale of goods and services within a free market.[3] Furthermore, we give attention to socially conscious rap music, or "progressive rap," and we pinpoint ways materialist and socially conscious hip-hop artists have given back to their communities. In the final section, we discuss why the hip-hop and Christian communities should join forces, and through this we hope to create a space for them to converse about how they might address poverty among African Americans as a matter of their communal obligations and in light of their particular set of resources—as a framing of their private relationship to their constituencies.

The Prosperity Gospel

The **prosperity gospel** or **"health-and-wealth** gospel" holds that *Christians can experience spiritual and material blessings or healing and prosperity through faith in Jesus Christ and through proper interpretation and application of scripture.* Although the prosperity message is most directly associated with the Word of Faith movement established by Kenneth Hagin, the prosperity message has a rich history and was influenced by urban African American religious innovators during the Great Migration, by New Thought materialists, by contemporary evangelicals, and by Pentecostal and Charismatic Movement leaders. African American religious leaders such as George Baker ("Father Divine") and Charles Manuel Grace ("Sweet Daddy") amassed large followings of African Americans in urban settings during the early twentieth century. Divine founded the Peace Mission Movement in Sayville, Long Island, New York during the Great Migration, when thousands of poor African Americans migrated from the South to the North. He taught his followers that he was God Incarnate and that he had come to establish heaven on earth. Grace established the

3. Chris Jenks, ed., *Core Sociological Dichotomies* (London: Sage, 1998), 383.

United House of Prayer for All Nations during this same period, and he assured his followers, who numbered between 27,500 and 3 million during the course of his ministry, that if they entrusted him with their money, they could live a good and prosperous life. Grace's organization owned somewhere between 100 and 350 churches throughout the United States. Grace personified the image of a prosperous minister as he lived extravagantly in mansions owned by his organization.[4]

While Father Divine and Sweet Daddy Grace preceded the Word of Faith movement by a couple of decades, Johnnie Colemon and Frederick Eikerenkoetter ("Reverend Ike") were immediate forerunners to the Word of Faith movement. They introduced **New Thought metaphysics,** *a philosophy that assures believers that they will experience social and economic prosperity by learning to recognize God in ordinary life situations and to apply positive thought principles.*[5] Colemon founded the Christ United Temple, a majority black Unity or New Thought congregation in Chicago in 1956, and she formed the Universal Foundation for Better Living denomination in 1974 after separating from the Unity Church due to having experienced racism within that church. Her establishment of a training school for ministers of New Thought metaphysics (the Johnnie Colemon Institute) and her television broadcast enabled her to spread New Thought teachings throughout the world. Colemon had nearly twenty-three churches in her denomination by the end of the 1980s. Likewise, Reverend Ike helped advance New Thought metaphysics by establishing the United Church and Science of Living Institute in 1969. Reverend Ike founded the Miracle Temple in Boston in 1965

---

4. Katherine Attanasi and Amos Young, eds., *Pentecostalism and Prosperity: The Socio-Economics of the Global Charismatic Movement* (New York: Palgrave Macmillan, 2012), 3–5; Milmon F. Harrison, *Righteous Riches: The Word of Faith Movement in Contemporary African American Religion* (New York: Oxford University Press, 2005), 134–35.

5. Harrison, *Righteous Riches*, 134.

and an additional New Thought metaphysics ministry in Harlem in 1966. He gave his followers practical tips for making money and encouraged them to aspire to live a prosperous life in the present, rather than waiting to experience happiness in heaven. Subverting the biblical passage in 1 Tim 6:10, he asserted, "The lack of money—not the love of money—was the root of all evil."[6]

Father Divine, Sweet Daddy Grace, Johnnie Colemon, and Reverend Ike laid the foundation for Kenneth E. Hagin Sr.'s Word of Faith movement, which holds that believers should: (1) be cognizant of their *blessed* identity in Christ, which is revealed in the biblical covenant between God and Abraham and throughout biblical scriptures; (2) engage in *positive confession*, or learn to "name it and claim it" by using the power of their tongue to manifest healing and prosperity in their lives; and (3) practice "sowing and reaping" by sowing a seed (giving an offering) and expecting God to generate a financial harvest.[7] The Word of Faith movement blends together evangelical, Pentecostal, and charismatic religious teachings.

The movement gathered impetus during the administration of President Ronald Reagan in the 1980s, the same historical period discussed in chapter two that was instrumental in the early development of hip-hop. Drawing on the individualism and "trickle down" philosophy that framed many political policies of the Reagan years, Word of Faith ministers, according to sociologist Milmon Harrison, taught poor believers that "sowing seeds," or giving their money to the church or more particularly to God was the key to escaping poverty and experiencing financial blessings and prosperity.[8] Successfully inspiring persons to give, many prosperity

6. Scott Billingsley, *It's a New Day: Race and Gender in the Modern Charismatic Movement* (Tuscaloosa: University of Alabama Press, 2008), 142.

7. Harrison, *Righteous Riches*, 8–12; Attanasi and Young, *Pentecostalism and Prosperity*, 111–12.

8. Harrison, *Righteous Riches*, 70–74, 150–52.

ministers raised substantial offerings and "amassed levels of wealth" that enabled them to enjoy the personal luxuries of life and purchase fine cars and houses for themselves.[9] They also constructed large houses of worship with various outreach and "broadcast facilities."[10] As a result of television broadcasting on Christian networks such as the Trinity Broadcasting Network (TBN), as well as broadcasts conducted via the Internet, Word of Faith movement leaders disseminated their faith message to an interdenominational and interracial television audience. Through expanding their reach, prosperity ministers established **megachurches**, defined as *churches that have memberships of at least two thousand and are housed in spectacular building on large campuses.*[11]

Important for our discussion, several African American televangelists who pastored megachurches played major roles in the advancement of the Word of Faith and prosperity message on TBN and other Christian broadcasting networks. For instance, Frederick K. C. Price was one of the earliest African American ministers to serve as a key figure in the Word of Faith movement. Based on a close relationship with Hagin and faithful adherence to Hagin's spiritual principles, Price says he was able to become debt free and experience financial prosperity.[12] Price believed that God could perform similar miracles in the lives of other believers if they were taught the word of God and how to exercise their faith. He explains in his book, *Prosperity on God's Terms*: "One of my ministerial assignments from God is to teach His Word in simple, direct, layman's terms so that anyone from anywhere with an open heart and mind can hear, learn,

9. Ibid., 151–52.
10. Ibid.
11. Ibid., 143; Jonathan L. Walton, *Watch This! The Ethics and Aesthetics of Black Televangelism* (New York: New York University Press, 2009), 2. We use both of these texts to construct our definition of megachurches.
12. Billingsley, *It's a New Day*, 109–110.

and profit thereby. . . . Faith, healing, the Holy Spirit, and, of course, prosperity are areas in which the Lord has led me to concentrate my *teaching* ministry."[13] In 1978, Price began to expand his ministry by delivering his prosperity message to millions of people via radio and television broadcasts. Based on this type of outreach, by 1987 Price claimed he was ministering to more than thirty-three million.[14]

In addition to Price, Creflo Dollar is a renowned African American televangelist and prosperity minister. He started the World Changers Church in 1984 in College Park, Georgia, at an elementary school cafeteria that he attended as a youth. In less than a decade, according to social ethicist Jonathan L. Walton, Dollar's ministry became one of the "fastest-growing congregations in the country," and Dollar became a prominent figure in the Word of Faith movement.[15] In 2004, Dollar expanded his U.S. reach by establishing a World Changers Church in New York.[16] Due to the strong level of interest, the church now has worship services in the auditorium at Madison Square Garden on Saturdays, with nearly five thousand persons in attendance each week. The pastor flies back and forth between his two churches on a private jet.[17] Dollar's close relationship and partnership with Kenneth Copeland, an established white Word of Faith televangelist, contributed significantly to his formation as a prosperity minister. He attended Copeland's "Believers' Voice of Victory" conferences, listened attentively to Copeland's cassette tapes, and absorbed Copeland's Word of Faith theology.[18] Dollar advances the prosperity message and Copeland's Word of Faith teachings during his sermons. For example, in "Made after His Kind," he

---

13. Harrison, *Righteous Riches*, 88.
14. Attanasi and Young, *Pentecostalism and Prosperity*, 112.
15. Walton, *Watch This!*, 148.
16. Ibid., 146–49.
17. Ibid.
18. Ibid., 147.

teaches that human beings are "gods" and have superhuman abilities just like their Creator.[19] He states, "I am going to say to you right now you are gods, little g. You came from God and you are gods. You are not just human, the only human part about you is this physical body that you live in."[20] Similar to teachers of New Thought metaphysics such as Reverend Ike, Dollar holds that people can "change or transcend their physical world" through developing a God consciousness or becoming "aware of the God in them."[21] Dollar has delivered dynamic sermons and written several Christian self-help books to advance Word of Faith teachings. Besides Price and Dollar, there are several other African American prosperity ministers that we could mention, such as Eddie Long, Juanita Bynum, and Leroy Thompson, who directly and indirectly embraced Hagin's Word of Faith prosperity message. Several of these ministers pastor large congregations and are televangelists and entrepreneurs.

Despite the obvious success, prosperity gospel teachings have been highly critiqued by some for: (1) being materialistic-driven and individual-centered; (2) being mainly preoccupied with the welfare of the Christian community and unconcerned with the well-being of non-Christians; and (3) ultimately resting on false premises and promises. Concerning the first point, the prosperity message resonates with American capitalism and has attracted many poor people who desire to escape poverty and live the American Dream. The prosperity gospel assures believers that they can experience individual success by accommodating to the American capitalistic system instead of seeking to advance an alternative economic system.[22] As it relates to the second point, some critics have argued

19. Ibid., 150.
20. Ibid., 151.
21. Ibid., 152.
22. Harrison, *Righteous Riches*, 148–50. Here, Harrison critiques the explicit endorsement of capitalism within prosperity-gospel churches.

that the prosperity gospel does not challenge poverty for the masses. Some prosperity ministers have adamantly held, "The best thing we can do for the poor is not join their ranks."[23] This perspective rests on an illusion that all Christians have equal access to the "keys" to wealth. That is to say, "if born-again Christians—as God's modern-day 'chosen people'—would but exercise the power inherent in their faith to 'name it and claim it,' then whatever they wanted would be theirs."[24]

These criticisms are not without value. The prosperity gospel in large part fails to challenge structural issues of poverty (the "poverty of the masses"). Nevertheless, despite these criticisms, it is important to note that some black ministers who espouse prosperity teachings have had significant impact on the economic development of black communities through the megachurches they established. This is because megachurches have often functioned as major businesses within the black community, as the pastor typically is not only the spiritual leader but also a business leader functioning similarly to a nonprofit CEO. The ministers often employ educated and experienced professionals in finance, business management, grant writing, and several other related areas, and they tend to have numerous professional ties with community and business leaders.[25] They also have often promoted economic development and financial empowerment and have encouraged members to strive to become self-sufficient rather than depend on government assistance and programs (consider our discussion of mutual-aid societies in chapter one).[26]

23. Ibid.
24. Ibid., 152.
25. Ibid.
26. See African American Women Empowered, "African-American Mega Churches," last updated January 31, 2011, http://awe-some.org/resources/BlackMegaChurches.htm. See also T. D. Jakes, The Potter's House website, http://www.thepottershouse.org; Bishop Eddie Long, New Birth website, http://www.newbirth.org; Creflo Dollar, http://www.creflodollarministries.org.

The Social Gospel

Whereas black prosperity gospel ministers often stress the health and financial well-being of individual Christian believers, some have focused on opposing oppressive social structures and improving the welfare of masses of persons mired in poverty. Over the course of time, we have come to call advocates of this stance *social gospelers,* and their approach the social gospel.

The **Social Gospel movement** is *a liberal theological Christian movement that originated in the early twentieth century in the United States and sought to improve oppressive social conditions by emphasizing salvation of social groups and working to advance the kingdom of God on earth.*[27] Several figures affected the Social Gospel movement, such as Shailer Matthews, Harry Emerson Fosdick, Washington Gladden, and Richard T. Ely, but Walter Rauschenbusch was one of the movement's most prominent leaders. This is because he "conceptualized the Christian social revolution in Christian thought."[28] His classic works, *Christianity and the Social Gospel* (1907) and *Theology for the Social Gospel* (1917), typify his theology of the Social Gospel movement. Rauschenbusch argued that the kingdom of God was central to the teachings of Jesus.

In the synoptic gospels, Jesus sympathized with the poor, and given Jesus' social and historical background, Rauschenbusch argues that poor persons considered him as being "a man of the common people" who was concerned about their needs and "never deserted their cause."[29] Yet Jesus' concern about "the least of these" in society and particularly his social teachings about the kingdom of God did

---

27. Walter Rauschenbusch, *Christianity and the Social Crisis in the 21st Century: The Classic That Woke Up the Church* (New York: Harper One, 2007), xviii–xxii.
28. Gary Dorrien, *Soul in Society: The Making and Renewal of Social Christianity,* (Minneapolis: Fortress Press, 1995), 6.
29. Rauschenbusch, *Christianity and the Social Crisis,* 68.

not become normative among later generations of Christians.[30] Later generations misunderstood the kingdom of God in at least four ways: (1) as being heaven or "merely a transcendent reality"; (2) as being the salvation of individuals; (3) as the body of Christ in general or the Roman Catholic Church (also known as "Puritan theocracy") in particular; and (4) as the "millennialist" eschatological hope of Christ's second coming.[31] Yet Rauschenbusch believed the kingdom of God was not any of these alone but instead was "the sum of all divine and righteous forces on earth."[32] He held that the mission of the church in modern times was to "wed Christianity and the Social movement, infusing the power of religion with social efforts, and helping religion to find its ethical outcome in the transformation of social conditions [systems, and institutions]."[33]

Although present in black communities long before this, the social gospel was one of the theological traditions embraced by civil rights leaders such as Martin Luther King Jr. King read Rauschenbusch's *Christianity and the Social Crisis* while he was a student at Crozer Theological Seminary.[34] Without a doubt, Rauschenbusch's Social Gospel movement helped provide a framework for King's ecclesiology, that is, his understanding of the purpose and function of the church.[35] Viewing the church through the lens of the social gospel and the Black Church tradition, King critiqued churches that focused only on individual salvation.[36] King argued, "The churches must become increasingly active in social action outside their doors. They must take an active stand against the injustices and indignities

---

30. Ibid., 27.
31. Dorrien, *Soul in Society*, 28–29.
32. Ibid., 30.
33. Ibid.
34. Lewis Baldwin, *The Voice of Conscience: The Church in the Mind of Martin Luther King, Jr.* (New York: Oxford University Press, 2010), 54.
35. Ibid.
36. Ibid., 80.

that the Negro and other non-white minorities confront in housing, education, price protection, and in city and state courts. They must support strong civil rights legislation. They must exert their influence in the area of economic justice."[37] King insisted that the mission of the church was not simply to lead individuals to experience eternal bliss in a futuristic heaven; however, the church should also seek to influence the kingdom of God by working with God to affect change in the lives of persons, "laws, structures, and institutions" in present times.[38] King viewed the kingdom of God on earth as being "synonymous" with the **beloved community,** an *ethical ideal that implied that the church should be the primary means by which humans are reconciled to each other and restored to fellowship with God.*[39]

After 1965, King came to recognize that combating economic injustice is more difficult than opposing racial injustice. He perceived American capitalism to be a root source of the problem of poverty in the United States.[40] While King acknowledged that some church members have participated in the struggle to serve the downtrodden and to give aid to persons from lower socioeconomic classes, he says, "Honesty impels me to admit that the church has often been on the side of the rich, powerful, and prejudiced, and some ministers have often turned to the Bible to find some erroneous justification for the preservation of the old order."[41] In essence, many churches acquiesced to American capitalism. He beckoned churches to not only give charitable resources to aid "the discouraged beggar on life's

37. Martin Luther King Jr., "America's Chief Moral Dilemma," Speech to Hungry Club, 10 May 1967, The King Center Archive, Atlanta; King, "The Role of the Church in Facing the Nation's Chief Moral Dilemma," Speech to the Conference on Christian Faith and Human Relations in Nashville, 25 April 1957, The Martin Luther King, Jr. Papers Project, Stanford University, Stanford, California; quoted in Baldwin, *The Voice of Conscience: The Church in the Mind of Martin Luther King Jr.,* 80.
38. Baldwin, *The Voice of Conscience,* 81.
39. Ibid.
40. Ibid., 94.
41. Ibid., 95.

highway and in life's marketplace," but also to "come to see that an edifice which produces beggars needs re-structuring."[42]

Despite its many prominent advocates, the social gospel has not been without its critics.[43] During the 1930s, ethicist Reinhold Niebuhr critiqued the social gospel for being utopian, idealistic, and overly moralistic. Niebuhr held that Rauschenbusch's vision for the kingdom of God was not "realistic enough in facing the political aspect of social change."[44] In his classic work, *Moral Man and Immoral Society: A Study in Ethics and Politics*, Niebuhr criticized Social Gospel Christianity for failing to understand the moral nature of human beings and political systems and institutions. (More discussion of Niebuhr's ethics will occur in chapter seven). In addition to being critiqued by neoliberal theologians, liberal theology was also critiqued by liberation theologians for not being radical enough, for having a middle-class orientation, and for surrendering to modern culture.[45] Black liberation theologian James Cone critiqued the social gospel for its connection to white middle-class liberal theology and its disconnection from black communities. Finding such theological thinking reconciliatory and "too moralistic," Cone disagreed with King's early efforts to pursue social change by appealing to the moral conscience of an economically divided and racist society. Cone argued King's sense of the Christian faith could work only when combined with the social critique offered by Malcolm X. In *Martin and Malcolm and America: A Dream or a Nightmare*, Cone highlights a growing connection between King's gospel and Malcolm X critique.

---

42. Ibid., 94.
43. Dorrien, *Soul in Society*, 235.
44. Robert T. Handy, *The Social Gospel in America: 1870–1920* (New York: Oxford University Press, 1966), 262.
45. Gary Dorrien, *The Making of American Liberal Theology: Idealism, Realism, and Modernity, 1900–1950* (Louisville: Westminster John Knox, 2003), 448–51; Gary Dorrien, *The Making of American Liberal Theology: Crisis, Irony, and Postmodernity, 1950–2005* (Louisville: Westminster John Knox, 2006), 133–43.

He notes that the King who embraced Social Gospel liberalism started to become more revolutionary a few years prior to his assassination.[46] King began to oppose poverty nationally and internationally, and he became more realistic in his assessment of America and stauncher in his critique of American capitalism.

Mindful of continuing economic injustice in the post-civil-rights years, some members of hip-hop communities have critiqued black Christian ministers and churches for not being concerned about the poor and for having a "pie in the sky" theological orientation that is only concerned about life in the hereafter. We now turn to what such advocates of hip-hop offer as corrective.

Materialistic Hip-Hop

Members of the hip-hop community and the Black Church have been highly critical of the hip-hop "bling" ideology, arguing that hip-hop culture breeds a sense of economic gain at all cost and in defiance of moral and ethical codes. In making this critique, they argue that the demand for economic cooperation advanced by Christ is replaced by a gross display of individual goods—"bling" over against charity.

As a matter of background, we turn to 1999, when the hip-hop group Cash Money Millionaires debuted the single "Bling-Bling."[47] The video for the song features the rappers B.G. and Lil Wayne driving luxury cars and wearing expensive jewelry, including gold, diamonds, and platinum. Quickly, "bling" became a popular term within hip-hop culture, used to mean *flashy materialistic possessions that signify individual economic prosperity.*[48] Pushing beyond its initial

46. James H. Cone, *Martin, Malcolm and America: A Dream or a Nightmare* (Maryknoll, NY: Orbis, 1991), 244–59, 513–35.
47. Christopher "B. G." Dorsey, featuring Bryan "Birdman" Williams, Tab "Turk" Virgil Jr., Bryan "Mannie Fresh" Thomas, Terius "Juvenile" Gray, and Dwayne "Lil Wayne" Carter, "Bling-Bling," single, debuted March 20, 1999.

entrance into the vocabulary of success, the notion of bling maintains a committed following. Albums such as 50 Cent's "Power of the Dollar" and "Get Rich or Die Tryin," released in 2000 and 2003 respectively, justify acquiring and maintaining material possessions by any means, including violent and criminal means.[49]

Preachers and laypersons were not the only ones upset by graphic depictions of acquisition like these. For instance, Martin Kilson, the first African American to become a full professor at Harvard University, states:

> The "hip-hop worldview" is nothing other than an updated face on the old-hat crude, anti-humanistic values of hedonism and materialism. . . . It is ironic, in fact, that black youth in poverty-level and weak working class families, who struggle to design a regime of self-respect and discipline in matters of education and interpersonal friendship, get no assistance whatever in these respects from hedonistic, materialistic, nihilistic, sadistic, and misogynistic ideas and values propagated by most hip-hop entertainers. The cruelty of the irony is compounded because many hip-hop entertainers come from working-class backgrounds, and yet lack awareness of the injury done to the life chances of themselves and their peers by the warped values that are the hallmark of hip-hop.[50]

While Kilson is right to critique materialism in hip-hop culture, his perspective has some flaws. He assumes that hip-hop is one singular entity, as if there is no variety within this cultural movement. Suggesting that hip-hop holds "warped values" ignores the possibility that values shift over time.[51] It also ignores the possibility that some

---

48. Emmett G. Price III, ed., *The Black Church and Hip Hop Culture: Toward Bridging the Generational Divide* (Plymouth, UK: Scarecrow, 2012), 87. The topic of bling has also been discussed in chapter three.

49. Curtis "50 Cent" Jackson, *Power of the Dollar* (unreleased album with Columbia Records, 2000); *Get Rich or Die Tryin'* (Shady/Interscope Records, 2003).

50. Martin Kilson, "The Pretense of Hip-Hop Black Leadership," *Black Commentator* 50 (July 17, 2003), http://www.blackcommentator.com/50/50-kilson.html. Cited in Derrick P. Aldridge, "From Civil Rights to Hip Hop: Toward a Nexus of Ideas," *Journal of African American History* 90 (Summer 2005): 227.

of those values have been inherited from the people in Kilson's (and previous) generations, including many black church members. Additionally, he does not adequately attend to *why* many hip-hop artists are attracted to bling. Furthermore, his critique does not adequately acknowledge how rappers' socioeconomic backgrounds affect their life options. Lastly, he does not acknowledge the link between bling and style, a concept discussed in chapter three.[52]

Though not all hip-hop artists were reared in poverty and some come from middle-class backgrounds, many hip-hop artists who grew up in underprivileged communities flaunt bling to indicate they have made it (accordingly to the American Dream) and have managed to escape poverty. Hip-hop artists and fans have often been attracted to certain styles of clothing and shoes such as Air Jordans, because in the words of Imani Perry, they seek to "recast" their status as inferior human beings and to "subvert" negative, racist depictions of black bodies.[53] Hip-hop mogul Russell Simmons explains, "Since black people crave success—a success historically denied us by racism or poverty—we wear these brands to celebrate whatever success we attain."[54]

Progressive or "Conscious" Hip-Hop

Some black church leaders have generalized all rap music as being materialistic, and this is based on limited acquaintance with progressive hip-hop artists who offer critical discussions of poverty

51. For more discussion on this issue, see Monica Miller's discussion of "buffering transgressions" in *Religion and Hip Hop* (New York: Routledge, 2012), 2, 135–37.

52. For more information, see Anthony B. Pinn's discussion of the "hermeneutics of style" in *Embodiment and the New Shape of Black Theological Thought* (New York: NYU Press, 2010), 138.

53. Imani Perry, *Prophets of the Hood: Politics and Poetics in Hip Hop* (Durham, NC: Duke University Press, 2004), 196–97.

54. Russell Simmons with Nelson George, *Life and Def: Sex, Drugs, Money, and God* (New York: Crown, 2001), 164.

in their music that push beyond materialism. There is a social and
political consciousness that is embedded in the historical fabric of hip-
hop culture and music. As we have mentioned earlier, during the
early days of hip-hop, pioneering rap artists Grandmaster Flash and
the Furious Five offered a remarkable social commentary and critique
of poverty in their inner-city community in their hit song "The
Message." In the first chapter, we emphasized how "The Message"
expressed the resentment and anger of people living in poor,
postindustrial communities. Here we want to add to that
commentary by saying "The Message" was also a *description* of the
conditions within these communities. "The Message" describes
urine-filled stairways and perpetual noise within these communities,
and when combined with the fact that opportunities are few and
far between in poor and underserved neighborhoods in the United
States, "The Message" expressed a deep feeling that one is stuck
within one's situation. Within these conditions, one feels as though
there is no way out, no choices that could lead to better life options.
Grandmaster Flash and the Furious Five told stories of their
experiences and struggles with urban poverty, and they used their
music to encourage and facilitate what Tricia Rose calls serious "social
reflection on poverty."[55]

However, Grandmaster Flash and the Furious Five are a part of the
early generation of hip-hop rappers. Many who follow conversations
regarding hip-hop culture have heard old-school hip-hop fans argue
that today's generation of rappers do not address social issues or
reflect a similar social consciousness as the old-school artists. Contrary
to this sentiment, there are rappers who critique socioeconomic
oppression. For example, in his song "Mathematics," released in 1999,
Mos Def (Yasiin Bey) identifies social and economic injustices that

55. Tricia Rose, *Black Noise: Rap Music and Black Culture in Contemporary America* (Middletown, CT: Wesleyan University Press, 1994), 18.

have kept many blacks mired in the cycle of poverty.[56] Throughout this song, Mos Def gives explicit attention to reasons why millions of blacks have been entangled in the prison industrial complex. He highlights the broad disparity between the unemployment rates for white and blacks, and he pinpoints how the government has invested more money in hiring law enforcement officers and has been apt to cut government programs that benefit the downtrodden. He explains that many poor persons have often resorted to selling drugs, abusing drugs, and committing robberies to escape and deal with poverty. Many of these persons become enmeshed in the "global jail economy." Critical of mandatory sentencing for drug abusers and of the three-strikes law, Mos Def argues that the prison system is undoubtedly about "business" and generating profits through exploiting a cheap pool of human capital rather than rehabilitation. For Mos Def, poverty and oppression are all about numbers.

Rappers such as Dead Prez, Common, KRS-One, the Coup, and Hieroglyphic have also provided social and political critiques of poverty. Though these artists may not come to mind when people think of mainstream hip-hop, groups like them are an integral part of hip-hop culture.[57] This lack of attention may be because social and political rap is not as popular as more commercial rap that glorifies a whole host of problematic stereotypes, but it bears repeating that these artists are not exceptions but comprise a critical mass of hip-hop artists; many hip-hop artists *do* offer critical commentary on poverty and social issues. Not all hip-hop music is materialistic or centered

---

56. Mos Def (Yasiin Bey), "Mathematics," recorded on *Black on Both Sides* (Rawkus, 1999).

57. For several additional examples of socially conscious rap music, see Aldridge, "From Civil Rights to Hip Hop." Aldridge mentions KRS-One, Ishues, Nas, Dead Prez, A Tribe Called Quest, Lauryn Hill, Poor Righteous Teachers, and Sister Souljah as examples of rappers who have "put forward an educational philosophy of liberation in their work." Aldridge, "From Civil Rights to Hip Hop," 232–41.

merely on pure financial gain. There is a socially conscious dimension of hip-hop culture.

There is another dimension that has not been acknowledged—namely, the existence of an **economic double consciousness** within hip-hop culture. By this, we mean *although many artists seemingly appropriate capitalistic practices through promoting bling in their music, many of these same artists have indicated a desire to participate in the struggle to combat poverty.* Economic double consciousness cuts across all hip-hop genres. An excellent example of this is reflected in the music and philosophical perspectives of Tupac Amaru Shakur (1971–1996). Tupac represents all of the genres (status, progressive, and gangsta), and this may have helped him become arguably the most well-known and influential popular figure of the late twentieth century. Although Tupac in some ways played into capitalism by sporting bling and participating in the system of American capitalism, he was also critical of American capitalism and of poverty in inner-city communities. Tupac's mentor, Mutulu Shakur, enabled him to deal with this contradiction by helping him to develop the philosophy of THUG LIFE, which is an acronym for "The Hate U Give Little Infants Fucks Everybody."[58] Thug Life, which Tupac referred to as a "contemporary version of black power" and which is discussed later in the ethics chapter (chapter seven), represents the "underground economic structure" that exists because of economic oppression. Talibah Mbonisi explains that pimping, drug dealing, and other illegal, underground professions exist "because people gotta feed their families and they can't do it because they are not allowed to participate in the capitalist structure in the United States."[59] This Thug Life underground economy, referenced by other scholars such as Sudhir Venkatesh, has its roots in political

58. Ibid., 244.
59. Ibid.

issues predating hip-hop and arising from the more militant side of the civil rights movement, Black Power.[60]

Kwame Ture (formerly known as Stokely Carmichael), a leader of the Student Nonviolent Coordinating Committee (SNCC, pronounced "snick") during the civil rights era, played an influential role in the development of the philosophy of Black Power. He defined **Black Power** as *a call for blacks "to unite, to recognize their heritage, to build a sense of community . . . to define their own goals, to lead their own organizations."*[61] In addition to Carmichael, other strong advocates of Black Power were Bobby Seale and Huey Newton, cofounders of the Black Panther Party. Seale and Newton were influenced by the revolutionary speeches of Malcolm X, especially his "Ballot or the Bullet" speech, which admonished blacks to pursue freedom "by any means necessary."[62] Tupac's parents were members of the Black Panther Party, and they highly respected Malcolm X's revolutionary rhetoric.[63] Tupac's Thug Life philosophy embraced the idea of doing whatever it takes to survive and to escape poverty. His philosophy holds that as long as economic injustice persists in black communities, the safety of communities and neighborhoods will be jeopardized. This is because many poor persons will inevitably do whatever they deem necessary to survive. Obtaining economic justice is the key to building stronger communities and safer neighborhoods. This was the position of many Black Power advocates, and it has continued as central for many within hip-hop culture.

---

60. Sudhir Alladi Venkatesh, *Off the Books: The Underground Economy of the Urban Poor* (Cambridge, MA: Harvard University Press, 2006).
61. Kwame Ture and Charles V. Hamilton, *Black Power: The Politics of Liberation in America* (New York: Vintage, 1992), 44; Aldridge, "From Civil Rights to Hip Hop," 241–43.
62. Bobby Seale, *A Lonely Rage: The Autobiography of Bobby Seale* (New York: Times Books, 1978).
63. Kara Keeling, "'A Homegrown Revolutionary'? Tupac Shakur and the Legacy of the Black Panther Party," *Black Scholar* 29, no. 2/3 (Summer/Fall 1999): 590–63.

Queen Latifah, Russell Simmons, Master P, Eve, and Nelly are hip-hop icons who have fought poverty through spearheading successful entrepreneurial ventures such as clothing lines, recording studios, and sports management companies that provide employment opportunities and feed local economies. Hip-hop figures such as Master P and Sean Combs grew up in the projects, yet they managed and invested their money well, often moving between the mainstream and underground economies, and eventually established their own record labels, No Limit Records and Bad Boy Records, respectively.[64] Not all have provided the same type of personal example of business savvy. For example, despite experiencing enormous financial success and raking in millions of dollars during the 1990s for several hit albums, MC Hammer accumulated massive debts and declared bankruptcy in 1996. Hammer financed an entourage of about two hundred people, possessed nearly seventeen cars, and owned a $30 million mansion.[65] Hammer's poor financial decisions and planning demonstrate that an excessive bling- and consumer-driven mentality may ultimately result in financial failure or "bankruptcy."

Desiring to help underprivileged persons in their communities, many hip-hop artists have generously devoted money to philanthropic endeavors and the establishment of nonprofit foundations such as LL Cool J's Camp Cool J, P. Diddy's (Sean Combs's) Daddy's House, Master P's P. Miller Food Foundation for the Homeless, Lauryn Hill's Refugee Project, the Christopher Wallace Foundation, and the Tupac Amaru Shakur Memorial

64. "Master P Biography," sing365.com, http://www.sing365.com/music/lyric.nsf/Master-P-Biography/1706779AB632A9CC482568C0002FCCB8.
65. Gordon T. Anderson, "Famously Poor: When Celebs Go Broke," *CNN/Money*, May 31, 2003, http://money.cnn.com; Keith Wagstaff, "Top Nine Celebrity Bankruptcies: MC Hammer," *Time*, February 14, 2012, http://business.time.com/2012/02/16/top-9-celebrity-bankruptcies/slide/m-c-hammer/.

Foundation.[66] These organizations are primarily geared toward helping impoverished communities and providing enrichment opportunities for young urban youth and inviting members of the community to volunteer their time helping youth in their communities. For instance, LL Cool J's Camp Cool J provides free sports activities, camping, and academic programs for underprivileged urban youth in New York. Sean Combs's Daddy's House provides academic instruction for teenagers on Saturdays, offers training on manhood/womanhood, and sponsors trips for urban youth to travel to Ghana and South Africa during an Urban Youth Tour. Lauryn Hill's Refugee Project conducts a mentorship program where each child is assigned two mentors (a college student and a professional). And the Tupac Amaru Shakur Memorial Foundation helps former inmates who are single mothers reintegrate into society.

As well as starting foundations, hip-hop artists have also utilized their platform to encourage the hip-hop community to engage in politics. For instance, P. Diddy, Russell Simmons, LL Cool J, and several other hip-hop figures endeavored to inspire members of the hip-hop community to vote during the Vote or Die Campaign of 2004 and Rock the Vote Campaign in 2008. Some hip-hop artists recognized that the political engagement of the hip-hop community is necessary to overcome social and economic injustice. Hip-hop artists supported the candidacy of Barack Obama because they desired to see change within the black community, the larger society, and the world. Russell Simmons states,

> Over the last few years I have begun to walk toward God or service to God, whether it is through promoting political initiatives that I believe could help the masses—from reforming the prison industrial complex

66. Murray Forman and Mark Anthony Neal, eds., *That's the Joint! The Hip-Hop Studies Reader* (New York: Rutledge, 2004), 318.

to increased involvement in electoral politics—or by focusing more on the numerous charities I am involved with. I am in a unique position to organize some Hip-Hop for the better of the masses and have lent my support to such people as Hillary Clinton, Al Gore, Reverend Al Sharpton, Andy Cuomo, Mark Green, and the Honorable Minister Louis Farrakhan [these are national, state, and local social action and political leaders].[67]

Several hip-hop artists, including Simmons, who grew up in poor urban communities have been eager to use their success and popularity to contribute to struggles against poverty. There are always exceptions; however, these efforts represent a huge cross-section of those within hip-hop. That is to say, while black Christians may have seen images of hip-hop artists flaunting their bling on television or discussing bling in their music, many probably are not conscious of the aforementioned community efforts and philanthropic endeavors initiated to combat poverty and strengthen underprivileged communities.

Ongoing Considerations

Poverty is an ongoing reality. According to the Bureau of Labor Statistics, the unemployment rate for blacks is nearly two times higher than the unemployment rate for whites.[68] Many blacks throughout the United States are disproportionately represented among the homeless, and many black families are but a few paychecks away from being homeless. Today many blacks still live in dilapidated communities, overrun with violence and illegal substance abuse.

---

67. Simmons, *Life and Def*, 219–21.
68. Bureau of Labor Statistics, "The Employment Situation—October 2013" news release, October 2013 statistics, Summary Table A. Household Data, seasonally adjusted, http://www.bls.gov/news.release/archives/empsit_11082013.pdf.

In this chapter, we have shown that black churches and hip-hop communities have employed strategies that respond to the problem of poverty. From the somewhat uncritical embrace of capitalistic practices in prosperity gospel and bling-bling, to the more critical perspectives of social gospel and conscious rap, these communities have offered somewhat overlapping responses to the issue of economic disparity. But such strategies have not provided responses that have resulted in a sustained decrease of poverty in African American communities. Although some have managed to escape the cycle of poverty, the hip-hop community and the Black Church both need to grapple with why masses of blacks are still in poverty in the twenty-first century. Artist and author Sister Souljah indicates that one of the major challenges with developing a movement to combat poverty is the conflicting relationship between consciousness and capitalism. She states, "It's very difficult to mix education and consciousness with capitalism. And most people, when confronted with an option, will pick money over everything else."[69] What will it take for blacks to escape poverty, and can their past performances speak to viable strategies for making a difference?

While this chapter has examined both the Black Church and the hip-hop community's responses to poverty and economic oppression, neither community can adequately respond to poverty without attending to interlinking issues of race and gender. Womanist theologian Jacquelyn Grant pinpoints that within the United States, poverty is "overwhelmingly black" and that poverty cannot be opposed without resisting racism.[70] She further argues "the racialization of poverty begin[s] with the proposition that Black people and other minority peoples bear the brunt of poverty in this

---

69. Angela Ard, "Organizing the Hip-Hop Generation" in Forman and Neal, *That's the Joint!*,312.
70. Jacquelyn Grant, "Poverty, Womanist Theology, and the Ministry of the Black Church," in *Standing with the Poor: Theological Reflections on Economic Reality*, ed. Paul Plenge Parker (Cleveland: Pilgrim, 1992), 49.

country; the feminization of poverty posits that overwhelmingly it is women who bear the burden of poverty."[71] The next chapter deals with gender dynamics and explores ways that the Black Church and the hip-hop communities have responded to patriarchy.

Study Questions

- What are the similarities between the hip-hop "bling" ideology and the prosperity gospel as taught in some black churches? How have members from both communities sought to respond to poverty in similar ways? In what ways do they differ?

- Evaluate the strengths and limitations of materialistic hip-hop music and prosperity message teachings. How have members from both communities been effective and/or ineffective in combating poverty?

- What are the similarities between socially conscious rap and progressive black Christian discourse? How have representatives from both communities endeavored to combat poverty?

- Evaluate the strengths and limitations of socially conscious hip-hop rap music and progressive black Christian discourse such as black liberation theology. How have members from both communities been effective and/or ineffective in opposing poverty?

- In what ways might these disparate communities work together to pursue economic justice?

71. Ibid., 52.

5

Black Churches, Hip-Hop, and Gender

This chapter examines the concept of gender as cast within hip-hop culture and the Black Church. It is not to be confused with the chapter on sexuality; a few important distinctions are necessary here. Gender and sexuality are distinct social and embodied realities, which are linked but nonetheless different categories of human life. Sexuality is often related to human anatomy, reproductive organs, and the body's capacity to both give and receive physical pleasure. **Gender** is *a social construct highlighted as standards and norms for appropriate* (read "acceptable") *male and female behaviors and attitudes.* Issues of gender are often associated with issues of **patriarchy,** which is *the privileging of men over women in virtually every aspect of interpersonal and social life.*

This chapter has three sections. First, we will discuss the dynamics of gender in the Black Church. While it can be argued that women dominate the rank and file of the Black Church, patriarchy still defines the parameters of women's position in the institution. Second, we make it a point to demonstrate the profound effects that hip-hop culture has on the self-understanding and self-awareness of black women within the culture. This musical genre has proven to be an important canvas on which black women make a statement about their place and role in the world. Hip-hop has afforded black women a creative venue to critique gender stereotypes and sexist thinking. Third, we entertain questions regarding the possible interchanges between black Christian communities and the creative visions, talents, and vivid storytelling of black female hip-hop artists as they work to defy the stereotypes cast against their womanhood and the limited perceptions of their "skillz." Some black churches and some hip-hop artists have offered indictments on patriarchal teachings and practices in order to more effectively address the inequalities of gender constraints in the lives of women and men.

Black Churches and Gender

It is typically argued that the Black Church has addressed—with mixed success—the spiritual, material, economic, and political well-being of African American communities. However, sexism and problematic gender hierarchies within churches have hurt the mission of these churches, because both prevent full recognition of the gifts and graces of the Black Church's *full* body. Often, black churches rely on antiquated, male-oriented notions of how to *be* in the church. Mindful of this problem, we should not be surprised that one of the predominant social issues confronting black churches, and thus preventing positive transformation, is the failure to address the plight of women or the churches' sexist and patriarchal teachings. Not only is this indicative of a moral failure, but it's a practical concern as well.

The cases of extraordinary black church women and their efforts on behalf of the Black Church's life and well-being are numerous and documented. Historian Evelyn Higginbotham's *Righteous Discontent* focuses on black women's presence and influence in black Baptist circles, arguing that these women were largely responsible for broadening the public arm of the church, making it one of the most powerful institutions of racial self-help in the black community.[1] Women like Ida Wells-Barnett, long before the large protests of the civil rights movement, were pioneering figures in using the church as the springboard to political action—exemplified in her relentless crusade to draft anti-lynching laws. Likewise, in *Jesus, Jobs, and Justice: African American Women and Religion*, historian Bettye Collier-Thomas argues that black women have been present in virtually every struggle for freedom, often taking substantial but largely unrecognized roles, yet over time, the church became the primary arena for them to assert authority and gain a voice.[2] For example, Nannie Burroughs used her resources and connections within the National Baptist Convention to open and operate the National Trade and Professional School for Women and Girls in Washington, DC. The church-related work of Wells-Barnett and Burroughs (fully cognizant of the scores of others unnamed) problematize the notion that only black male clergy have been on the frontlines of the church's growing public engagement with the world.

Brooks-Higginbotham and Collier-Thomas's attention to black women in the story of the Black Church's life and development prompts an acknowledgment of the multifaceted nature of black religious leadership—a leadership that is embodied in both men and women and goes far beyond any kind of normative understandings of gender and/or gender roles. Yet, despite the grand examples of black women's enterprising agency in creating a place for themselves

1. Evelyn Brooks Higginbotham, *Righteous Discontent* (Cambridge, MA: Harvard University Press, 1993).
2. Bettye Collier-Thomas, *Jesus, Jobs, and Justice: African American Women and Religion* (New York: Knopf, 2010).

within the very ranks of church leadership, these churches have often included teachings and creeds meant to impose the silence of women. Many black women served their religious communities without full denominational support in part because much church doctrine and many church leaders advocated domesticity and "true womanhood." This resulted in public leadership and church leadership being left to men. In short, in church contexts, it was often the case that, on the basis of the Bible and other teachings of the church, women were told their proper place was in the home. They were to raise moral children and keep the home smoothly running so that these men were prepared to conduct public work.

Not all women (and not all men for that matter) embraced this patriarchal take on black women's work, and in rejecting this limited role, they pushed for inclusion in the work of churches. When we are mindful of this, it becomes much easier to see the ways in which women have always been *central* to the church's development and activity in the communal uplift of blacks. African American women have been tireless contributors to church educational ventures, served as organizers for the launching of the Women's Club Movement, and have been primary agents in the political organizing of black freedom movements.[3] Sociologist and womanist scholar Cheryl Townsend Gilkes asserts the indispensability of black churchwomen to the health of black communities: "Black women have remained committed to an institution that exists largely because of their extraordinary investments of time, talent, and economic resources . . . I have concluded that black women are fundamentally correct in their self-assessment: 'If it wasn't for the women,' the black community would not have had the churches and other organizations that have fostered psychic and material survival of individuals and that have

---

3. See Paula Giddings, *When and Where I Enter: The Impact of Black Women on Race and Sex in America* (New York: Morrow, 1996).

mobilized the constituencies that have produced change and progress."[4]

Despite academic treatments and the historical evidence available, black women's roles, functions, and vitality in the life of their church communities have been taken for granted by both male clergy and female churchgoers.[5] Working to correct this omission, womanist theologians, such as Delores Williams, are steadfast in their determination to ensure that black women's experiences are central to black religious thought and ecclesial life. In *Sisters in the Wilderness: The Challenge of Womanist God-Talk*, Williams criticizes African American churches and their male leadership for inadequate responses to sexism and **homophobia** (*fear or hatred of same-sex loving persons*). Furthermore, Williams encourages black women to "refuse to accept any perspective that does not take seriously black women's experience as a source–that does not take seriously African-American women's oppression and their intellectual, social, and spiritual history."[6]

Among other things, liberating and restorative spaces within black church communities demand recognition of the full humanity and personhood both men and women. This is one of the primary tenets of womanist thought. **Womanism**—based on a term coined by Alice Walker in the 1980s,[7] and appropriated by black female religious studies scholars[8]—encompasses *theological, ethical, literary methods that make the experiences of black women in North America central to its intellectual process.* Womanist scholars have called for an ecclesial

4. Cheryl Townsend Gilkes, *If It Wasn't for the Women* (Maryknoll, NY: Orbis, 2000), 7.
5. Ibid., 248.
6. Delores S. Williams, *Sisters in the Wilderness: The Challenge of Womanist God-Talk* (Maryknoll, NY: Orbis, 1993), 213.
7. See Alice Walker, *In Search of Our Mothers' Gardens: Womanist Prose* (San Diego: Harcourt Brace Jovanovich, 1983).
8. Stephanie Y. Mitchem, *Introducing Womanist Theology* (Maryknoll, NY: Orbis, 2002), 55–57.

commitment to the ways in which rigid gender constructions affect women's understanding of their identities and, further how they diminish women's capacities to see themselves as vital members of church life and the larger public sphere. "Having church" in this way, as Karen Baker-Fletcher has noted, embodies an appreciation—an insistence upon the shared collaboration between all ages, races, generations, and genders. As we elaborate upon the cultivation of additional spaces for contemporary black churches to ponder problems with gender inequality and sexism, the way forward must involve a new understanding of the notion of community that is more intentional about the inclusion of female participants and their various gifts and talents.

Hip-Hop and Gender

Most people associate hip-hop with an overwhelming masculinity.[9] Rap music has always elicited many different responses from the enthusiast and critic alike. It has often been praised for its honest portrayal of communal struggle(s) against dehumanization, its acute insight(s) into the problems and potential of black life in America, and its unabashed criticism of political, social, and economic problems that promote the status quo at the expense of black communities. However, there are shortcomings to its depiction of urban life in that it often embraces biased social structures and notions of gender as well as tactics of violence. Rapper Ice-T, for example, drew much criticism from former Vice President Al Gore's wife, Tipper Gore, former President George H. W. Bush, and others in the aftermath of the L.A. riots for his song "Cop Killer"—a heavy-metal

---

9. Cheryl L. Keyes, "Empowering Self, Making Choices, Creating Spaces: Black Female Identity via Rap Music Performance," in *That's the Joint! The Hip-Hop Studies Reader*, ed. Murray Forman and Mark Anthony Neal (New York: Routledge, 2004), 265.

revenge fantasy featuring a verbal assault against the Los Angeles Police Department.[10]

The graphic attention to violence is easily noted and challenged. However, undercurrents of gender bias and problematic social structures are more difficult to gauge. That is to say, it is often the case that such problems are difficult to detect in critiques because critics often rely upon simplistic reductions of the art form. This is a mistake; as journalist Kevin Powell notes, "It is wrong to categorically dismiss hip-hop without taking into serious consideration the socioeconomic conditions that have led to the current state of affairs" in urban communities.[11] But missing from this important corrective is attention to the manner in which hip-hop culture and the larger society may disagree on socioeconomics but agree on gender dynamics within the United States.

Negative responses to Hip-Hop are sometimes geared toward our deep uneasiness with the human body as what we earlier defined as a material reality that both gives *and* receives pleasure (physical body) and represents social and cultural meaning (discursive body). For example, Nelly's infamous "Tip Drill" video, featuring bevies of thong-wearing women gyrating and clapping their buttocks, left little to the imagination and further solidified the disturbingly commonplace tendency of male artists' capacity for female sexual objectification. Both the lyrics of the song and the music video contain misogynistic aspects. The song gleefully explores the commodification of women's bodies for men's enjoyment. Furthermore, these videos present a totalizing interpretation of black

10. See, for instance, "Trans World Music Drops Ice-T Album," *Albany Times Union*, June 19, 1992, available at http://find.galegroup.com/ezproxy.rice.edu, Gale Doc. CJ156610676; "The 1992 Campaign; Vice President Calls Corporation Wrong for Selling Rap Song," *New York Times*, June 20, 1992, Gale Doc. A174892309.
11. Mark Anthony Neal, "I'll Be Nina Simone Defecating on Your Microphone: Hip-Hop and Gender," in Forman and Neal, *That's the Joint!*, 247. See also Ernie Paniccioli and Kevin Powell, *Who Shot Ya? Three Decades of Hip Hop Photography* (New York: HarperCollins, 2002).

women's *lack* of agency, as they are viewed from the vantage point of being perpetual playthings of the libidinal whims of men. Given this portrayal of female embodiment and personality, clearly, there is much to be desired—particularly when one considers the significance of rap music in contemporary society—for "there is no denying the fact that hip-hop's grip on American youth allows for the circulation of sexist and misogynistic narratives."[12]

The problem with much of the public opinion on hip-hop, particularly religious opinion, as we have stated previously, is the simplistic response. It is the tendency of some to cloud the complexity of rap music's profound and affirming message(s) and expression(s) by uncritically dismissing the music outright for its gritty components.

For all its faults and shortcomings, similar to churches, hip-hop culture, particularly in the form of rap music, has remained a critical medium through which marginalized communities have found a sense of place, wholeness, and self-affirmation in the face of a society that has largely benefited from the inverse of these collective efforts toward well-being. There is also a sense in which Hip-Hop enables marginalized communities to undo the negative representations of themselves by drawing on creative responses to their experiences in order to carve out a fuller sense of identity and material well-being structured on their own terms.

Hip-hop has spoken to a variety of issues that demonstrate its validity as a cultural art form. It represents an effort to get the language "right" regarding the misrepresentation of black ability, intellect, and solidarity.[13] As such, hip-hop has created space to express pride, to examine social structures, to cultivate political consciousness for the purposes of communal uplift, and to engage

---

12. Neal, *That's the Joint!*, 247.
13. This is not to downplay hip-hop's popularity beyond the borders of the United States. To be sure, hip-hop culture has spread across the globe, and there is virtually no region that has not, in some way, been influenced.

in the kinds of self-affirmation that strengthen a group's capacity to insist on agency and full humanity.[14] This spiritual, psychical, and mental clarity that rap music has afforded marginalized communities is no less apparent in the lives of black women artists. Vivid reflections on black female empowerment, social critique, and progressive sexual politics within black female rap might suggest strategies for responding to these issues as they exist in churches, offices and job spaces, and individual family structures.

Very little attention has been given to how female artists have made strides in dismantling patriarchal structures. We view such artists as pioneering representatives of a **black feminist hip-hop aesthetic**—by this, we mean simply *an approach on the part of female rappers that is focused on creating music that offers a direct assault on sexism and gender inequalities within black communities*. With time, whether through the rhythmic and acrobatic moves of B-girl and fly-girl dancers, or the vocal prowess and political consciousness of female emcees, rap music provided black women an avenue through which they challenged the predominately masculine artistic expression within rap music.[15] Tricia Rose has noted that black women rappers are critical figures in the process of black female identity formation because they have the unique ability to "interpret and articulate the fears, pleasures, and promises of young black women whose voices have been relegated to the margins of public discourse."[16] Such marginalization from the public eye is critical in that these restrictions render black women voiceless and without

14. See Gayraud Wilmore, *Black Religion and Black Radicalism: An Interpretation of the Religious History of African Americans* (Maryknoll, NY: Orbis, 1992).
15. Leola A. Johnson, "The Spirit Is Willing and So Is the Flesh: The Queen in Hip-Hop Culture," in *Noise and Spirit: The Religious and Spiritual Sensibilities of Rap Music*, ed. Anthony Pinn (New York: New York University Press, 2003), 154.
16. Tricia Rose, *Black Noise: Rap Music and Black Culture in Contemporary America* (Middletown, CT: Wesleyan University Press, 1994), 146.

identity in this sphere. Male rappers' assessment of black women, whether colleagues or not, have largely deemed black women (or women generally) as objects of sexual gratification and enemies.

When female emcee Lana Michelle Moorer, better known as MC Lyte, first came on the scene with her 1988 debut album, *Lyte as a Rock*, hip-hop enthusiasts were confronted with a very different understanding of the central actors within the drama of hip-hop's development. Prior to MC Lyte's emergence, young black men drove the expression of the art form. MC Lyte, through substantial lyricism, tackles themes such as female independence and sexual freedom as a way of addressing destructive remnants of what cultural critic Tricia Rose has referred to as the "gangsta-pimp-ho trinity" within commercialized rap. MC Lyte is by no means the only example of this trend; Queen Latifah, with her Afrocentric declaration of the power and prestige of black women as royalty, British artist Monie Love, and many others have demonstrated a new standard of black female hip-hop culture.[17] However, we choose to focus on Lyte because of her prominence as a pioneering figure of the black feminist hip-hop ethos. By looking closely at MC Lyte, we are able to tell a rich story about women who have produced music filled with empowering messages, insisting upon the full humanity of black women on spiritual, material, physical, and emotional levels.[18]

The pro-woman lyricism of MC Lyte offers a direct confrontation to male rappers who attempt to stunt female agency and/or claim women as property. A review of Lyte's collected albums reveals her well-deserved reputation for exhibiting a heightened awareness of the pitfalls of gender restrictions, as well as for harsh raps that are highly critical of men who use such restrictions to manipulate

---

17. Keyes, "Empowering Self," in *That's the Joint!*, 266–67.
18. Joan Morgan, *When Chickenheads Come Home to Roost: My Life as a Hip-Hop Feminist* (New York: Simon and Schuster, 1999), 61.

women. *Lyte as a Rock* is one of the most striking examples of black hip-hop feminism. It explores and exposes the interior lives and thoughts of many women who are pushed to the bottom of society yet still find a way to redirect the course of their self-understanding and bodily movement. In discussing a range of topics, including romantic courtship, individual empowerment, and the display of bravado for her rap skills, Lyte inverts common understandings of female space, voice, and agency, and "cast[s] a new light on male-female sexual power relations and depict[s] women as resistant, aggressive participants."[19]

If it is true, as Kid from the rap duo Kid-N-Play noted, that women in the rap game have to "work twice as hard to get half the credit,"[20] then in the face of that reality, Lyte's "I Am Woman" reveals that she is undeterred. "I Am Woman," in which Lyte echoes the women's liberation theme by Helen Reddy, quells any notion that she is unable to perform with the same degree of creative genius and verbal tenacity as her male musician colleagues.[21] Most telling about this song is the audaciousness of Lyte's self-confidence. In a society that expects women to be submissive, the lyrics here contradict patriarchal notions of female personality—that is, conceptions of women based on a male-dominated society. The disregard MC Lyte shows for the "rules" of male-dominated hip-hop society, through her confidence in her emcee skills, can serve as a reminder to all young women that, with a bit of self-assurance as well as knowledge of one's value, it is possible to succeed and be recognized even within a community that deems you less valuable.

When considered from the overall place of black women in contemporary society, MC Lyte's commentary provides an insightful

19. Ibid., 155.
20. Ibid., 146.
21. MC Lyte, *Lyte as a Rock* (East/West Records, October 25, 1990), compact disc.

read of glass-ceiling politics within hip-hop culture. In doing so, she demonstrates how progressing through the networks of rap culture as a woman in many ways mirrors the gender and racial discrimination that characterizes workforce experiences for women of color—thereby criticizing male rappers and the larger societal framework that produces sexism or patriarchy, which then gives rise to material inequalities between men and women. Despite the odds, MC Lyte argues that women can be themselves and thrive, whether as teachers or professors, as CEOs of Fortune 500 companies, or as rhyming emcees.

In "Paper Thin," MC Lyte wrestles with and playfully reverses gender politics—this time by commenting upon the problems of infidelity, male dishonesty, and all the complexities that emerge within the power dynamics of heterosexual relationships. Tricia Rose cites the song as an example of black women's experiences with insincere men paying lip service to them while seeking romantic escapades with other women.[22] This is an experience that MC Lyte then uses to develop her own "strategy" through which she navigates future relationships with men in a more aggressive, proactive manner.[23] In "Paper Thin," Lyte redefines the relationship on her own terms, dictating how and when sexual encounters will occur on the basis of her own standard. We agree with Tricia Rose that this song can serve as an anthem for legions of black women who suffer the emotional pain and humiliation of broken relationships.[24] It speaks to intentional and self-directing reversals that expand the nature of women's empowerment in heterosexual relationships.[25] MC Lyte uncovers the indispensability of self-love and self-care for black women. Her exhortation for black women to have the presence

22. Rose, *Black Noise*, 161.
23. MC Lyte, *Lyte as a Rock*.
24. Ibid.
25. Rose, *Black Noise*, 161.

of mind, courage, and self-esteem to love themselves into healthier relationships and life options is at the heart of black feminist hip-hop.[26]

MC Lyte's music embodied a tenacious defense of black women's personhood at a time when such a move was simply not the norm. In declaring herself worthy of respect and love, unwilling to subject herself to any mode of debasement, confident in the empowering features that accompany the constructing of her voice, MC Lyte offers profound insights into black female identity and agency that are useful for women (and men) both inside and outside of churches. Her musical gifts highlight alternative forms of black women's representation that reclaim black women from distorted perceptions premised on false gender constructions. In short, MC Lyte offers a road map to women who seek to define themselves on their own terms.

Ongoing Considerations

Black women who are attacked and pushed to the margins from outside their community due to racial classification and class hierarchies also face the additional strain of sexist belittlement. This situation explains why so many black male clergy downgrade women's abilities and capacities for being instrumental participants in the leading and expanding of the mission of the Black Church. The reality of sexism and patriarchal condescension is just as pervasive in hip-hop culture. The disconnect between the large numbers of black female parishioners in contrast to the lack of black female church leadership is quite similar to the dearth of talented female emcees, as well as the lack of their due recognition.

26. Morgan, *When Chickenheads Come Home to Roost*, 44.

As black Christian communities and hip-hop communities suffer from a woeful lack of attention to female subordination and the corresponding lack of participatory agency, it seems that one viable effort toward resolution could involve a comparison of notes in order to continue addressing sexism and patriarchy. We find it beneficial to envision this conversation as one of mutual exchange, and this mutual exchange, as we have demonstrated here, can begin with a recognition of both movements' shared commitment to the well-being of their respective communities.

Hip-hop culture has provided a platform to critique and challenge the problems that affect the interplay of black life and American political institutions. This is also true of black Christian institutions, which have, through political, economic, and educational endeavors, provided a vocabulary and model for action. We believe that engagement between these two communities on the issue of gender disparities can potentially create a more holistic, egalitarian religious community that draws upon its collective resources to address contemporary struggles by pushing for "brothers to honestly state and explore the roots of their pain and subsequently their misogyny sans judgment."[27] After all, "we have to do better for ourselves. We desperately need a space to lovingly address the uncomfortable issues of our failing self-esteem, the ways we sexualize and objectify ourselves, our confusion about sex and love and the unhealthy, unloving ways we treat each other. Commitment to developing these spaces gives our community the potential for remedies based on honest, clear diagnoses."[28]

27. Morgan, 80.
28. Ibid., 81.

Study Questions

- Do you agree with our claim that black churches and hip-hop communities are sexist? Why or why not?

- In what ways does sexism and gender discrimination negatively affect the relevance of African American churches and hip-hop communities in the twenty-first century?

- In what ways can churches and hip-hop communities do more to address sexism?

- How might hip-hop feminism be a powerful agent in the black Christian communities' efforts to become more egalitarian for their female parishioners? How might the strategies offered by African American Christian women and preachers be a powerful agent in the hip-hop community's efforts to become more egalitarian as well?

- What prevents male clergy from being more receptive to female leadership and participation within black Christian communities?

- What prevents hip-hop from being more egalitarian?

- How can the church do more to reach young adults in order to inspire them to embrace more progressive gender politics?

6

Black Churches, Hip-Hop, and Sexuality

In this chapter, we explore the issue of sex and sexuality in black churches and hip-hop culture (particularly rap music). For the purposes of this book, we define **sex** as *the many ways humans use their bodies to give and receive physical pleasure, usually through their genitals.* **Sexuality** is *the process of making sense of what is the proper way to handle the body's ability to give and receive physical pleasure.* In other words, sex involves the act of "doing it," and sexuality is how we make sense of the *right* (or appropriate) ways of "doing it." Sex and sexuality are very connected to each other, so for the rest of the chapter, we will use the term *sex(uality)* when talking about both of these terms to highlight this deep connection between these two concepts.[1] (When we are speaking of only one or the other, we will use each word appropriately.) In chapter 2, we said the body has two dimensions: a physical, "fleshy" dimension and a discursive, "symbolic" dimension. Sex(uality) is directly connected to

---

1. Anthony Pinn, "Embracing Nimrod's Legacy: The Erotic, the Irreverence of Fantasy, and the Redemption of Black Theology," ch. 9 in *Loving the Body: Black Religious Studies and the Erotic* (New York: Palgrave Macmillan, 2004).

our physical bodies, as it revolves around how we give and receive physical pleasure and how we understand the proper context for that process. In this chapter, we claim that sex(uality) operates in part, in both black churches and hip-hop communities, as a response to a racist and patriarchal society—an effort to manage and control what the body produces and gives in the context of sexual pleasure as a way of changing how the larger society depicts black people. We also argue that although there are differences in the way sex(uality) functions in black churches and in hip-hop communities, both communities tend to present sex(uality) as heteronormative in orientation and homophobic in practice. By way of definitions, **heteronormativity** is *the privileging of heterosexuality as the normal and therefore most—if not only—appropriate sexual orientation.* **Homophobia** is *the fear and/or hatred of same-sex loving persons.*

While sex(uality) is explicitly about how bodies give and receive physical pleasure, it is also about power.[2] In her book *Sexuality and the Black Church*, theologian and Episcopal priest Kelly Brown Douglas claims that the power aspect of sex(uality) is connected to racism and patriarchy.[3] According to Douglas, black sex(uality) has been largely controlled by, or at least framed by, the dominant society's ways of behaving and doing. By demeaning black sex(uality), the dominant society is also demeaning black humanity.

Black Churches and Sex(uality)

Sex(uality) within African American churches is a sensitive subject,[4] and its complexity results in black church leaders and laypeople

---

2. Kelly Brown Douglas, *Sexuality and the Black Church: A Womanist Perspective* (Maryknoll, NY: Orbis, 2006), 19–25. See also Veronique Mottier, *Sexuality: A Very Short Introduction* (New York: Oxford University Press, 2008), 119–23.
3. Douglas, *Sexuality and the Black Church*, 23.
4. Ibid., 67.

advocating a variety of—at times contradictory—approaches to the topic. In this section, we will discuss two approaches. The first involves defining sex(uality) in terms of heterosexual and monogamous marriage. Related to this, many black Christians interpret Adam and Eve's joining together as the proper mode of marriage, and therefore marriage itself is usually understood as a heterosexual institution. As a result, black churches taking this approach usually ignore or reject non-heterosexual relationships. The second approach (which is also the least popular) entails embracing black sex(uality) in an expansive and nonjudgmental fashion. When we say "embracing black sex(uality)," we are referring to black churches being open to homosexual and bisexual men and women as part of the family of Christ, with equal value and importance.

Extending the conversation started in chapter two on the body, we will call the first way of handling black sex(uality) the "politics of sexual respectability." Earlier we discussed the politics of respectability in terms of how black Christians—particularly black women—dressed and behaved in order to change whites' perceptions of them. In this chapter, we use the term *politics of sexual respectability* to talk about how black church members and leaders handle black sex(uality) in order to resist certain perceptions about black sexual desire. In other words, black churches emphasize the "reform of individual [sexual] behavior and attitudes" in order not only to conform to traditional sexual standards of Christianity, but to also show society that blacks are civilized and deserving of respect and dignity.[5] We will call the second way of handling black sex(uality) the "embrace of sexual difference." By embracing multiple forms of sexual relationships, this second approach emphasizes that there is no *one* right way of having sex.

5. Evelyn Brooks Higginbotham, *Righteous Discontent: The Women's Movement in the Black Baptist Church, 1880–1920* (Cambridge, MA: Harvard University Press, 1994), 187.

The politics of sexual respectability limits understanding and expression of sex(uality) to monogamous heterosexual marriage. As many black church members and leaders might claim, the Christian tradition, through its doctrine and holy text, the Bible, labels the marriage bed the one place where Christians are to enjoy sex. For example, the book of Hebrews states, "Marriage is to be held in honor among all, and the marriage bed is to be undefiled; for fornicators and adulterers God will judge" (Heb. 13:4, NASB). Furthermore, through many influential Christian thinkers such as Augustine, Thomas Aquinas, and John Calvin, the more general Christian tradition has, over time, developed an approach to sex(uality) that limits sex(uality) to the marriage bed.[6]

While their defining of sex(uality) in terms of heterosexual marriage has been restrictive and demeaning in particular ways, black churches have seen it as allowing black men and women to resist attacks on their sexual being by showing the dominant society that they can govern their lives and their bodies in a civilized and respectable manner over against typical, negative depictions of black sex(uality). For instance, one of the many ways whites demeaned black sex(uality) was through the development of stereotypes like the "black buck" and the "Jezebel." The black-buck stereotype depicts black men as violent, sex-hungry predators with (metaphorically) oversized genitals and insatiable sex drives. The Jezebel stereotype depicts black women as sex-hungry seductresses who are always ready and willing to lure men into their beds.[7] Both stereotypes helped to paint a picture of African Americans as largely guided by their sexual desires and thus having a more animalistic, barbaric, and/or nonhuman nature. The politics of sexual respectability responds to

6. Mottier, *Sexuality*, 18–24; Douglas, *Sexuality and the Black Church*, 25–27.
7. Douglas, *Sexuality and the Black Church,* 36–40, 45–47.

these kinds of representations by policing when and where black men and women express and satisfy sexual desire.

One graphic example of the politics of sexual respectability at work in black churches is prophetess Juanita Bynum's "No More Sheets" sermon. The context for the sermon is that after she had attended Pastor T. D. Jakes's singles conference for two years, she was asked to speak at the same conference in 1997. Bynum preached about the spiritual dangers of sexual promiscuity. By telling her own "sinful" sexual story of having had multiple lovers, she sought to "teach others despite her own personal cost."[8] Tied to this was her take on the subject of marriage in which she encouraged women to establish a strong relationship with God and practice celibacy until they got married. Bynum's sermon prescribes a conservative sexual lifestyle, and her message of theological redemption from sexual sinfulness through a stronger commitment to God reflects sexual discipline and denial as benchmarks of Christian conduct made more compelling through a personal narrative. The moral of the story: the politics of sexual respectability allowed for a woman like Juanita Bynum to move from humble beginnings to a dignified and honorable lifestyle.[9]

While the politics of sexual respectability might offer a way for black Christians to lead more civilized and dignified lives, it has a very big side effect. In a word, it tends to either overlook or reject men and women who are not heterosexual. Along these lines, as cultural critic Victor Anderson has claimed, black churches have been progressive in their approaches to civil and human rights, but more conservative in their attitudes toward homosexuals. As a result, "Black churches

---

8. Monique Moultrie, "Between the Horny and the Holy: Womanist Sexual Ethics and the Cultural Productions of No More Sheets" (PhD diss., Vanderbilt University, 2010), 123.

9. Someone might suggest that her subsequent marriage history might contradict this notion, but Prophetess Bynum still enjoys a relatively comfortable and secure lifestyle. See, for example, her biography on her website, which chronicles her continued success and fame: http://www.juanitabynum.com/index.php/about-dr-bynum. See also Monique Moultrie's discussion of Bynum in her dissertation, "Between the Horny and the Holy."

constitute a surrogate world that may tacitly 'accept' Black gays and lesbians into their fellowship on the basis of them being silent regarding their sexuality, while their gifts and talents are exploited by the churches in their roles as musicians, choir leaders, ushers, and teachers of youth."[10] Within the politics of sexual respectability, black church leaders and laypersons can welcome gay men and women—as long as they are willing to hide their sex(uality) and look the other way when their humanity is attacked in sermons and prayers. "I marvel," writes Anderson, "that so many Black gays and lesbians continue to maintain their faith in their churches even as their very lives and bodies are Sunday after Sunday ridiculed, trivialized, and preached against as abominations."[11] This demand for silence is often replaced by direct confrontation with and rejection of those who do not fit the normative sex(uality) of black churches. This homophobia, wherein black Christians treat black gays and lesbians in a negative fashion, is marked by "tirades as if gay and lesbian people do not deserve love and respect as human beings, although [these Christians] paradoxically proclaim that as Christians they love everybody."[12]

One of the many reasons homophobia is perceived as venomous revolves around the manner in which many African American men and women see homosexuality as a danger to the stability of black families as well as an attack on black masculinity.[13] By publicly and loudly denouncing the so-called perverseness and sinfulness of homosexuality, many black churches employing the politics of sexual respectability are attempting to protect the stability of the black

10. Victor Anderson, "The Black Church and the Curious Body of the Black Homosexual," in *Loving the Body: Black Religious Studies and the Erotic*, ed. Anthony Pinn and Dwight Hopkins (New York: Palgrave MacMillan, 2004), Kindle ed., location 3866.
11. Ibid., location 3857.
12. Douglas, *Sexuality and the Black Church*, 87.
13. Ibid., 88; Elijah G. Ward, "Homophobia, Hypermasculinity and the US Black Church," *Culture, Health, and Sexuality* 7, no. 5 (Themed Symposium: Female Genital Cutting, September–October 2005): 493–504.

family and more traditional notions of black manhood. Hence, to be male and gay in these contexts can really mean that one is not necessarily a "man," and this preoccupation with manhood indicates the pervasive presence of patriarchy in black church communities. While we discussed patriarchy in chapter 5, we here highlight patriarchy in terms of society's preoccupation with what it means to be a man or a woman, and how these gender roles influence black sex(uality). From Donnie McClurkin to Eddie Long,[14] preachers have often endorsed homophobia in their teaching and preaching. Furthermore, their megachurches speak (or in Long's case, spoke) to the prevalence of heteronormativity and homophobia in black churches.[15]

Many members of the LGBTQ (lesbian, gay, bisexual, transgendered, and queer) community are fighting for marriage equality—that is, the ability for non-heterosexual people to get legally married. As the preceding discussion suggests would be the case, some of the fiercest opponents of marriage equality have been black churches. When President Obama publicly offered his support to the LGBTQ community, some of these churches announced their disappointment in and disgust for him because they were trying to "save the family unit."[16] By regulating when, where, and with whom black men and women can have sex, churches employing the politics of sexual respectability seek to operate within the confines of the

14. For Donnie McClurkin, see Peter Hamby, "Obama Supporter: 'God Delivered Me from Homosexuality,'" *CNN Politics*, October 29, 2007, http://politicalticker.blogs.cnn.com/2007/10/29/obama-supporter-god-delivered-me-from-homosexuality/. For Eddie Long, see, for example, YouTube, http://www.youtube.com/watch?v=UItGijdsCf8. This video features a snippet of Eddie Long's most controversial antigay sermon.
15. Ward, "Homophobia, Hypermasculinity and the Black US Church," 494.
16. See Billy Hallowell, "Black Pastors Launch Anti-Obama Campaign to Convince African Americans to Withdraw Support for the President," *The Blaze*, August 1, 2012, http://www.theblaze.com/stories/2012/08/01/black-pastors-launch-campaign-to-convince-african-americans-to-withdraw-support-for-obama-over-gay-marriage-stance/.

biblical text and the Christian tradition, as well as protect themselves from attacks by the dominant culture.

However, not all black churches employ the politics of sexual respectability. Though their numbers are smaller, there are black churches open to multiple expressions of black sex(uality) by explicitly (and fully) embracing LGBTQ members.[17] Rejecting the relative silence or outright denunciation of homosexuality or bisexuality present in the politics of sexual respectability, these churches seek to support a more nurturing and affirming space for spiritual growth and for community. These "welcoming" churches emphasize the fact that all human beings are equally deserving of God's love and salvation.[18] This, however, does not mean all restrictions on sexual expression are denounced. For example, in these churches, gay women and men can—and do—participate in long-term monogamous relationships and get married (when it is legal to do so) and may highlight monogamy as an important aspect of healthy homosexual relationships (as it is advanced in heterosexual relationships). Nonetheless, in rejecting the more popular and pervasive notions of black sex(uality) as limited to the confines of *heterosexual* monogamous marriage, members of these churches "felt healed of the suffering and rejection that had burdened them . . . these church members [create] new possibilities for a Christian way of life in which homosexuality was seen as natural, normal, and potentially moral."[19]

However, even in embracing multiple sex(ualities), open and affirming black churches have highlighted monogamous and permanent relationships as the most appropriate space for sexual activity, thereby maintaining some social codes endorsed by their

17. Krista McQueeney, "'We are God's Children, Y'all': Race, Gender, and Sexuality in Lesbian- and Gay-Affirming Congregations," *Social Problems* 56, no. 1 (February 2009): 154.
18. Ibid., 169.
19. Ibid.

opponents.[20] In this regard, both the politics of sexual respectability and the embrace of sexual difference share a fundamental similarity: they regulate black sex(uality) by claiming that proper sex(uality) is limited to the confines of more stable and monogamous relationships. As we will see in the next section, hip-hop artists handle black sex(uality) not by regulating black bodies, but by highlighting black sexual freedom.

Hip-Hop and Sex(uality)

While black churches handle sex(uality) by regulating bodies, hip-hop communities, like earlier blues communities, often deal with sex(uality) by graphically highlighting and celebrating the body's ability to give and receive physical pleasure within a variety of spaces and places. As we have repeatedly noted throughout the book, hip-hop culture in general, and rap music in particular, has served as a space for freedom of self-expression and self-making. In this case, it involves embracing sexual freedom rather than restricting black sex(uality) to limiting notions of monogamous, stable relationships. Yet, like church communities that utilize the politics of sexual respectability, hip-hop communities are largely framed by patriarchy and heteronormative behavior. As we noted in chapter 5, hip-hop is largely a man's game, dominated by the interests and desires of men, and this has ramifications even with hip-hop culture's efforts to free sexuality from restrictive arrangements.

We highlight this paradox by turning again to a song highlighted in the chapter before this one: Nelly's "Tip Drill" video. In a sea of thong bikinis, a fully dressed Nelly raps about the "tip drill," the refrain for which focuses on women whose faces are extremely unattractive but whose bodies—particularly the buttocks—still

20. Ibid., 157–66. Here, McQueeney discusses "strategies" that an open and affirming black church employed in order to live out their Christian lifestyles.

stimulate Nelly sexually. Furthermore, a "tip drill" is someone whom a man will pass on to his friends; in other words, after he finishes with her sexually, he will encourage his friends to also have sex with the woman.[21] When this is put together with the images of droves of women with little to no clothes on, wagging their backsides in front of the camera, we realize that one of the most dominant representations of sexual experience in hip-hop has to do with what visual and physical pleasures the female body can provide for men. Although there are many more examples of patriarchy at play in depictions of sex(uality) in hip-hop—ranging from Sir Mix-a-Lot's "Baby Got Back" to Lil Wayne's more recent song "Love Me"[22]—we must understand this within the larger context of the dominant society's depictions of black sex(uality).

As we noted already, black men were often deemed animalistic and barbaric, largely guided by lust. Instead of attempting to reverse this depiction (as is the case in the politics of sexual respectability), some rappers embrace the stereotype fully. By recounting numerous sexual exploits with beautiful women, these rappers project themselves as men who are exceptional lovers, "pimps" and "playas," whose sexual prowess makes them better than others.[23]

We will not rehearse here what we said in our chapter on gender, but it is important to note that artists like Salt-n-Pepa, Lil' Kim, and Khia have used hip-hop as a space for freely expressing their sexualities in ways that are contrary to what Lil Wayne and others offer. In Lil' Kim's videos, for example, we are constantly met with men on their knees, subjecting themselves to her desires and whims.

---

21. Nelly, "Tip Drill," recorded on *Da Derrty Versions: The Reinvention* (Derrty Entertainment, 2003).

22. Sir Mix-a-Lot, "Baby Got Back," recorded on *Mack Daddy* (Def American, 1992); Lil Wayne, "Love Me," recorded on *I am Not a Human Being II* (Young Money, 2012).

23. See Tricia Rose's insightful discussion of sexism in hip-hop culture in her book *The Hip Hop Wars: What We Talk about When We Talk about Hip Hop—and Why It Matters* (New York: Basic Civitas, 2008), 113–31, 167–86.

This is exemplified, for example, by her video "How Many Licks." In this video, images and the written word highlight Lil' Kim's ability to use the male body as an object of her own sexual desires and pleasures.[24] We do not cite these examples to suggest that there is sexual equality within hip-hop. Again, as we said in our gender chapter, hip-hop is also largely guided by patriarchy. But we do offer Lil' Kim as a way of showing how sex(uality) in hip-hop is premised on freely expressing and discussing one's sexual experiences in ways that both affirm and critique the sexual politics status quo.

While it is often the case that discussion of sex(uality) takes place in a song from either the perspective of the male artist or the female artist, as the preceding examples suggest, there are also examples of a dialogue—a shared arena for exploring the dynamics of sexual identity and expression. An example of this is the song "Magic Stick," a duet performed by Lil' Kim and 50 Cent. In the song, both artists discuss how their genitals are "magic"—that is, they can sexually please anyone.[25] Having these magical genitals allows for Lil' Kim and 50 Cent to brag about their sexual exploits in ways that allow both male and female to occupy more dominant positions in sexual activities and relationships.

The expression of prowess is not without its challenges or ways in which the proclamation enforces or reifies sexuality. While 50 Cent is able to define his manhood in terms of the quantity and quality of women he has had, Lil' Kim reminds her listeners that she is not a whore and largely limits her conversation to how wonderful she is in the bed with one person. Men in hip-hop are able to define their manhood through sexual conquests, while women like Lil' Kim define their femininity not only through at least an implied limit

24. Lil' Kim, "How Many Licks?" Vimeo, http://vimeo.com/m/41649363 (video).
25. Lil' Kim featuring 50 Cent, "Magic Stick," recorded on *La Bella Mafia* (Shady/Aftermath, 2002).

but also through the ability to satisfy partners—something that rarely comes up for men in hip-hop, who concentrate on being satisfied.[26]

Hip-hop is also largely heteronormative and homophobic. Countless classic and not so classic rap lyrics play on homophobia as a theme. Notwithstanding figures like Frank Ocean, who recently came out to at least imply that he once fell in love with a man, the tides of hip-hop's homophobia and heteronormativity are very slowly, if at all, turning. For instance, it remains the case that one of the harshest criticisms leveled at a male rapper is that he is "gay." Think in terms of the song "Ether," in which Nas calls Jay-Z out on his sexuality,[27] and in his most recent song, "Lift Up Your Skirt," Lord Jamar calls Kanye West gay for wearing a kilt.[28] By denouncing other rappers as homosexual, these "dis" tracks are aimed directly at the manhood of other men, and thus equate homosexuality with a lack of masculinity.

Although there is a lot of heteronormative and homophobic behavior in hip-hop culture in general and rap music in particular, certain gay hip-hop artists and fans have created a space for themselves. Long before Frank Ocean came on the scene, there was a thriving gay Hip-Hop community. While satirists like Aaron McGruder might poke fun at the idea of a gay rapper,[29] the group D/DC (which stands for "Deep Dick Collective") enjoyed popularity in gay hip-hop circles in the early to mid-'90s. Challenging long-held assumptions that hip-hop sex(uality) was heterosexual, these men rapped as openly black gay men, articulating their own stories

26. Nicki Minaj's feature on Usher Raymond's song "Lil Freak" (LaFace, 2010) puts her in the subordinate position of pleasing Usher by participating in a bisexual threesome with him and another woman.

27. Nasir Jones, "Ether," recorded on *Stillmatic* (Columbia, 2001).

28. Lord Jamar, "Lift Up Your Skirt" (independently recorded, accessed on YouTube: https://www.youtube.com/watch?v=lSJrBeHu4ug, September 15, 2013).

29. See *Boondocks*, a cartoon series featuring a black family, developed by Aaron McGruder. In reference to the discussion in chapter six, check episode 6 in season 1 and episode 15 in season 2.

and struggles.[30] Furthermore, to our knowledge, at the time of the writing of this book, the most popular openly bisexual woman rapper is Nicki Minaj. Yet even though she identifies as bisexual, this is often used to acquiesce to the whims and lusts of men.[31] If we listen, for example, to Minaj's feature on Usher's single "Lil Freak," we realize that Minaj's bisexuality serves to heighten Usher's sexual pleasure; she is willing to bring other women to Usher so that Usher can watch and participate in Minaj's sexual activities with these other women. Minaj's bisexuality may fall outside of a strict understanding of heteronormativity, but when we realize that she is acquiescing to Usher's whims, it becomes clear that she might be stuck within the patriarchal system.

Ongoing Considerations

Before we jump the gun and lambaste artists for their patriarchy, heteronormativity, and homophobia, it is necessary to understand that, as with black churches, this articulation of black sex(uality) emerges in part as a response to attacks on black sexual desire. This does not mean hip-hop gets a free pass (any more than black churches should receive one). Tricia Rose makes this clear enough: "Artists who are this sexist, this hateful, toward black women should become radioactive to listeners and, thus, inactive on radio. They should become pariahs, not messiahs. And their performances should bring them shame, not fame."[32] But even as we agree with Rose, we also acknowledge that these practices and orientations do not come out of thin air.

30. D. Mark Wilson, "Post-Pomo Hip-Hop Homos: Hip-Hop Art, Gay Rappers, and Social Change," *Social Justice* 34, no. 1 (2007): 117–40.
31. Usher, "Lil Freak."
32. Tricia Rose, *The Hip Hop Wars*, 130.

Discussing the effects of the dominant society's attacks against black sex(uality), Kelly Brown Douglas writes, "The White cultural attack . . . has rendered the Black community virtually impotent in its ability to conduct frank, open, and demanding discourse concerning matters of sexuality."[33] To a certain extent, she is correct. Both hip-hop culture and black church culture are largely heteronormative, homophobic, and patriarchal. To ignore or denounce members of the black LGBTQ community, to denounce homosexuality, and to demean one's manhood or one's womanhood on the basis of patriarchal and homophobic practices makes it quite easy for people to feel disconnected. It also makes it more difficult to be open and honest about sexual attractions, which can lead to dangerous and unhealthy sexual activities to the extent sexual engagement has to be hidden.[34] In the long run, by repressing homosexuality and bisexuality, black churches and hip-hop communities alienate themselves from some of the very people who may be closest to them.[35]

33. Douglas, *Sexuality and the Black Church*, 67.

34. See, for example, Victor Anderson, "Masculinities beyond Good and Evil: Representations of the Down Low in the Fictional Imagination of Alphonso Morgan's Sons," *Ameriquests* 6, no. 1 (2008): http://ejournals.library.vanderbilt.edu/ojs/index.php/ameriquests/article/view/137/153. Here Anderson suggests that men on the "down low"—that is, men who secretly have sex with other men while living publicly straight lives—are just as much a product of their own lusts as a result of the homophobia of black communities. Many people attribute the rise in HIV/AIDS rates to DL men.

35. Although he is lesser known to the larger American public, Bayard Rustin was one of the masterminds of the civil rights movement in the mid-twentieth century. Not only was he less well known than his counterparts (Jesse Jackson, Ralph Abernathy, and of course Martin Luther King Jr.), Rustin's sexuality is a lesser-known fact of contemporary notions of the civil rights movement. We bring this up to show how some of the most important people in our lives could be hiding a significant part of who they are all because we may have been insensitive in our speech or uncritical in our religious and theological positions.

Study Questions

- Hip-hop and Christianity share certain similarities and also many differences concerning sexuality. List a number of the similarities, and list their differences. Which list is easier to make?

- Are patriarchy, heteronormativity, and objectification issues that do more harm than good when addressed? Why or why not?

- What might the similarities between black churches and hip-hop on the issue of sex suggest about points of possible dialogue between the communities?

- Can you think of a moment when you've been a victim of or participated in patriarchy? If so, and you're within the Black Church, what from hip-hop might help you respond to that experience or experiences? If you're in hip-hop, what could the Black Church offer you?

7

Black Churches, Hip-Hop, and Ethics

In previous chapters, we gave attention to particular issues and concerns that join and (at times) separate hip–hop and black churches. Undergirding each chapter is an underlying question of what we should do or how we should behave in the world in light of the issue—race, sex(uality), and so on—at hand. This chapter gives explicit attention to behavior by exploring various ethical viewpoints that have emerged in hip–hop and black churches as they attempt to "do the right thing." We have chosen to think through certain ethical perspectives with an eye on how they interact with different social settings and contexts and how they, in turn, help to shape social life and options. Such a task will certainly leave out more than it captures, because the sheer variety of ethical outlooks emerging from within hip–hop and black church communities is so vast.

Mindful of this limitation, we think through three widespread, overlapping ethical dispositions within black churches and three prominent, intersecting hip-hop ethical standpoints. This chapter does not assume any ethical or moral high ground and therefore is not seeking to justify any particular ethical position. Instead, we work to hold in tension various ethical outlooks. But first we set context by offering definitions. In brief, ethics—to be ethical or act ethically—means to "do the right thing."[1] So we define **ethics** as *action guided by a variety of life experiences, beliefs, and/or community concerns.* At face value, ethics is a matter of what we ought to do in light of particular situations needing resolution.

What is the right thing? Many Christians find in the Bible (and church doctrine) answers to such questions. For instance, commandments like "Thou shalt not kill" help to situate a Judeo-Christian ethical foundation. The New Testament imperative of loving one's neighbor (as one loves oneself) provides another ethical framing. Yet ethics involves more than this frame of reference. Not all Christian communities interpret the Bible in the same way (e.g., literal interpretations vs. metaphorical importance of Scripture) or follow it with the same fervor; this is how during the civil rights movement both sides of the conflict could proclaim a Christian base. (Note: Both members of black churches and members of the Ku Klux Klan use the same doctrinal foundation, the Bible, on Sunday mornings. What separates one group from the other, religiously, is only interpretation of biblical scripture.)

Furthermore, longstanding translation disagreements and the social and cultural differences between the biblical writers' world and today produce challenges. Just as there is something called the "Black" Church that is an outgrowth of particular experiences, ethics is equally shaped by social context. For instance, although one of the Ten Commandments clearly states, "Thou shalt not steal," who defines what it means to "steal"? What counts as theft for a person denied the legal right of ownership, as was the case for enslaved

---

1. For an example of this popular definition, see, for instance, Robert Wandberg, Roberta Brack Kaufman, and Millie Shepich, *Ethics: Doing the Right Thing* (Edina, MN:Capstone, 2000); David W. Gill, *Doing Right: Practicing Ethical Principles* (Downers Grove, IL: InterVarsity, 2009).

Africans? During the nearly 250 years of U.S. slavery, many of the enslaved made a distinction between "stealing" and "taking." Stealing amounted to securing from another enslaved person without permission, while taking involved "appropriating from white folks" what was owed to the enslaved anyway. As theologian James Cone notes, ethics for the enslaved meant "to do the right thing" as "was necessary to stay alive in bondage with dignity."[2] When we delve a bit deeper, it becomes plain that social contexts and experiences shape not only the decisions people make, but also the way people judge those decisions. The number of options that a person even believes are possible and the choices a person or group thinks are available are also influenced by context and experience.

The distinction made between stealing and taking offers an important first snapshot of the different components present in what we call an **ethical framework**, which is *the sum total of (1) social context—the social experiences a person or group faces, (2) norm clarification—the definitions of and concerns for a community based on these social experiences, and (3) criteria of evaluation—the religious or philosophical beliefs and objects used to make sense of those experiences within (and across) communities*. In brief, ethical frameworks are made up of what persons or groups experience, how persons or groups come to define themselves and their duties in light of those experiences, and essential guides (e.g., the Bible) used in the process. Any particular ethical framework will give varying degrees of attention to each of these three components, yet all three are present in any framework.

Discussing ethical frameworks instead of "ethics" offers a way to compare and contrast individual and communal concerns in a productive fashion by guarding against simply debating morality, or

2. James H. Cone, *God of the Oppressed*, rev. ed. (Maryknoll, NY: Orbis, 1997), 191–92.

what gets labeled "right" and "wrong." Without a doubt, constructive critical comments about right and wrong are necessary. Nonetheless, rather than making a simple cost-benefit analysis of the ethical failings or successes of hip-hop or black churches, more helpful for our discussion is to look at how different people in different places and with different concerns act in the world—with their own tools and with the wisdom born from their experiences—and why they act in particular ways.

Black Churches and Ethics

The moral codes (i.e., what is "right" and "wrong") of black churches are drawn from the Bible and enhanced by church doctrine and creeds. And in like manner, these codes are easily gathered from sources like the Bible, for within many black churches, the Bible offers the foundation and blueprint for acceptable ethical frameworks. However, social factors like racism, sexism, heterosexism, and poverty influence interpretation of Scripture and bleed into what is perceived as the best way to behave in the world. It is important to keep in mind that biblical texts were used to support and to critique slavery, to endorse sexism and to challenge sexism. Mindful of the previous chapter, we should note that some black churches have addressed the issue of gay marriage by fighting for the equality of all based on biblical mandates to love one's neighbor and based on biblical passages such as Gal. 3:28 that emphasize social inclusivity. Other black churches, however, have actively fought against gay marriage based on biblical passages such as Lev. 18:22 that claim homosexuality is a sin or an abomination. Here is the rub: both responses are based on the Bible.

To push this discussion forward, we offer three Christian ethical frameworks. For the sake of argument, these ethical frameworks when taken together can be understood as representing systems of conduct. As is common practice, such systems are named or categorized. Here we argue for the following three naming possibilities as a way of unpacking ethics within black church circles. They are not the only options, nor are they all-inclusive, but they do offer a way of thinking about the form and function of ethics. They are: an *ethic of formation*, a personalized *ethic of impossibility*, and an *ethic of liberation*. These particular names are meant to summarize the overall purpose of the particular approach to ethics. However, other names could be and are in fact used to capture the same sense of proper behavior and actions. So more important than the actual naming of the system of ethics is the fact that black churches have applied their frameworks to a range of issues, and this application has involved contradictory positions and attitudes—but all premised on what these churches understand as Christian duty and biblical obligation.

Ethic of Formation

By way of definition, an **ethic of formation** *takes its ethical guidelines from the Bible—including aspects of both the Hebrew Bible and the New Testament—and seeks to bring about the kingdom of God on earth through proper action in the world.*[3] Lines from the Lord's Prayer, "Thy kingdom come, thy will be done, on earth as it is in heaven," show the connection between ethics, the Bible and Jesus Christ. We have defined ethics, and by "formation" we mean to say the process by which "Jesus take[s] form in His Church" so that the church is robust and righteous enough to realize the kingdom of God on earth.[4] Some churches apply this ethic to an understanding of the kingdom of

---

3. Though this definition is original, it follows from and is inspired by Dietrich Bonhoeffer's characterization of formation ethics.

4. Dietrich Bonhoeffer, *Ethics*, ed. Eberhard Bethge and trans. Neville Horton Smith (New York: Macmillan, 1965), 83.

God here on earth, while others presume the kingdom will fully be achieved only at the end of history.[5] This work to bring about the kingdom of God, whether on earth or in an alternate space, is meant to provide the final solution to human misery and suffering, to human misdeeds and injustice, by bringing all human behavior in line with the will of God, guided by life-affirming rules and regulations.

Stepping outside black churches for a moment, one of the most famous proponents of this ethical system is the German theologian and pastor Dietrich Bonhoeffer, exemplified in his political commitments before and during World War II. His commitment to an ethic of formation remained unwavering even as his convictions (and their implications for fighting against the Nazis) led him to be murdered by the Nazis because of his participation in a plot to kill Adolf Hitler.[6] Stepping back, we must note that Bonhoeffer perceived life as difficult and full of gray ethical areas. Apathy, indifference, and not knowing exactly how to determine right from wrong reflected ethical dilemmas that led many Germans to comply with the Nazi vision of producing a global superior Aryan race based within a German empire. This led Bonhoeffer to state that the church was guilty of murder in its silence.[7] The rise of Adolf Hitler and the Third Reich, from Bonhoeffer's perspective, required a rereading of the Bible and an aggressive application of its teachings stripped of any allegiance to the trappings of church politics and compromises. So understood, for Bonhoeffer, the Bible offered a way to correct a social setting that had been turned upside down.[8] Applying "ethics as formation" to his social context, Bonhoeffer wrote, "Concrete

---

5. Ibid., 84.
6. David F. Ford, *The Future of Christian Theology* (Hoboken, NJ: Wiley, 2011).
7. Else Marie Pederson, Holger Lam, and Peter Lodberg, *For All People: Global Theologies in Contexts: Essays in Honor of Viggo Mortensen* (Grand Rapids, MI: Eerdmans, 2002), 107.
8. Dietrich Bonhoeffer, *Life Together and Prayerbook of the Bible*, Dietrich Bonhoeffer Works (Minneapolis: Fortress Press, 2004), 144.

judgments and decisions will have to be ventured here. Decision and action can here no longer be based on the personal conscience of the individual. Here there are concrete commandments and instructions for which obedience is demanded."[9]

Many African American Christians were inspired by Bonhoeffer, just as he had been inspired by the Black Church during his brief time at Union Theological Seminary in New York City. In Bonhoeffer, many African American Christians found a way to confront evil and maintain a commitment to the fundamental truths of the Christian tradition and the Bible. Dr. Martin Luther King Jr. is certainly one who saw in Bonhoeffer's ethics a way forward. That is to say, for African American Christians like King, the church at its best was understood to provide a community for ethics, and the Bible offered agreed-upon criteria for right actions to be known and implemented.[10] Deeply concerned with the kingdom of God on earth, black churches in line with civil rights strategies and struggles embraced King's sense of the "beloved community."[11]

Beyond the grand schemes of Bonhoeffer's work and the civil rights movement, simple examples of this ethic in practice include any moments in which the Bible is appealed to for its guidance in the pursuance of the kingdom of God. Within this ethic, a balanced commitment to sacred text and community produce the guiding ethical rules in any given social setting. Communities upholding this ethic are committed to obedience to God (as they understand God) and a notion of community as kingdom-building. This ethic plays out across a variety of churches, including this-worldly denominations that focus on overall social uplift and otherworldly

9. Bonhoeffer, *Ethics*, 88.

10. Willis Jenkins, *Bonhoeffer and King: Their Legacies and Import for Christian Social Thought* (Minneapolis: Fortress Press, 2010), 142.

11. Vincent L. Wimbush, *African Americans and the Bible: Sacred Texts and Social Structures* (New York City: Continuum, 2001), 133.

varieties, including Pentecostal denominations. Expressed in a variety of ways, one significant feature of this ethic is that it promotes the idea that when the faithful are "doing the right thing" inside church walls, the larger society will benefit in terms of the model provided by the church, and from church members continuing to "do the right thing" outside of church walls.[12] That is to say, though the inspiration for this ethical stance is Jesus Christ taking form in the church, at its root the ethic of formation focuses on the church and building it as an authoritative means of addressing the larger society. Whether through a focus on suffering or on well-being, the church's ability to influence the larger society is paramount.

Though this ethic of formation is influential within black churches, not all communities hold to it. In fact, many black Christians have been influenced by a personalized ethical framework, which pushes against some of the claims of the ethic of formation. We turn now to this perspective.

Ethic of Impossibility

One of the most famous U.S. Christian thinkers is Reinhold Niebuhr, who appeared on the cover of *Time* magazine in 1951 and was cited by President Barack Obama as one of his "favorite philosophers."[13] Reinhold Niebuhr's influence on American Christianity is immense. His central concern was to interrogate the usefulness of the Bible in determining how to "do the right thing" in society. The conclusions he drew from his studies set the stage for explaining an ethical framework no longer based on biblical ideals of what can and should happen, but rather based on what the Bible indicates about right action impossible without divine action.[14] If an ethic of formation

---

12. Peter J. Paris, *The Social Teaching of the Black Churches* (Minneapolis: Fortress Press, 1985), 8.
13. David Brooks, "Obama, Gospel and Verse," *New York Times*, April 26, 2007, http://www.nytimes.com/2007/04/26/opinion/26brooks.html.

attempts to "do the right thing" by bringing about the kingdom of God, an **ethic of impossibility** *is concerned with the human inevitability of doing the wrong thing without God's intervention and assistance*. That is to say, the previous ethical framework entails a sense of human shortcoming and sin, but human flaws are highlighted in the ethic of impossibility. By "impossibility," we mean our *inability to escape sin, to fully arrive at the kingdom of God on our own without divine intervention.* For Niebuhr, every attempt at the kingdom of God brings with it the "imperfection of [human] knowledge" and an egoistic arrogance that such an effort is possible, making every attempt "impossible."[15]

For him, the tragedy of World War II points to the deep damage human arrogance and unjustified optimism can do, so this ethic of impossibility is meant to provide an alternative that recognizes the shortcomings of human nature. Elements of this ethic are seen in older Christian ideas as well, including the hugely influential St. Augustine of Hippo's doctrine of "original sin," which suggests that humans are born in sin, with a limited and warped spark of God in us as a result of the sin of Adam and Eve. Hence, sin is inescapable because it is part of our nature.[16] What becomes important in this context of sin is recognition of our complete and utter dependence on the grace of God—the only means by which we are able to overcome sin.[17] The ethic of impossibility highlights human shortcomings. It requires action in the world but recognizes the limitation of our reach because of our flawed nature.

Black churches holding to this ethical perspective push a sense of human frailty while also noting the manner in which God provides

---

14. Reinhold Niebuhr, *An Interpretation of Christian Ethics* (New York: Harper & Brothers, 1963), 19.
15. Ibid., 36, 52.
16. Daniel L. Migliore, *Faith Seeking Understanding: An Introduction to Christian Theology* (Grand Rapids, MI: Eerdmans, 2004), 154–59.
17. Niebuhr, *An Interpretation,*55.

a way for us to do good work that advances the individual and the community. Stated candidly, this ethic of impossibility begins with awareness that humans simply cannot achieve Jesus' ethical stature.[18] In fact, as Niebuhr explained this ethical stance, even the suggestion that human action could produce the kingdom of God is to be "dishonest" about human possibilities, to commit the sin of pride (this is most certainly connected to our conversation about poverty in chapter four, where we noted that Niebuhr critiqued the Social Gospelers for thinking that the kingdom of God could be achieved on earth). He labeled such thinking "egoism," saying that this "egoism is always destructive."[19] This has implications for the previously discussed ethic of formation. The ethic of impossibility understands ethic of formation as inherently sinful. To the extent that a proper Christian ethic can be achieved, its usefulness rests on explaining the impossibilities of making total sense of the relationship "between the loving will of God and the will of man."[20]

This ethic of impossibility uses its biblically based interpretation of sin as a means of understanding the social world as naturally problematic, incapable of being fully responded to in a way that would bring about fully the kingdom of God. In sum, such efforts on the part of humans to achieve clear and consistent advancement on the individual and collective level are an *impossible possibility*, meaning impossible on our own and possible only through the intervention of Christ. Hence, it is an impossible possibility.[21]

Some African American Christians advance a system of ethics that highlights and privileges the certainty of Christ's intervention on our behalf, and they do so because they understand God's very nature to

18. Ibid., 35.
19. Ibid., 38.
20. Ibid., 23–24.
21. Ibid., 36.

be aligned with human liberation. The ethics of liberation, discussed next, exemplifies such a synthesis.

Ethic of Liberation

Like the previous two systems of ethics, this third option begins with an interpretation of the Bible. However, an **ethic of liberation** highlights and interprets liberating threads in Scripture, especially the belief in Jesus' "preferential option for the poor."[22] Liberation ethics begins with *an awareness that God is on the side of the oppressed and dispossessed, and that ethics should involve a commitment to the liberation of the oppressed from bondage in all forms.*[23]

While such an ethic of liberation is presented in subtle ways through the history of black churches, one of its first academic proponents is theologian James Cone. For him, an ethic of formation may be well intentioned, but the kingdom of God will not be brought about if anyone is excluded from that kingdom, whether on earth or in heaven. That is to say, this first form of ethics does not provide enough explicit attention to God's privileging of the oppressed and does not necessitate attention to the here and now, which is of fundamental concern to thinkers like Cone. Accordingly, the ethic of formation could very well reproduce the status quo.[24] Conversely, an ethic of impossibility is too quick to excuse the ethical mistakes made by individuals and communities, leading Cone to characterize Reinhold Niebuhr and others as perpetuating an "invisible" racism in their work.[25] As with the ethic of formation, this again has the potential to perpetuate the status quo. If humans cannot

---

22. Laceye Warner, "Reconsidering Evangelism: Lessons from Black Liberation and Womanist Theologies," in Linda Elaine Thomas. *Living Stones in the Household of God: The Legacy and Future of Black Theology* (Minneapolis: Fortress Press, 2003), 71–82.

23. James H. Cone, *God of the Oppressed*, rev. ed. (Maryknoll, NY: Orbis, 1997), 183–85.

24. Ibid., 183.

25. Ibid., 184.

escape their sin, then social problems and conditions such as racism or sexism can be justified as unavoidable. Viewing social problems as certain evils, which cannot be vanquished, may make it difficult for some to justify strong efforts to oppose them.[26]

For Cone, God demands nothing less than the liberation of the oppressed from bondage. Cone describes an ethic of liberation this way: "To live as a Christian simply means being what God has made us, namely, liberated creatures committed to the freedom of humanity."[27] Nothing less than this constant attention to liberation will produce an adequate Christian ethic workable in the contemporary world. For Cone and other liberation theologians, debating ethical frameworks as if there were competing options is to ignore the cries of those in the wilderness of racial and gender oppression, people and communities alienated because of their race, income level, sexual preference, and other factors.[28] Ethics involves "deciding between the old and the new age," the age of oppression and the age of freedom.[29] Here, freedom is of central import.

The clear distinctions we have drawn between these three modes of ethics are for the sake of discussion, to allow investigation. However, in practice, the situation is more complex in that churches today tend to form ethics in ways involving a blending of aspects of all three types. During the last decades of the twentieth century, Black Church ethical platforms were confronted by new challenges. Popular culture had always infiltrated churches and pushed against the moral codes and ethical frameworks assumed by these churches, yet hip-hop culture has offered a somewhat compelling ethical challenge in part because it arises as black churches (like other

26. This criticism is taken up by Traci West and James Cone in their discussions of Reinhold Niebuhr cited in note 24.
27. Cone, *God of the Oppressed*, 199.
28. Ibid., 190.
29. Cone, *God of the Oppressed*, 206.

churches in the United States) are facing numerical decline and a lessening of their influence. Hip-hop culture promotes complex and layered ways of being in the world that at times embrace but at other times run in full contradiction to what is proposed by churches. Confrontation between these two, black churches and hip-hop culture, regarding proper ethics in the contemporary world has been unavoidable. Next, we explore the ethical frameworks offered within the context of hip-hop culture.

Hip-Hop Ethics

The ethics of hip-hop are displayed not only through the manifestations of the culture—music, dress, and language—but as well by the realities of the daily lives of those within the urban landscape of America. This section will discuss various modes of ethics within hip-hop; some ethical approaches will mirror those in the church, and others will be completely divergent. Again, however, it is our purpose to find a space or spaces where the ethics of the church and the hip-hop community can find or at least develop some common ground.

Ethic of Rebellion

Any discussion of ethical frameworks must begin with awareness that social factors are the starting point for hip-hop ethical frameworks. As we discussed in our analysis of history in chapter 1, these social influences include economic conditions within cities; a waning significance of traditional religious, educational, and other cultural institutions; and a growing drug epidemic that brought about a sanctioned police assault on many African Americans. Though not all hip-hop artists or fans know firsthand such conditions, these realities have had an enormous collective impact on the ethical sensibilities found within hip-hop culture in general and rap music in particular. These social issues produced a situation in which a generation of young black women and men were left thinking that the institutions charged with helping them were causing as much (or more) harm as good. For instance, some argued black churches were more interested in telling young people what to do than in helping to meet their needs by providing basic necessities. Furthermore, schools resembled prisons, with regimented schedules and bars over windows and doors, producing a sense of "custody and control" more so than addressing the learning needs of students.[30] Law enforcement agencies, charged with protecting citizens, began to do so much harm through racial profiling and violence that they could not be trusted.[31] To this end, the hip-hop "community" formed, as people were systematically alienated from other institutional types of community. These young people took it upon themselves to provide the resources and creative outlets necessary to sustain them in this situation. What emerged from this was an **ethic of rebellion** that *pushes against any sort of constricting understanding of right action as offered by social institutions.*[32]

Epitomized by the life and work of Tupac Shakur, the ethic of rebellion played out in his conception of Thug Life, which we discussed in chapter 4. Here we discuss Thug Life as an ethical framework that throws open ethical possibilities and options over and against the narrow confines of life in the late twentieth century. Feeling the weight of racism, narrow understandings of sexuality and the body, and repressive ethical statements about what can and cannot happen with respect to sexuality, Tupac resisted traditional

30. Loic Wacquant, "Deadly Symbiosis: When Ghetto and Prison Meet and Mesh," *Punishment & Society* 3, no. 1 (n.d.): 95–134, 108.
31. Mickey Hess, *Icons of Hip Hop: An Encyclopedia of the Movement, Music, and Culture* (Santa Barbara, CA: ABC-CLIO, 2007), 302.
32. This ethical formation is inspired by Anthony Pinn's concept of an ethic of perpetual rebellion, as discussed in Anthony B. Pinn, *Terror and Triumph: The Nature of Black Religion* (Minneapolis: Fortress Press, 2003).

religious ethical frameworks. In fact, when asked about religion, he responded, "I think some cool motherfuckers sat down a long time ago and said, 'Let's figure out a way that we can control motherfuckers.'"[33] Responding to what he registered as the ethical failure of these institutions and the larger society, Tupac's own ethical sensibilities valorized a "Thug Life" based on individual expression and awareness that life under these conditions was hardly bearable; hence, people are free to do what is necessary to survive in an absurd world. So conceived, an ethic of rebellion carries with it a righteous anger at the establishment. If the same society that created his alienation wanted to label him a thug, then the "thug life" they would get! If society wanted to charge Tupac with a crime, then he would use the opportunity to stand up in a courtroom and remark that the justice system had not been just to him, that it (and the larger society it represented) did not care about him.[34]

While one of its most notable spokespersons, Tupac is not the first to advance the ethical merit of rebellion. One must also keep in mind the celebration of this ethical posture in songs by N.W.A. such as "Fuck tha Police" and "Real Niggaz." In these songs, the group employed an ethic that not only rebelled against law enforcement, but also reappropriated the very term *nigger* into something ethically powerful. When the group was rhetorically asking, "Why do I call myself a nigger?," its answers included the difficulty associated with obtaining a good job, police harassment, and the inability to change racist conceptions of black skin. Owning the label of "nigger" offers a moment for recognition in a racist world. N.W.A. carved out its ethical sensibilities and pushed against the larger society and anything that would stand in the way of being heard or recognized.

33. s0liD1337, "2pac Talking about His Belief in God and Religion," YouTube, July 26, 2010, http://www.youtube.com/watch?v=MnmLl6Fm1MM&feature=youtube_gdata_player.
34. Pejjj, "Shock G Talking About 2Pac: Speech in Court," YouTube, May 29, 2008 (citing *Thug Angel*), http://www.youtube.com/watch?v=kbaf_OzA5pc&feature=youtube_gdata_player.

Ethic of Doubt

Being heard and recognized gets to the heart of hip-hop ethical frameworks. If one general statement might be made about why hip-hop emerged at all, it could be said that a group of young people was tired of being ignored and not heard, not recognized by social institutions that appeared to be more concerned with determining right and wrong than with actual people. Out of this need to be seen and heard, the ethic of rebellion took shape. But it was not the only ethical platform. Connected to the ethic of rebellion but more focused on a radical ongoing interrogation of the ideas and practices inherited from normative institutions emerged an **ethic of doubt**. Whereas an ethic of rebellion tends to push against society while also seeking to secure the "goods" associated with the larger society, an ethic-of-doubt platform can be thought of as *a nontraditional ethic that calls into question those things inherited from the social and cultural institutions of the larger society.*

This ethic of doubt is also **postmodern**, meaning it grows out of *an awareness that the motivations and methods used to make sense of the world come unraveled when tested*—a test offered over and over again by hip-hop culture. That is to say, this ethical platform works based on an underlying assumption that there is no Truth with a capital *T*; rather, truth is contextual and open to debate. Hence, this ethic of doubt calls into question the philosophical and religious foundations people use when constructing their ethics. Common, a well-known rapper and actor, expresses this postmodern sensibility in his verse on the track "The Truth."[35] In the song, Common highlights how religious and social institutions do not tell the truth, only time (in other words, his experience) does. People can lie; institutions can be

35. Common, "The Truth feat. Common and Talib Kweli," on Pharoahe Monch, *Internal Affairs*. Priority Records, 1999.

wrong or misguided in their assertions or ethical frameworks; and only time will be able to tell whether these people or institutions were more "right" or "wrong." Ethical concerns are determined through personal and collective histories, through awareness and analysis of change over time.[36] Common's point is not to suggest that ethics or "doing the right thing" should be abandoned, but rather to assert that his ethics (and his sense of what is real or right) will unfold from his own experiences and his understanding of those experiences.

Concerns and social issues like racism, homophobia, and poverty require hard questioning in order to produce useful action. As part of this process, blame has to be placed at the feet of those who are guilty of perpetuating injustice. Often, the culprits are traditional religious leaders and institutions, or at least, many religious leaders are deemed to perpetuate these social concerns. For instance, noting the "false prophets" who tell youth they are sinners, Common's verse from "The Truth" calls into question pastors and church leaders. For Common, these "vendors of hate," progenitors of human oppression have him battling "his own mind state," causing him and others to interrogate themselves as problems rather than solutions to problems. Yet Common's ethic of doubt calls this institutional ethical practice into question and says no to such detrimental mind games. For Common and this ethic of doubt, truth does not come from religion.[37] Similar in certain respects to those advancing an ethic of impossibility, Common and others like him produce ethics from recognition that because of the inability, the impossibility of religion to do proper work that it often claims to do, ethical platforms must develop apart from traditional religion. Religion prevents individuals from being able to look inward in a positive light. Through this ethical doubt, the "truth" is revealed.

36. Common with Adam Bradley, *One Day It'll All Make Sense* (New York: Atria, 2012), 57.
37. Common, "The Truth."

By this, figures like Common mean to expose the way religion and religious ethics get in their own way. That is to say, religion often flies in the face of its often-stated concerns for human growth, love, and acceptance. In this sense, rather than rebel, the ethic of doubt helps individuals sift through life strategies to determine what is useful and what is not.

Ethic of Embodiment and Style

The **ethic of embodiment and style** *relates the importance of personal style and artistic creativity to proper action.*[38] Philosopher Friedrich Nietzsche once wrote, "To 'give style' to one's character—a great and rare art! It is practiced by those who survey all the strengths and weaknesses of their nature and then fit them into an artistic plan until every one of them appears as art."[39] Few quotations better capture the ethic of embodiment and style, as artists adhering to it "survey" their "strengths and weaknesses" and respond to them through personal artistic style.

Within the ethic of embodiment and style, the body takes the role of the Bible as the foundation for ethical determinations. While in chapter two we discussed how hip-hop communities used dress to convey a message to the world, here we focus more on how style and dress are understood in terms of "doing the right thing." In this regard, bodies are "read" like the pages of Scripture.[40] Upon this awareness, bodies are registered as a blank canvas, an expanse of possibilities that play out through stylistic choices. And from these choices—who is the "freshest" or the "flyest"—communities are

38. Anthony B. Pinn, *Embodiment and the New Shape of Black Theological Thought* (New York: NYU Press, 2010), 138.
39. Friedrich Wilhelm Nietzsche, *The Gay Science: With a Prelude in Rhymes and an Appendix of Songs* (New York: Vintage, 1974).
40. Pinn, *Embodiment*, 22.

determined and sustained. Early examples of this within hip-hop include Adidas sneakers often worn with robust, ostentatious colors and laces meant to simultaneously signal inclusion in a community and yet uniqueness within that community. Here, ethics is aesthetics as it focuses on a need and demand to be recognized, where "bodies in time and space" meet up with "creative impulse[s]" that "allow for a full range of life pursuits."[41] That is to say, what we ought to do—the question of ethics—involves an answer tied to what one wears and how one moves through the world with style and flair.

With this particular ethical platform, attention shifts from what is said about action in the world to how one presents one's body as the main mode of "doing" in the world. It insists on uniqueness and personal style. Hence, ethics comes to be defined as the choices people make to fit into a group or community, as well as to stand out from that (or other) groups. Other examples include tattooing, the wearing of certain types of jewelry, creative hairstyles, and other artistic accessories, including gold or platinum "fronts" (metallic teeth coverings). "Jesus pieces" and crosses worn by hip-hop "heads" serve as a reminder that these hip-hop ethics are never (fully) disconnected from the institutional ethics discussed earlier in this chapter and moments of social injustice marking our social landscape. For example, these two—religious imagery and social injustice—blend together as rapper Plies recently shifted from a "Jesus Piece" to a "Trayvon Martin" piece. Having already written a tribute song to Trayvon Martin (itself making references to Christian commitments), Plies made a necklace bearing the face of Trayvon and wore it in tribute to him and his memory.[42] With this mode of ethics, "doing" involves modification of the body in some way, shape, or form. It has

---

41. This ethic of embodiment and style is inspired by Anthony Pinn's discussion of a hermeneutic of style found in ibid., 138.

42. See, for instance, Plies, Plies. *We Are Trayvon*, Atlantic/Slip-n-Slide, 2012; "Plies Chain Tribute to Trayvon Martin,," 2014, https://www.youtube.com/watch?v=ECGBcKG7wbA.

to do with the manner in which bodies occupying time and space with a particular "look" shape how they are perceived and ways in which they are approached and addressed. In a way, this third ethical platform is worn, carried on the body.

In the long run, these hip-hop ethical frameworks might offer insight into who is and is not recognized within Black Church ethical frameworks and in this process, might help black Christian communities to "do the right thing" when they engage hip-hop. To paraphrase cultural critic Michael Eric Dyson, understanding the similarities and differences between Black Church ethics and hip-hop ethics might help both communities bear witness to two of the most lasting and influential aspects of black culture—to see and hear each other.[43]

Ongoing Considerations

In cities across the United States, thousands of youngsters (often black and brown) are killed each year. For instance, in 2010, the U.S. murder rate of people aged ten to twenty-four was approximately 7.5 per 100,000. This alone is enough to make both black churches and members of the hip-hop community pause. These rates increased among males, jumping to 12.7 per 100,000, while African American rates skyrocketed to 28.8 murdered per 100,000.[44] In other words, the principal demographic popularly associated with hip-hop faces the threat of murder at rates disproportionate to an already problematic

43. Michael Eric Dyson, *Between God and Gangsta Rap: Bearing Witness to Black Culture* (Cary, NC: Oxford University Press, 1997).
44. Centers for Disease Control and Prevention, "Homicide Rates among Persons Aged 10–24 Years: United States, 1981–2010," *Morbidity and Mortality Weekly Report*, July 12, 2013, http://www.cdc.gov/mmwr/preview/mmwrhtml/mm6227a1.htm?s_cid=mm6227a1_w.

national average.[45] The social context that breeds rebellious, doubtful, and embodied ethics is tragic and in a literal sense death-dealing.

At the time of this writing, many in the United States are involved in a heated debate over gun control in the aftermath of the brutal murders that took place at Sandy Hook Elementary School on December 14, 2012. The very contentiousness of this debate exemplifies the violent society within which black Christians and hip-hop enthusiasts live. Yet intense interest in increased gun regulation stemming from tragedies such as Sandy Hook has not been matched by equal energy regarding African American and Latino young people murdered daily in places like Detroit and Chicago. What should be done to protect, to safeguard life? Both black churches and hip-hop communities note and respond to the ethical challenges of life in the United States, and they do so in ways that overlap but also conflict. What we have presented in this chapter entails a brief mapping of some of the ethical frameworks found within black churches and hip-hop communities. As we have presented these platforms, the issues addressed in earlier chapters shadow the conversation, in that ethics has something to do with the recognition of injustice and efforts to combat those circumstances inside and outside of churches, alike.

Mindful of what we provide in this chapter and what was said in earlier chapters, it should be evident that not only do both groups have much in common, but there is much that separates them, and this tension might offer fruitful points of conversation and connection. However, in the next chapter, we recognize that the discussion of hip-hop and black churches must extend beyond the

---

45. Amanda Paulson, "Youth Homicide Rate Hits 30-Year Low, but It's Not Good News for Everyone," *Christian Science Monitor*, July 16, 2013, http://www.csmonitor.com/USA/Society/ 2013/0716/Youth-homicide-rate-hits-30-year-low-but-it-s-not-good-news-for-everyone.

borders of the United States. Both are global, and in the next chapter, we tackle the scope and implications of this internationalization.

Study Questions

- The six ethical frameworks discussed here often overlap. Can you think of instances when you have made ethical decisions that were based on more than one of these frameworks working together?

- What would you consider an ethical failure? What framework discussed is guiding your understanding of "failure"?

- How can churches and hip-hop community members have more productive conversations about what to do about pressing social problems like racism, poverty, sexism, and homophobia?

- In what ways do concerns over recognition inform hip-hop communities and members of African American churches?

- How can the life and legacy of Tupac Shakur teach hip-hop and black churches something about how ethics are created and what those ethics should look like in twenty-first-century America?

8

Black Churches, Hip-Hop, and Globalization

Overall, the four sections of this chapter seek to unpack the global expansion of both the black church and hip-hop. The first section provides a comprehensive definition of globalization. The second section treats French hip-hop as a case analysis in that this cultural form will be explored in detail with the goal of making generalizations concerning the globalization of hip-hop culture. The third section explores globalization of the Black Church through the lens of African American foreign mission activity in Africa in general and West Africa in particular, and this brings the chapter full circle back to French hip-hop. Ultimately, this section reveals how African American missionary activity influenced the cultural form of hip-hop, specifically as displayed in French Christian hip-hop. In this way, French Christian hip-hop captures within its content and structure interconnections between hip-hop and the Black Church created by means of the dynamics and mechanisms of globalization. Finally, the last section discusses a few points worth considering when thinking about the ways in which globalization plays out beyond the issues raised in this chapter.

Defining Globalization

Emerging in popular use in business and political circles during the 1980s as a way to name the flow of capital across various countries around the globe, **globalization** is currently defined in terms of its economic, social, political, and cultural ramifications. In this regard, it speaks to the expansive web of exchanges of all sorts that cut across national borders and in this way merging the world. For the purpose of this chapter, **globalization** represents *accelerated flows or intensified connections—across national and other boundaries—of commodities, people, symbols, technology, images, information, and capital, as well as disconnections, exclusions, marginalization, and disposition.*[1] This definition stays true to the term's capitalist origin but also includes a social dimension.

Additionally, globalization seen in this way emphasizes three elements worth noting. First, globalization connects by forming links that may be integrative in that separate local realities are conjoined, creating a single entity. Or it links by way of forming networks of global interdependency, which is the second element of globalization.[2] These mutually dependent global alliances are both formed and maintained by the flows and connections presented in our definition. It is important to note that interdependency between participating parties does not always mean equal distribution. For example, the formation of global alliances, much like those contained within hip-hop and the Black Church, may lead to a relationship of interdependence that privileges one member over the other. This leads to marginalization and deliberate exclusion. Finally, globalization, in addition to creating connections and interdependent

1. Mwneda Ntarangwi, *East African Hip Hop: Youth, Culture, and Globalization* (Champaign: University of Illinois Press, 2009), 2.

2. Geoffrey B. Cockerham and William C. Cockerham, *Health and Globalization* (Cambridge: Polity, 2010), 10–11.

networks, is a process that in some cases leads to the creation of **glocal** products;[3] various examples of such products will be explored later in this chapter. These creative products take into consideration *global and local characteristics*—hence the term *glocal*. This process is representative of the connective nature of globalization. However, going glocal quite often leads to "disconnections, exclusions, and marginalization," as noted previously.

Hip-Hop and Globalization

In the foreword to *The Vinyl Ain't Final*, historian Robin D. G. Kelley speaks about the genealogy of hip-hop. He states:

> Contrary to recent media claims, hip hop hasn't "gone global." It has been *global*, or international at least, since its birth in the very local neighborhoods of South Bronx, Washington Heights, and Harlem. While the music, break-dancing, and graffiti writing that make up the components of hip hop culture are often associated with African-American urban youth, hip hop's inventors also included the sons and daughters of immigrants who had been displaced by the movement of *global* capital [emphasis added].[4]

Kelley goes on to establish connections between hip-hop pioneers like DJ Kool Herc and graffiti artist Taki 183 and their countries of origin, Jamaica and Greece, respectively. As discussed earlier, DJ Kool Herc innovated the way turntables and break beats were used at parties; however, Taki 183 is a mysterious figure most may not know. Taki 183 is one of the original taggers of the New York City subway system.[5] Kelley's insight allows him (Kelley) **to** recognize the presence of explicit interconnections within and between the local

3. Roland Robertson, "Glocalization: Time-Space and Homogeneity-Hetereogeneity," in *Global Modernities*, ed. Mike Featherstone, Scott Lash, and Roland Robertson (London: Sage, 1995).

4. Dipannita Basu and Sidney J. Lemmelle, *The Vinyl Ain't Final: Hip Hop and the Globalization of Black Popular Culture* (London: Pluto, 2006), vi.

5. Alan Light, ed., *The Vibe History of Hip-Hop* (New York: Three Rivers, 1999), 36–37.

terrains of the South Bronx, Washington Heights, and Harlem. In effect, Kelley makes the point that what we have been discussing is and has always been made from and within a global context.

More importantly, he acknowledges the presence of implicit transnational links embedded in the founding fabric of hip-hop. **Transnationalism** can be defined as *a localized phenomenon or product that developed under multi-national or multi-cultural (ethnic) influence.* The recognition of this global element in the foreword of an edited volume that focuses on the globalization of this cultural art form is important for a couple of reasons. First, it posits hip-hop genealogy as one characterized by a localized form of transnationalism. That is, this cultural form's origin can be traced back to local neighborhoods of New York City, but its participants represent multiple nationalities. The local, then, is not a singular American representation but multidimensional in regard to the participation of various ethnicities in the movement. Secondly, Kelley's acknowledgment of the international roots of hip-hop establishes New York City as the point of origin. It is from this locale that the movement globally expands to countries like Cuba, China, Turkey, Nigeria, and France. Just as Americans come from all places, such is the genealogy of the cultural product of hip-hop born in America.

When we examine the development of hip-hop in countries outside of the United States, the three elements of globalization (creating integrative links, interdependent networks, and glocal products) are easily identified. What will follow is a case study analysis of hip-hop culture in France—specifically, an examination of the introduction and maturation of French rap music. This analysis will provide an example of the progressive globalization of hip-hop.

One of the reasons why French hip-hop is important to this conversation is that outside of the United States, France places second in the global sales of hip-hop music. The current-day notoriety of hip-hop stems from very humble beginnings. Surprisingly, one of the initial contributors to the hip-hop movement in France is none other than the "Master of Records," Afrika Bambaataa. He is primarily known as a pioneer of hip-hop and the founding father of the Zulu Nation, but little has been written about Bambaataa's involvement in the globalization of hip-hop, particularly in France. Yet in 1984, he formed a French chapter of the Zulu Nation. Bambaataa discusses the global spread of his organization in a 1998 interview in which he notes that the Zulu Nation "started in the black and Latino community, and then it started spreading out to the different communities, throughout the tri-state area, and then throughout the United States, and then throughout the world."[6] While break-dancing is the first hip-hop element to enter into the cultural landscape of France, it is through the Zulu Nation that Bambaataa exposed the youth of Parisian *banlieues* (suburbs) to hip-hop as a way of life.

French rap during the first decade of its inception adopted the styles of African American rappers. This mimicry period, however, wanes at the beginning of the 1990s, when up-and-coming rappers decide to assess their lyrics in light of their cultural context. Rappers like Assassin and Ministère AMER acknowledge that the social conditions of U.S. rappers do not quite align with those they face in France. For example, the former speaks candidly about how the conjoining of their ethnicity and ancestry (familial country of origin) with other social factors like economic disparities serve as markers that marginalize them within French society. The acknowledgment of such discrimination would become the building blocks for the formation of what is known as the hard-core movement. Hard-core artists are adamant about separating themselves from American

6. Bill Brewster and Frank Broughton, *The Record Players: DJ Revolutionaries* (New York: Grove/Atlantic, 2011).

gangsta rap. It is important to state here that French hard-core hip-hop artists have a stereotypical perception of gangsta rap, which is quite different from the one that was presented in chapter two of this book. **Hard-core rap** accordingly is *a vehicle to popularize and vent the anger and the frustrations of many disadvantaged or sometimes mistreated individuals and to defend the cause of the poorest and least socially integrated segments of French society.*[7] For its advocates, hard-core rap espouses a sociopolitical ideology that moves beyond the privileging of drive-by shootings, slinging dope, and gaining material wealth at any expense. In this way, hard-core rap signals one of many attempts by French rappers to escape the adoption period and move into a period of appropriation in which artists maintain some American stylistic elements but not at the expense of the implementation of local social, political, and ethnic contexts. In short, French hip-hop goes glocal.

Not only does the glocalization of French hip-hop set it apart from its American counterpart, but the presence of ethnic and religious diversity adds to the uniqueness of this cultural art form in France. French rappers like Lord Kossity, Red One, and MC Solaar represent multiple ethnic groups who are either immigrants or the children of those who immigrated from the Caribbean and Africa, respectively. Also, women MCs like Diam (Greek and French) and Princess Aniès (Taiwanese and French) represent populations of mixed heritage living in Paris. Historian Charles Tshimanga establishes a connection between the presence of these multiple ethnic groups, globalization, and identity politics in France. "Ongoing globalization," he writes, "continues to bring different cultures and ethnic minorities to the banks of the Seine. Their arrival in France challenges the very

---

7. André J. M. Prévos, "Postcolonial Popular Music in France: Rap Music and Hip-Hop Culture in the 1980s and 1990s," in *Global Noise: Rap and Hip Hop Outside the USA*, ed. Tony Mitchell (Indianapolis: Wesleyan, 2002), 44.

concept of nation-state and its identity and the significance of transnational cultural values."[8] Identity politics, then, becomes a central theme in the lyrics of many French rappers. For example, French rapper Kery James—the son of Haitian parents— in 2012 released a song entitled "Lettre à la République." (Letter to the Republic). He exclaims that French politicians are "pillagers of wealth, murderers of Africans, torturers of Algerians . . . the colonial past is yours, you chose to link your history to ours."[9] James offers a critique of the French government. More importantly, however, he recognizes Algerians and their French-born children in particular and Africans in general as marginalized members of French society. Africans here represent those of Arab ancestry from North Africa and those of African descent from the Caribbean. For him, they are the target of societal oppressive forces, quite often seen in the form of economic disparities and violence. James's lyrical protest laced with identity politics caused a major stir in the French political arena. The root of this tension goes beyond his inclusion of identity politics in that his Islamic religious orientation played a role in the negative perception of the movement by some political and social circles in France.

Religious diversification, much like that of ethnic diversity, adds to the uniqueness of French hip-hop. For instance, La Fouine and Canardo are hard-core rappers of Moroccan descent who lace their rhymes with Islam, while Diam and Abd Al Malik symbolize a growing number of hip-hop artists converting to Islam. The former converted to Sunni Islam, while the latter found solace in Sufism.

8. Charles Tshimanga, "Let the Music Play: The African Diaspora, Popular Culture, and National Identity in Contemporary France," in *Identity and Uprising in Contemporary France*, ed. Charles Tshimanga, Didier Gondola, and Peter J. Bloom (Bloomington: Indiana University Press, 2009), 271.

9. Hishaam Aidi, "Don't Panik! Islam and Europe's 'Hip Hop Wars,'" *Aljazeera*, June 5, 2012, http://www.aljazeera.com/indepth/opinion/2012/06/20126310151835171.html.

Sufism, according to Abd Al Malik, is "about love and the awareness of the spiritual nature of every human being."[10] He expresses this way of life in both his music and his autobiography, entitled *Sufi Rapper: The Spiritual Journey of Abd Al Malik*. While Sunni and Sufi Islam compose a significant portion of the religious landscape included in French hip-hop, other religious sensibilities, including that of **pharaohism**, a term coined by André Prévos, also find expression in this medium.[11] This term speaks to *a religious ideology premised on mythological images of Egyptian pharaohs and systems of numerology.* The French hip-hop group IAM (Imperial Asiatic Men) is a promoter of this particular religious form: "IAM's pharaohism is the clearest attempt so far at the creation of a new type of religious space, but not a church, at least in the sense that the word has come to be accepted by compilers of dictionaries. This new religious space is closer to a type of messianic space organized by the symbolic representations outlined by the artists."[12] IAM offers fans another religious option—one that moves beyond mere architectural boundaries and affords a more fluid conception of religion.

Rappers who embrace the Christian faith also diversify the landscape of French hip-hop. LSD, Drick-C, and the trio group Dernier Rempart (Last Stand) are only a few examples of the growing number of hip-hop artists who label themselves Christian rappers. The growth of French Christian rap is due to the presence of black Pentecostal churches, such as the Deeper Life Bible Church and the Redeemed Christian Church of God, in *banlieues* north of Paris.[13] It

---

10. Carmel Wroth, "French Rap Star Abd Al Malik Inspires Change among Inner City Youth," *Odewire*, April 1, 2009, http://www.theoptimist.com/channel2/french-rap-star-abd-al-malik-inspires-change-among-inner-city-youth/french-rap-star-abd-al-malik-inspires-change-among-inner-city-youth.
11. Prévos, "Postcolonial Popular Music in France," 49.
12. Ibid.
13. Baptiste Coulmont, "Capitals and Networks: A Sociology of Paris' Black Churches" (paper presented at conference on African Churches in Europe, Brussels, December 2010).

is important to note that "black" is utilized in the French context to symbolize the actual color of the individual. Thus, black churches in the Parisian context are spaces occupied by African Christians or those of African descent, including African Americans. Parisian black Pentecostal spaces and the surrounding *banlieues* where they are located serve as catalysts driving the French Christian rap scene. These *banlieues* are characterized by poverty, crime, and violence, and Christian rappers, much like their secular counterparts, protest these deplorable conditions. For example, members of Dernier Rempart on their latest album, *Rien n'est impossible* (Nothing Is Impossible) rap about suicide, sexuality, and economic hardship. However, the Lord, whom they refer to in French as *l'Éternel*, is the driving force behind surviving life's turmoil generally and societal woes. They pay homage to the Lord's helping hand in songs like "L'eternel est mon berger" (The Lord Is My Shepherd) and "Unité, Combat, Victoire" (Unity, Fight, Victory)."

In the end, French rappers, whether they profess a specific religious identity or discuss societal ills facing those of African descent in a hard-core manner, are universally deconstructing and reconstructing a more complicated depiction of French identity. For these French hip-hop artists, it is time for France, in the words of rapper Abd Al Malik, "to realize that diversity is part of French identity."[14] Hip-hop in France acts as a vehicle by means of which members of marginalized populations articulate views on issues such as identity, economic disparities, political injustices, and social inequalities. French artists create a glocalized version of this cultural art form, which is representative of "a distinctive syncretic manifestation of

---

14. Scott Sayare, "A Rapper and Poet Pushes for a New French Identity of Inclusion," *New York Times*, August 24, 2012, http://www.nytimes.com/2012/08/25/world/europe/rapper-abd-al-malik-pushes-for-new-french-identity.html?pagewanted=all&_r=0.

African American influences and local [French] indigenous elements."[15]

The Black Church and Globalization

Like hip-hop, the Black Church displays characteristics of globalization identified earlier in this chapter. Specifically, the global spread of the Black Church illustrates how globalization acts as a connective process joining local communities in varying geographical spaces (e.g., ghettos of the United States and *banlieues* of France) and, at times, in a transnational manner. To examine the manifestation of these predicates of globalization at work in the Black Church, this section reconstructs a historical map of its role in foreign missionary efforts, with a specific focus on Africa.

On February 6, 1820, Daniel Coker along with ninety other African Americans boarded the *Elizabeth* with hopes of spreading the gospel to Africa. That same year, his work began with the organization of the first African Methodist Episcopal (AME) church in Sierra Leone. Over the next eighty years, the AME church's presence would extend beyond Sierra Leone to locations such as Liberia and South Africa. This expansion was not without its critics. For instance, Bishop Daniel A. Payne opposed missionary activities in Africa for practical reasons. He maintained that the "A.M.E. Church did not have the financial resources to support adequately an African mission, even in just one country."[16] Whether endorsed or opposed, the AME Church did not represent the only African American Christians to venture into Africa. The African Methodist Episcopal Zion Church sent missionaries to Liberia in 1876. African American Baptists followed suit in 1883, when William Colley and five

---

15. Mitchell, *Global Noise*, 3.
16. Stephen Ward Angell, *Bishop Henry McNeal Turner and African-American Religion in the South* (Knoxville: University of Tennessee Press, 1992), 136.

members of the black Baptist Foreign Mission Convention headed to Liberia. By 1900, the Baptists had established missionary stations in west, south, and central Africa. Combined, by the turn of the century, these major constituents of the Black Church "sponsor[ed] seventy-six missions in Africa and educate[d] thirty African students."[17]

Finally, in 1926, at the insistence of Mother Elizabeth "Lizzie" Robinson, the Church of God in Christ (COGIC) formed the Home and Foreign Mission Board for the purpose of joining this push to "save" the continent of Africa. It is important to note the instrumental role women play in COGIC African missions. Not only were women like Beatrice Lott, Dorothy Webster, and Elizabeth White responsible for breaking missionary ground in Africa, but by 1960, COGIC, due to the tireless efforts of these women, had built three churches, appointed a residential bishop to serve over the Liberian mission complex, and established schools along with a clinic. Currently, COGIC boasts over 132 churches in South Africa alone. Additionally, COGIC has established several African districts including the Southern Nigeria Ecclesiastical Jurisdiction. Institutional networks such as these represent concrete realities of globalization. Specifically, these relationships are interdependent in that they are not one-way but represent a "mutual engagement on a global scale."[18]

Ethicist Peter Paris, in his renowned work *The Social Teaching of Black Churches*, offers an explanation for this early and continual interest in the evangelization of Africa by African Americans, which is worth quoting at length: "A major impetus for their involvement

---

17. Ogbu U. Kalu, "Early African American Charismatic Missions and Pentecostal-Charismatic Engagements with the African Motherland," in *Afro-Pentecostalism: Black Pentecostal and Charismatic Christianity in History and Culture*, ed. Amos Young and Estrelda Y. Alexander (New York: New York University Press, 2011), 213.

18. Dale T. Irvin, "Meeting beyond These Shores: Black Pentecostalism, Black Theology, and the Global Context," in Young and Alexander, *Afro-Pentecostalism*, 240.

in foreign missions was to help civilize Africa, which they thought would contribute significantly to racial uplift both symbolically and politically. We see here a striking similarity between the task of bringing up the race from the degradation of slavery and that of bringing Africa out of 'heathenism' and 'uncivilized' culture. The theological and *ethical* substance of their foreign mission enterprise thus differed little from that of their white counterparts."[19] Paris's explanation highlights the ways social conceptions of race served as one of the primary reasons African Americans participated in the evangelization of Africa. In this way, race (especially the relational concept of race as treated in chapter three) connects people of African descent living in different geographical locales. Mission efforts such as those outlined briefly in this chapter highlight race, Christianity, and the connective function of globalization.

In addition to racial affinity, missionaries of the Black Church were driven by an ethical obligation, which is again premised on race. They have sought, as presented in the previous chapter on ethics, "to do the right thing" by introducing Christianity to their African brethren as a part of their divine obligation and calling. According to Paris, this ethical impetus to free Africans from the chains of "heathenism" places the motives of African American Christians in the same category as those of "their white counterparts." Unlike whites who often engaged in foreign missions that preserved and helped to create the system of white supremacy, African American Christians viewed their missionary work as executing God's will to uplift black people. Known as the "Blackman's Burden," this sacred responsibility calls for some African American missionaries to, in the words of Ogbu Kalu, "make Africa a Garden of Eden again and to enable black people to prove a sense of worth and ability."[20]

19. Peter Paris, *The Social Teaching of the Black Churches* (Minneapolis: Fortress Press, 1985), 79.
20. Kalu, "Early African American Charismatic Missions," 212–13.

In addition to these motives for missions, a more practical reason for the missionary activities of African Americans must be considered. Some African American Christians sought sociopolitical and religious freedom in Africa. That is to say, they saw movement to Africa as a way to escape the secondhand citizenry they faced in the United States. For example, African American women such as Amanda Smith decided to abandon their roles as domestic servants in order to "work among her brothers and sisters in Africa."[21]

As was witnessed with hip-hop, there is a performative dimension to the globalization of religious culture. So left to examine is the nature of religious expression encouraged by missionaries. In other words, there were various reasons for undertaking missions, and there were various ways in which proper religious devotion was to be expressed. While COGIC missionaries, like their counterparts, sought to utilize Christianity as a means to garner respectability for the race as a whole, the evangelization of Africa also entailed a new space for religious expression.[22] For COGIC, devotion to the faith at home and abroad conjoins sanctification with the evidential presence of the Holy Spirit, which is manifested through practices such as glossolalia (i.e., speaking in tongues) and dance. Initially, early COGIC missionaries desired to curtail the dance activities of Africans. Not recognizing the spiritual significance of African dance, African American COGIC missionaries labeled it a profane, sexualized form of movement.

Eventually, a compromise was reached. Africans kept dance, but missionaries supplied a Christian rationale for dance. According to COGIC founder, Bishop Charles H. Mason,

21. Calvin White Jr., *The Rise to Respectability: Race, Religion, and the Church of God in Christ* (Fayetteville: University of Arkansas Press, 2012), 80.
22. Kalu, "Early African American Charismatic," 212–13.

The people of God do not dance as the world dances, but are moved by the Spirit of God. So you can see that it is all in the Spirit of God and the glory of God. It is not to satisfy the lust of the flesh, or the carnal appetite as the world dances, but only to glory God and satisfy the soul. The world dances of the world, about the world and to the world. The children of God dance of God, for God and to the praise and glory of His name. They have the joy of the Spirit of the Lord in them.[23]

Mason's rationale is twofold. First, he provides a justification for COGIC's inclusion of dance in its doctrine and ritual activities. Second, Mason's recognition of a distinction between secular, indigenous dance and sacred, Christian dance allows "African converts to continue the practice of dancing, but only as a sign of the reception of the Holy Spirit."[24] In short, African dance becomes Christianized. This Christianized African dance, similar to French hip-hop, represents a glocal product. Specifically, it combines a local African "indigenous" element of dance with a global Pentecostal "holy" dance.

The glocalization of African dance is only one example of how the Black Church missionary enterprise in general and African American Pentecostal missionary activities in particular influenced African Christianity. There are also musical developments that merit some consideration. We highlight for this reason **hiplife** and **praiseco** as examples of glocal cultural products created through the establishment of global ties between African Americans and Africans. Both are products of the 1990s. Hiplife is *a syncretic mix of highlife (a hybrid musical form composed of jazz and Christian hymns) and hip-hop.* Hiplife music can be heard throughout West Africa; however, it is mainly associated with Ghana. In her work *Hiplife in Ghana*, cultural studies scholar Halifu Osumare highlights the relational ties

---

23. White, *The Rise to Respectability*, 89.
24. Ibid.

between global and local elements found in hiplife. "Hiplife's story," she explains, "is one revealing tension between *globalization* and *localization*, neocolonialism in today's transnational capitalism, and hip-hop's youth agency that facilitates young Ghanaians finding their voice within a traditional society" [emphasis added].[25] Thus, hiplife is a glocal platform that allows youth to articulate their political and social thoughts within Ghanaian society as well as in Nigeria and Senegal.

Like hiplife, praiseco *incorporates Christian elements with indigenous music; but, unlike the former, the latter specifically infuses Pentecostal gospel music with African sensibilities.* Also noteworthy is the fact that praiseco, a West African Pentecostal musical form (also accompanied by a specific form of dance), also bridges hip-hop sensibilities. It conjoins an "African appropriation of the gospel" that was introduced by "the charismatic missionary vision" of African American Pentecostals with the African American musical form of hip-hop.[26] No longer did "the born again Christian need to patronize the club house because Christian music and praise songs were using the same rhythm and words."[27] Praiseco blurs lines of distinction between sacred and profane (i.e., popular) music. The manner in which West African Pentecostals have incorporated secular hip-hop into its sacred musical structure offers yet another example of glocalization.

Not only are the 1990s an important decade to consider in the formation of musical glocal products like those of hiplife and praiseco, but also during this time period, various West African missionary enterprises established themselves in the United States and Europe. African Pentecostals in particular established churches in both the

---

25. Halifu Osumare, *The Hiplife in Ghana: West African Indigenization of Hip-Hop* (New York: Palgrave Macmillan, 2012), 2.
26. Kalu, "Early African American Charismatic Missions," 211, 213.
27. Ogbu U. Kalu, "Holy Praiseco: Negotiating Sacred and Popular Music and Dance in African Pentecostalism," *Pneuma* 32 (2010): 36.

United States and Europe. For example, the Nigerian-based Redeemed Christian Church of God (RCCG) opened parishes in American cities such as Miami, Sacramento, and Chicago, as well in European countries like Germany, England, and France. Regarding the latter, currently there are over twenty RCCG parishes scattered throughout Paris proper and in the suburbs of the city. The rapid establishment of these ecclesiastical spaces is due to what RCCG leaders call "reverse missions."[28] According to these leaders, "The rise of African churches in the northern continents is a reversal of the Christian mission because Africans, once the beneficiaries of the Western Christian missionary enterprise [including Black Church foreign missions], are now evangelizing the former heartlands of Christianity."[29]

The churches resulting from reverse missionary activities are concrete representations of the connective function of globalization. They symbolize the flow of Christian ideas—like those introduced by African American Christians—across geographical boundaries. This flow, in turn, creates transnational and interdependent networks. But even more, churches like those of the RCCG, especially in France, are conduits for glocal musical forms like praiseco.[30] The exchanges within these areas are intriguing because they highlight the ways in which the growing presence of African Pentecostal churches like the RCCG has affected hip-hop and how French Christian rappers have in turn integrated into their lyrics a Pentecostal-charismatic form of Christianity. For instance, Manou Bolomik, who is known as the "pastor rapper," incorporates charismatic Christianity into his music. Songs like "Un seul nom" (One Name) and "Ô Lord" posit

28. Richard Burgess, Kim Knibbe, and Anna Quaas, "Nigerian-Initiated Pentecostal Churches as a Social Force in Europe: The Case of the Redeemed Christian Church of God," *PentecoStudies* 9, no. 1 (2010): 103.

29. Ibid.

30. Tshimanga, "Let the Music Play," 252.

Jesus as a guide and a source of power for those seeking to lead a sanctified, holy life. Regarding this approach, Manou states, "I talk about God and Jesus, but especially the choices they give us to do."[31] He goes on to say, "I speak to a rising generation of young people in France who feel bad about themselves."[32] In addition to spreading charismatic Christianity to French youth, some Christian rappers integrate musical forms like praiseco into the stylistic structure of their songs. Elements of praiseco, for instance, find expression in the music of rap group Leader Vocal (Vocal Leader). The songs "Jazzolude" and "Funkylude," on the group's latest CD, entitled *L'odeur du sang face B* (The Smell of Blood Side B), combine elements of jazz, funk, Pentecostal gospel music, and secular hip-hop.

Ongoing Considerations

At this point, the chapter comes full circle in that French Christian hip-hop is a product of globalization that points to the establishment of global/transnational networks (African American missions and African reverse missions) and glocal products (black Pentecostal-influenced Africanized Christianity, hiplife, and praiseco). To this end, French Christian hip-hop contains within its DNA a genomic map (record of inheritable traits) that provides a preliminary outline of how globalization plays out in both churches and hip-hop.

While the formation of glocal creations and global networks represent similarities between the globalization of the Black Church and hip-hop, there is also one major difference worth noting. Scholar of hip-hop and religious studies Elonda Clay, in an essay entitled "Subtle Impact," touches on how this difference plays out in the Black Church. She states, "The church has historically participated in

31. Patrice Sanchez, "Pau: Le pasteur qui fait des concerts rap AVEC Jésus," *Sud Quest*, March 28, 2013.
32. Ibid.

black people's struggle for economic, educational, and environmental justice. In order to continue this ministry into the twenty-first century, . . . the Black Church will need to search for ways to offer a fresh and authentic witness in communities impacted by globalization."[33] The Black Church, according to Clay, must be more relevant. This involves possessing a sense of elasticity that will allow the Black Church, much like French hip-hop, to act as a glocal product, not just a contributor to the actualization of glocal creations. French hip-hop, unlike the Black Church as it stands, possesses a malleability that allows it to act as a cultural form bending and shaping itself in accordance with various communities of concern.

The question confronting black churches, particularly if they take seriously the reach of hip-hop, involves an interrogation of their traditions and practices that either help or hinder their ability to talk beyond their walls and social customs. Within hip-hop, there is a similar question demanding attention: What does it mean for hip-hop culture to extend and speak beyond one particular geographic context? As black churches confront challenges to identity and function as a consequence of globalization, hip-hop culture likewise must confront and consider the nature and impact of its global reach, which includes the creation of glocal products that possess characteristics of both hip-hop and the Black Church.

33. Elonda Clay, "Subtle Impact: Technology Trends and the Black Church," *Journal of the ITC* 31 (2003–2004): 155 and 174.

Study Questions

- List and discuss three elements associated with globalization.

- The 1870s are known as the golden period of Black Church missionary activity in Africa. What is the connection between the missionary activity of African American Christians and the eventual formation of glocal products like praiseco music?

- What are some similarities and differences between U.S. hip-hop and French hip-hop?

- What is the primary difference between globalization and glocalization? How does this difference play out in hip-hop and the Black Church?

9

A Relationship between Black Churches and Hip Hop?

While we have presented the perspectives of black churches and hip-hop, mostly in the form of rap music, on a variety of timely issues, we have not brought them into formal conversation. That is, we have provided an introductory sense of how both respond to these issues, but we have not done this in an explicitly comparative way. Our goal has been to provide useful information that readers might then use to bring hip-hop and Christian religious communities together within their own contexts, to whatever extent they deem useful. This book, in that sense, is a guide—a source of information, by definition—as opposed to being a statement on how black churches and hip-hop culture should interact and what should be desired as the outcome of that interaction. Thus far, we have not provided a blueprint concerning how black churches and hip-hop culture might foster useful synergies, nor have we wrestled with the plausibility of sustained interaction between the two.

While not pretending to provide that type of blueprint, we do want to offer some thoughts concerning the plausibility of relationship—mutually beneficial exchange and partnership—

between religious organizations such as black churches and hip-hop culture. These reflections are meant to give some sense of what might be at stake in forging that type of interaction between the two, and what barriers to such a relationship might exist. In this way, this chapter summarizes much of what has been said in earlier pages and examines whether hip-hop and the Black Church can be in relationship. As previous chapters have shown, hip-hop, in numerous ways, is more than a generational difference in how young people encounter and interact with the world. While some baby boomers may not get it, hip-hop is more than culturally superficial practices and productions. Rather, it, like Black Church teachings and practices, is a way of life for many, a means by which to view the world and act in accordance with that vision. Yet, as is the case with black churches placed in numerous competing denominations, not even this vision and the accompanying praxis of hip-hop culture are singular. Instead, there are various ways to embrace hip-hop, and there are numerous paths through hip-hop culture traveled by adherents around the globe.

It would be years after hip-hop's initial success, before people within Black Church culture concerned themselves with it as anything more than a negative challenge to moral and ethical sensibilities that were assumed to have sustained black communities for centuries. We do not recall very many ministers pushing themselves and their congregations to embrace the challenge and potentialities lodged in the twists, turns, and lyrical complexities of hip-hop culture until a few years back. Ministers like Rev. Efrem Smith cut against the grain in their high regard for hip-hop and its potential to transform the church.[1] Still, black churches were also

---

1. See: Efrem Smith and Phil Jackson. *The Hip-Hop Church: Connecting with the Movement Shaping Our Culture* (Downers Grove, IL: InterVarsity, 2012). See also http://www.efremsmith.com/category/blog/about/, accessed October 17, 2013.

slow to embrace other cultural innovations (e.g., gospel music and casual dress), fearing that doing so would open them to immoral behavior, yet they came around. So too, black churches have slowly altered their relationship to hip-hop culture. In short, times have changed, and now a turn toward hip-hop as a source of church renewal is a serious consideration.

There is no doubt that positive change in light of pressing historical issues is a hallmark of black churches at their best. One need only reflect, for instance, on the impact of the social gospel on black Christianity. Perhaps this is one way to unpack theologically the gospel bluegrass tune "Let the Church Roll On." Gospel bluegrass is a form of music with roots that reach into Appalachia as well as African American musical aesthetics. Often related to country music, gospel bluegrass speaks to Christian experience and commitment. In this particular song, the lyrics speak to the idea that the church is more than the sum of its parts. If particular church leaders, such as deacons, do not behave in accordance with God's standards, they must be dismissed so that the church can be all it is meant to be. One, by extension, could argue that embrace of hip-hop is another of those necessary developments—a new way of being in line with the will of God—that must be endorsed. If some fail to do so, well, "let the church roll on" without them.

For many churches with an aging membership, a productive relationship or embrace of hip-hop culture is a lifeline. This more-open approach to hip-hop culture, particularly rap music, is a far cry from earlier and graphic denouncements by figures such as Rev. Dr. Calvin Butts. As readers will recall, Butts in 1993 responded to explicit lyrics in rap music through a public protest during which he was prepared to steamroll over CDs to prove his point that violence (of any kind) in rap music would not be tolerated. He did not use the steamroller, but the implication was enough to make his point. It may seem incongruous that Butts, a Christian pastor, fought violent imagery in music with a ritual act of destruction; however, is not the basic message of the Christian faith tied to the violent death of a prophet—the death of Jesus the Christ? Mindful of this, Reverend Butts's threat of violence to safeguard spiritual well-being is not too far off of the basic message of the gospel: new claims to life come through the violent death of an innocent figure. Nonetheless, this is nuance, and it does not do much to explain why a violent act against hip-hop would have been the moral and ethical approach. A better way is possible: in place of a visceral response framed through rigid morality, ministers and scholars mentioned in the other chapters of this book suggest engagement, cooperation, as a more useful approach.

Bending to Embrace

Again, engagement between musical forms and black Christianity is old, dating back to a struggle over the correctness of spirituals, or what Bishop Henry McNeal Turner of the African Methodist Episcopal Church labeled "cornfield ditties," over against more socially comfortable hymns.[2] This process of conflict continued through the troubled relationship between black Christian socio-theological sensibilities and the gospel music, with churches fearing the sway of the blues-influenced gospel music might create an opening in churches for other worldly (and devil-influenced) activities and behaviors. In each case (and the list of examples could continue), black churches were confronted with theological and ritual restructuring as a matter of continued relevance and appeal. They were faced with new cultural developments and new

2. See Henry McNeal Turner, *Respect Black: The Writings and Speeches of Henry McNeal Turner* (New York: Arno, 1971).

technologies that could, as they believed, enhance their mission or result in their demise.

Hip-hop is the most recent example of this dilemma. In a word: if you rap it, will they come and bring glory to God? Or will they come and cause confusion and a loss of righteousness? Such a dilemma! Yet ministers such as Marlon Hall are confident hip-hop offers a transformative moment: "No phenomenon has the potential to mirror the gospel of Christ like Hip Hop. The church of Christ and the Hip Hop movement share a passion for human interest and sensitivity to human pain. They have an influence that stretches like a rubber band beyond cultural contexts, continents, and time. When it comes to human development, they have a connection that is indivisible and a future that is undeniable."[3]

Wrestling with this challenge is the stuff of legend in many church circles, and stories concerning personal engagement with musical intolerance abound. Churches are forced to confront a question: What of hip-hop speaks to the core of the Christian faith? Some undoubtedly argued that spirituals, hymns, or gospel music give glory to God and are theologically in line with the gospel message. Perhaps this is one reason theologian James Cone could argue that the blues are secular spirituals.[4] But is this the case with hip-hop? some Christians ask, with images of gangsta rappers haunting them.

Whether the conversation is about the spirituals, gospel, or hip-hop, when it's time for churches to absorb them, there is a protective turn whereby the more troubling dimensions of the new musical form's worldview are contained and rendered of little consequence. This entails a theological safeguard against the more troubling challenges to the Christian faith. For instance, some churches

3. Cheryl Kirk-Duggan and Marlon Hall, *Wake Up: Hip Hop Christianity and the Black Church* (Louisville: Abingdon, 2011), 4.
4. James H. Cone, *The Spirituals and the Blues* (Maryknoll, NY: Orbis, 1992).

concerned with hip-hop might limit consideration to obviously Christian modalities of rap music. But what of the larger cultural ethos out of which even Christian rap emerges? Can it be so easily dissected and removed from the larger culture of hip-hop?

Popular artists like the late Tupac Shakur, whose ideological leanings call into question the safe assumptions of black Christian moral sensitivities, cannot be so easily absorbed into church thought and activity. Even when one, as Michael Eric Dyson does, projects Tupac Shakur's sensibilities as a marginal and prophetic take on the Christian faith, his theological platform raises substantial concerns. One might agree with Dyson, in that "it is a central moral contention of Christianity that God may be disguised in the clothing—and maybe even the rap—of society's most despised members."[5] Yet what does one do, for instance, with Tupac's celebration of the "Black Jesuz" who serves as the patron saint of "Thugs"? This is a saint from the 'hood who condones the thug's raw lifestyle rather than critiquing it. Does the core of Tupac's theological position, the Black Jesuz, challenge at a fundamental level the core of the black Christian commitment? Is there a christological dissonance at play here that prevents absorption of more troubling but no less religious modalities of rap music? That is to say, can one use Tupac Shakur's music to praise the Lord? Does his musical autobiography serve as a proper testimony of God's goodness and of grace? To this end, it seems fitting to conclude with the rebellious words of a thug that are cast at churches but equally applicable to hip-hop: "If the churches [and hip-hop] took half the money that they was making and gave it back to the community, we'd be 'ight."[6]

5. Michael Eric Dyson, *Holler if You Hear Me: Searching for Tupac Shakur* (New York: Basic Civitas, 2001), 209.
6. See Eddie S. Glaude Jr., *In a Shade of Blue: Pragmatism and the Politics of Black America* (Chicago: University of Chicago Press, 2007).

Here's the point: what is important is not so much what church leaders think is appropriate within hip-hop culture—what they select and what they leave behind. More important is the musical taste of the community churches seek to bring into the fold. If the idea is to utilize hip-hop in Christian practice as a way to increase black churches' appeal to young adults, churches must acknowledge that the musical tastes of this desired audience include more than Christian rap. In a word, the young people sought by churches will typically bear in their cultural memories an expansive understanding of rap music that is not limited to biblical lessons and moral pronouncements. Those who limit their consumption of rap to Christian modalities are probably already in the church.

It may be the case that any relationship between black churches and hip-hop will involve forced Christianization of a cultural form, or the placing of a certain theological stamp on a culture not always friendly toward church theology. This is a hard point for churches to accept, although we do not know that it really matters much to hip-hop culture, where the margins of social existence are a familiar and comfortable home.

Cultural Mappings

Hip-hop as a culture involves a mapping of reality, complete with signs, symbols, vocabulary, grammar, style, and so on. It presents a particular picture of the world (worldview) that is at times gritty and without the comfort of a sure sense of progress so prevalent in many church circles. This understanding of the world, from our perspective, is not so easily transferred to church settings, which have their own cultural context. It is not easy, but we are not suggesting it is impossible.

While both Black Church culture and hip-hop culture are concerned with the creation of ways to acknowledge and celebrate life, they differ in some significant ways. For example, Black Church culture assumes a faith-based reading of events, a posture toward the world that often, as philosopher of religion Eddie Glaude has noted, fails to fully appreciate the tragic nature of life. In contrast, hip-hop culture is often aggressively attuned to the tragic dimensions of existence, at times to the point of despair. Black churches often argue, "God is on the throne, and all is well," but hip-hop in the form of rap music is not always convinced there is merit to this assumption.

As we have noted elsewhere in this volume, the styles of Black Church culture and hip-hop culture intend to make visible black bodies beyond the confinements of sensory-based discrimination, but with differing levels of comfort with moral ambiguity. Hip-hop culture might be to Black Church culture what some black literature's raw and gritty depiction of life was to black uplift literature and its moral arrangements. Think in terms of Harlem Renaissance graphic depictions of desire for inclusion in U.S. society unfulfilled over against the tales of respectability lodged in slave narratives. It is this struggle for inclusion within a society hard-pressed to grant it that Harlem Renaissance writer Langston Hughes experienced when lamenting deferred dreams.[7]

In significant ways, hip-hop culture and its influence raise challenges that cut to the core of how we perceive and discuss the importance and beauty of black bodies. While black churches believe beauty in human history exists as a reflection of divine beauty, hip-hop culture's influences and embodied, stylistic representations and ideas of beauty often say something very different. One sees this, for example, in the paintings of Jean-Michel Basquiat, a graffiti artist turned art world darling during the 1980s. As art historian Richard Powell notes, Basquiat's tendency toward the presentation

7. Langston Hughes, "Harlem," available at Poetry Foundation: Poems and Poets, http://www.poetryfoundation.org/poem/175884, accessed May 14, 2014.

of body organs on the exterior of black figures was meant as a critique of racism and the superficial nature of U.S. existence.[8] He painted the body exposed, unprotected, and unreal in a way that runs contrary to traditional Black Church theological understandings and the construction of black bodies in religious circles, where the debate over the physical versus the spiritual is still heated. This is not how the typical body is presented in churches' stained-glass windows. So is the black body in the pew the same black body as framed by hip-hop culture? (We have in mind the understanding of body presented earlier—the body as both biochemical reality and discursive construction.) Are people understood in the same way in these two cultures? Are human nature, purpose, and function the same in these two cultures, and if not, what then? That is, do churches establish different moral and ethical frameworks that require a different way of thinking about and shaping these bodies? And are those frameworks at odds with those provided in hip-hop culture?

There are ways in which one can connect questions of theodicy, or the problem of evil, to significant concerns facing black Americans: What can one say about divine justice in light of human suffering? More to the point, what can one say about divine justice in light of the suffering encountered by African Americans? Or even more focused, what can be said about divine justice in light of those suffering unto death due to poverty and other forms of injustice? The answers given by black churches and by hip-hop culture often differ, and this poses, we believe, a challenge for churches wanting to relate to hip-hop. For many black Christians, the church's response involves an appeal to divine intervention marked by recognition of the image of God in each of us: God will make a way out of no way, and we are refined by the suffering God allows us to endure,

8. Richard J. Powell, *Black Art and Culture in the 20th Century* (New York: Thames and Hudson, 1997), 167.

is the way that thinking goes. For many within hip-hop culture, the response is more unsettled and awash in a type of comfort with paradox. There is something telling in Michael Dyson's assessment of this theodical arrangement. Rappers and hip-hoppers alike, he writes, "are attempting to negotiate the dominion of death and the sovereignty of suffering by rejecting its ultimate logic—of the utter finality of existence—and insist on an immortality of expression that is undiminished by physical displacement."[9] Yet, while Dyson's vantage point is a prophetic Christian faith wed to radical democracy, hip-hop culture's take on theodicy is culled from its relationship to the blues—and the rough corners of life—containing an irreverence often foreign to the black Christian context.

Hip-Hop Churches?

If the preceding points are accepted, questions must be asked: What does it mean for black churches to embrace hip-hop? What are some implications of claiming to be a "hip-hop church"? And do hip-hop and black churches share a common language that allows for exchange across their differences?

For long stretches of African American religious history, there has been an assumption that the language of Christianity (e.g., redemption, sin, and so on) served as a fundamental commonality bringing together African Americans in and outside churches. Hip-hop culture brought this assumption into question, and perhaps the inability to assume this shared language is what promotes a mode of theological-social discomfort, a tension church folks want (need?) to resolve. In fact, does not church doctrine seek to resolve tensions and produce commonality? That still leaves us with the question of how

---

9. For a parallel discussion, see Josef Sorett, "Believe Me, This Pimp Game Is Very Religious: Toward a Religious History of Hip-Hop," *Culture and Religion* 10, no. 1 (2009): 11–22.

to resolve this tension without collapsing into subjugation of one of these two modalities of culture—black churches and hip-hop culture.

We believe attempting to resolve this tension can be productive, and in regard to this topic, it might suggest new and imaginative modalities of ritual and theological thinking. Yet, unfortunately, subjugation of difference is a relative easy move, one employed too often. The initial rejection of hip-hop by some religious leaders speaks to this desire to end tension and foster the dominance of Christianity. A similar move has taken place within the context of hip-hop's rejection of certain dimensions of black church life. In making this argument, we are not endorsing either culture—church or hip-hop; neither are we suggesting one over the other as an acceptable approach. We are, in fact, comfortable with paradox and tension. Instead, we are only pointing out a common approach to the tension between Black Church thinking and hip-hop thinking. This tension, this paradox, is productive for dialogue. If we are making any normative claims at all, it is that these paradoxes offer a starting point not for resolving them through dialogue, but for simply recognizing that the tensions suggest a commonality, a location offered by unresolved social issues that rest as the "common ground" on which the hip-hop community and black church communities might converge.

When Hip-Hop Can't Be "Saved"

Embedded in our remarks is a challenge faced by those seeking to transform black Christian culture and practice vis-à-vis hip-hop. This challenge involves an appropriate response to those who oppose contact with hip-hop on what they label theological and moral grounds. We label this dilemma a matter of passive projection of Black Church problems onto hip-hop, and this is done to preserve the Black Church's status quo without having to wrestle with its internal problems. In biblical terms, one might refer to it as the speck/log syndrome. As Jesus laments when speaking about the shame in judging people, "Why do you look at the speck of sawdust in your brother's eye and pay no attention to the plank in your own eye? How can you say to your brother, 'Let me take the speck out of your eye,' when all the time there is a plank in your own eye? You hypocrite, first take the plank out of your own eye, and then you will see clearly to remove the speck from your brother's eye" (Matt. 7:3-5, NIV). That is to say, housed in a somewhat aggressive response to hip-hop culture might be a theological sleight of hand—an effort to distract from the real issues—whereby shortcomings of black Christianity are bracketed and safely put away through quick attention to the moral and ethical defects of hip-hop culture. Put another way, some church members opposed to hip-hop culture might be saying, in effect, do not look at the problems we have (the log), let's concentrate on the problems displayed in hip-hop culture (the speck). They see the speck in the metaphorical eye of hip-hop but fail to see the log in the metaphorical eye of black churches.

We are not so naive as to offer an apology for hip-hop culture that does not acknowledge its numerous difficulties and shortcomings. Clearly, many strands of hip-hop culture, as we have noted throughout this book, involve a bleakness stemming from surrender to the worst impulses of human behavior, such as sexism, homophobia, radical materialism, and so on. However, what distinguishes surrender to these base impulses within the context of hip-hop culture from a similar surrender in Black Church culture? We cannot imagine that there is need to rehearse the list of indiscretions, phobic responses, and non-liberative agendas that litter the history of African American Christianity in general and black churches in particular.

Ongoing Considerations

There is often a failure to realize the manner in which dialogue with hip-hop culture might afford an opportunity to confront these warts on black churches in ways that cannot be couched in theological sleight of hand. For example, did aggressive attacks on hip-hop by figures such as Rev. Dr. Calvin Butts and C. Delores Tucker serve as a dramatic redirect—a shift away from the violence often found within Black Church settings? Gangsters are not limited to hip-hop culture; the same singular framing of life options and self-serving posture toward the world are expressed in the destructive behavior of too many church leaders, those who justify greed and manipulation through questionable appeals to special knowledge and special relationship to the divine. Too many church leaders, like more-questionable figures in hip-hop culture, share the lament "Pimpin' ain't easy."

The objectification of women and the xenophobic response to sexual orientation expressed in hip-hop culture were first championed in black Christianity and justified by narrow readings of Scripture celebrated in an unquestioned fashion in all too many black congregations. Yet authentic and effective exchange with hip-hop might change churches for the better, might afford opportunity to see churches at their creative best, but might also afford confrontation with their shortcomings. This, however, involves more than the incorporation of hip-hop as ritual practice within the existing framework of church thought and life.

We are suggesting a multidirectional response by which the similarities and differences between Black Church culture and hip-hop culture are used as a creative stratagem for the transformation of thinking and activities. Such an appreciation, we argue, marks the best of Black Church tradition—keep in mind, for example, the transformation in Black Church thinking resulting from its encounter with the social gospel. The dingy corners of Black Church life have been exposed on a variety of occasions and on a variety of fronts, but it would be willfully ignorant to suggest there is not much more work to do. There are demonic pronouncements against our human family that must be acknowledged and corrected with a deep tenacity guided by an attitude of care and hope. Perhaps sustained and nuanced attention to hip-hop culture might provide a way of getting at these issues. This is not to say transformed black churches provide the answer to all life questions or that these churches are a necessary component of the landscape of black communities. Rather, we argue that for as long as these churches exist, they ought to avoid doing harm, and hip-hop also should avoid doing harm.

There is a complexity at work, one first expressed in the blues, through its ability to both disrupt and help reconstruct religious sensibilities and commitments. In a similar fashion, as Michael Eric Dyson remarks, the ways in which hip-hop meditates on "fate, judgment, death, and God" might force "us to contend with the ultimate truths and proclamations of the gospel" in ways that enhance the integrity of black Christianity for those who embrace Christianity. When addressed without bad intentions or without limited self-awareness, hip-hop culture might serve as an alternate **hermeneutic**—a new *lens through which to view and confront the more deformed and deforming aspects of Black Church politics and practice.* In turn, this mutual exchange may provide mechanisms and means by which hip-hop can tackle its shortcomings.

If nothing more, the discourse concerning productive exchange between black churches and hip-hop culture might result in a deeper appreciation for the margins or outposts of our existence, the outlying areas of our life maps where creativity is the norm and where vocabulary and grammar shift and change to better reflect the felt nature of life. In other words, consideration of hip-hop that pushes beyond superficialities might help us appreciate the importance of looking at issues from the vantage point of the least privileged, those excluded from the status quo. Allow a stating of the obvious: "Hip-hop don't stop" and "Praise the Lord" will never be synonymous theologically; that much is certain. But if those influenced by each proclamation free themselves for conversation, they may discover something of value.

The authors of this volume have differing opinions regarding the importance, viability, and meaning of churches, but on this point, we are in agreement: at this current moment, churches are still part of the religio-cultural landscape of the United States and still demand critical attention. Hip-hop also holds a key place in popular imagination. So with respect to linkages between the two, we can hope against hope that both the Black Church and hip-hop, as cultural realities, will see the opportunity available to them.

Study Questions

- Give an example of how black churches have responded to musical innovations over the course of their history.

- Based on this chapter, what would you list as one of the ways black churches have responded to the moral and ethical outlook of hip-hop culture?

- What is meant by the speck/log argument?

- Is it possible for black churches to embrace hip-hop culture? If yes, why? If no, why not?

10

The Cipher

Ci·pher (sfr) *n.* **1.** One having no influence or value; a nonentity. **2.** **a)** A cryptographic system in which units of plain text are arbitrarily transposed or substituted according to a predetermined code. **b)** The key to such a system.[1]

Contributor One

In hip-hop, the cipher is a locale where artists of various backgrounds, social concerns, training, and skills come together in a linguistic battle of wit and passion, where respect is awarded for having the courage to speak up and for having used that moment to learn, entertain, and engage one another on equal footing. The cipher, in hip-hop, is where known and unknown artists congregate around an impromptu circle—sometimes on street corners, sometimes in more "sanctioned" spaces—and the participants and viewers are forced to listen and be heard.

The topics of active listening and being heard direct us to the heart of the cipher. If you pause over the definitions at the beginning of this chapter and spend a bit of time thinking about what they mean,

---

1. This definition is a paraphrasing derived from selected meanings of the term found at http://www.thefreedictionary.com/cypher.

then images of hip-hop, of alienated and marginalized youth might spring to mind. You might envision the faces of your daughters and sons or grandchildren. To truly understand a cipher and what it involves is to think about the way people with no voices find creative ways to speak, to let their own voices be heard over the clutter from all those around them. So yes, you might find yourself thinking of many of the youth you know. Or you might think of someone like Trayvon Martin, whose body and mind many deemed of little value or influence, or you may think of many of the other stories you have read in the pages of *Breaking Bread, Breaking Beats.*

Despite the differences we have discussed throughout the book, hip-hoppers and many church members share this feeling of the cipher, of having little or no influence or value in the eyes of another, of being a nonentity. Appealing to the cipher as both a means of connection and a blueprint for dialogue, we hope to decode hip-hop culture for a wide range of audiences, particularly religious leaders and students focused on religion and church-based issues.

Check out the second definition of the cipher: a code. It is a whole collection of otherwise arbitrary signs and symbols that come together to help people make sense of their environment. That is, a cipher is something that reveals knowledge and meaning to people who participate within it. You might think of the Bible as a code, or a cipher, for understanding and responding to the world in which we live. By this point, you might have a sense that many within the hip-hop community respond to the world by appealing to hip-hop, or music, or dance, or graffiti as their way of understanding the world.

Even within hip-hop, the cipher is a special place. Thinking about the two definitions of the cipher, the hip-hop cipher is more than a circle; it is more than a collection of noisy young people. The cipher is a place where people within a community come together to renegotiate the values and meanings that constitute a community. A cipher is where the keys to community are both coded and decoded, where people come to know themselves and their own desires, as much as they learn how to present those desires and ambitions to others in a way that is helpful and not harmful. It seemed, then, that the hip-hop cipher might have something to say about all of the tensions and confusions and frustrations that accompany churches and young people coming together.

We have modeled this book and this chapter on the cipher because it is a model for learning about and creating a type of community where knowledge is produced and reproduced as people come together to make sense of their world. For us as the authors, that "world" we are making sense of is this very book project; for hip-hop heads, their world might include police brutality or drug use or absentee parents. The cipher is where these worlds collide and are remade with a greater awareness of the challenges we face. With this in mind, we conclude with brief sections written by the Writing Collective members, noting their experiences within the cipher created by the writing process.

Contributor Two

When volunteering to help underprivileged persons in downtown Houston improve their life options, I have seen and met persons of all races, including whites, blacks, Hispanics, and Asians who are homeless and jobless. I have had several real conversations with senior citizens, adult men and women, and young teenagers who are sleeping on sidewalks and park benches. I have noted that poverty is a social concern that not only affects black Americans; it affects all Americans.

Although this book mainly looks at hip-hop and the Black Church through the lens of African American history and culture, when dialoguing with members of the collective, I have been forced to reconsider how the issue of poverty reaches across races, sexes, ages, and nations. I acknowledge that there is a strong link between racial and economic oppression, but I know from my experience that poverty is by no means merely "a black thing." Furthermore, while women, especially women of color, are victims of economic injustice, poverty does not only affect women and their children in the United States; men also are mired in poverty. Additionally, poverty reaches across ages and touches young and old alike. Lastly, though much of our book focuses on the Black Church and hip-hop within the context of the United States, poverty is a global concern. In order for the Black Church and hip-hop community to come together and "do the right thing" and combat poverty, both communities must engage diverse groups within and outside their communities, especially poor persons, who often lack a strong voice.

Acknowledging and empathetically listening to the views and voices of others is not easy. Doing this requires diligent hard work and effort. One challenge our collective had to work through when engaging each other was working through our disagreements about various matters, including changes to the manuscript, writing tasks and responsibilities, and our different outlooks and culturally located viewpoints. At times, we succumbed to the temptation to make prejudgments about why we were disengaged from the collaborative process, failing to attend a meeting or fulfill a particular task on time. Nonetheless, we worked through our disagreements and conflicts by being patient with each other and keeping our lines of communication open. We went back and forward via e-mail threads, telephone conference calls, and face-to-face meetings. We were able to complete this collaborative project only by learning to work as a team. We hope that this book, born out of our knowledge and experience, aids members of the Black Church and hip-hop by providing them with tools to collaborate on several important issues affecting our community, our nation, and our world.

Contributor Three

Ciphering is dangerous. When one is searching for the code that might unlock a doorway to greater understanding and self-awareness, the stakes are always high, and vulnerabilities exist around every corner. After weeks and weeks of writing the tightest lines, to be delivered as if they were freestyle, I'm wearing the freshest gear. Walking to the corner where the cipher will commence, my mind picks apart the latest verse from Nas, spelling out to myself where he went wrong and when his lyrics were on point. Just smellin' myself.

Arriving at the cipher, ready to do battle, I come ill equipped. See, I thought the cipher was *about* battling, being the best you can and showing the world your skills at the expense of everybody else in the cipher. But then I get there, and I see something else is going on. We're all trying to make it. We're all trying to get signed by the people who barely have the courage to watch the cipher, much less jump in to spit a few bars. Here we are nonetheless, ciphering, folks looking at me like "Did he just say that?" and me looking back, knowing that my line was tight. Rhyme after rhyme, tearing down the group, about to get paid.

Lookin' behind the cat across from me while sister next to me spits bar after bar of what I must admit is amazing, I see the record execs. I see money falling out their pockets, the twinkle in their eye. I want to get signed. We all want to get signed. Soon I'm up again, ready to impress. I can smell the success. Waxing so poetic that I'm impressing myself, I can't shake the execs peeping the scene. My palms sweat. My voice cracks, and I lose the flow. Cat next to me picks up the slack, laughingly punching me in the arm, knowing what happened.

He's been there before. We all have. We've all had moments where the quest for success had us stumbling over the things that were going to get us there, the things about us, the things that defined us, each other, the cipher. Turning around, walking back home, I notice my mind shifts gears from my attempt to pimp myself out to the ones who held me up when I let myself down—the ones I thought I was battling.

See, the cipher is a place where the unknown become the known, to be sure. But I had it twisted, and the cipher brought me back around. The cipher's not about battling; it's about building—building yourself, building others, building the world in the image of creativity. And that building doesn't start with tearing down. It starts with embrace. I'd gotten it twisted. I thought to build (a career, a book, a church, a relationship), you had to destroy. I thought the cipher was where that happened. I was wrong. I was wrong like black churches are wrong when they judge hip-hop kids. I was wrong like Tyler, the Creator when he markets his rape lyrics as satire. I was wrong to forget that the only way to be seen by a society or profession or group that does not see you, that sees you as a nonentity, is not to wave your hand, but to see others not seen in a new light, learning and cultivating trust and respect in the group, the cipher. Only then is it even worthwhile to be seen by anyone else.

Ciphers are about building. And building can be dangerous. You never know what the end result will turn out to be. But I'm thankful for this reminder. I'm thankful for building. I'm thankful for the cipher. And I'm humbled in the sight of the product we've built together.

Contributor Four

Music in a very general sense has the unique ability to capture the best and worst of a people's (or a person's) culture; religion has this same gift (or curse). That is the essence of this work. In that, it is the ultimate purpose of this book: to take what is best and what is worst in the Black Church and within hip-hop and find a space where conversation and growth can take place.

Hip-hop and the Black Church can stand on their respective merits and history as institutions that begrudgingly know of each other but won't speak to each other. They can accept the lie that they do not need each other and can address the issues that plague them as institutions separately and independently. That lie however, will eventually rot the core of the institutions and leave scores of mentally dead and spiritually devoid young people in their wake. As institutions that claim to be organically created and sustained, they may not ultimately be able to survive this lie.

So these bitter neighbors must confront each other; they must speak, and they must find a place in which to work together before they both, as institutions, render themselves obsolete. No longer is hip-hop the thing those kids are doing on the street corner, nor is the church to be ignored and dismissed as rhetoric for those "born-agains." They are both human movements, which reflect the very best and worst of humanity and therefore must recognize and respect each other's strengths and weaknesses and work toward some semblance of experiential commonality. That is to say, there are similar problems that need to be dealt with, so perhaps these communities can come to some agreement on how to deal with said problems.

That is what this conversation hopes to achieve—to wrestle with similar problems held by diverging communities. To, in essence, form a community focused on a future bright with promise instead of one darkened by oppression, ignorance, and intolerance. How else will these institutions see themselves into the future, if not by breaking down the barriers they themselves threw up? It is hip-hop and the church that marginalize their women, the poor, and homosexuals; therefore, hip-hop and the church must resolve to solve these problems or risk falling into obscurity.

Ultimately, it is our hope, as a collective community of people and as people from diverging communities, that this conversation will take place in a fruitful and worthwhile fashion. This book is the baton, and it is now being passed to the church and the street corner so they may complete this relay for the good of all communities involved and the human collective.

Contributor Five

As scholars, we often write about what is near and dear to us; I took on the initial research for the sexuality chapter because, on many levels, I have struggled with my own understanding of what proper sex means. In undergrad, I used to say all of the right religious things about sexuality: don't do it unless you're married, homosexuality is a sin, etc. I said the right things until I ended up having sexual encounters of my own that fell outside of the Christian code of sexual ethics. What many black churches *don't* preach is how pleasurable sex is and how connected it makes you feel to another person. And after having candid conversations with my own friends, I realized that I wasn't on my own; we all yearn for intimacy, and sex is one of the most powerful ways to be intimate with another person.

I worked on the issue of sexuality because, from my perspective, both hip-hop and Christianity do one of two things, or maybe even a combination of both: (1) they take away the intimacy completely, turning men and women into sex objects; or (2) they tell us what kind of intimacy is appropriate, taking away certain kinds of intimacy. As a result, sex is repressed in many African American communities, and people end up making a whole bunch of decisions that may go against their well-being. In researching this chapter, I hoped to shed light on the fact that the issues I highlighted are damaging to the very people we say we love and are committed to. Pastors cannot get away with cheating on their wives while simultaneously denouncing homosexuality; this is conflicting behavior that sends the community confusing messages, which have serious implications. And hip-hop artists can't produce videos with a woman's backside plastered across the screen and then hide behind "artistic license." I worked on this issue because I think it's time these two movements—movements I love and hold very dear—become more accountable to the communities with which they are concerned.

In my research and writing this text with other people, I realized that my desires had to be molded to fit in with the goals of the rest of the writers. But more than this, I realized that I had to trust my teammates to have my back when I could not be there to make my concerns known. One of the most powerful things I learned in working with a significantly diverse group of other writers and thinkers is that I could not do it all. In the dialogue I hope we have sparked with this book, I would like for the two communities to figure out very practical ways in which one could take up the slack for the other.

One of the most memorable music videos I saw was by Ludacris, I think, where he was talking about Atlanta. And while I don't remember the lyrics to the song, I do remember seeing the face of famed Atlanta-area megachurch pastor, Creflo Dollar, flash across the screen. And one of the most memorable songs I heard was G.O.O.D. Music's "Higher," where rapper and Christian preacher Ma$e dropped one of the baddest verses I've heard in a while. I appreciate these experiences, because they signal that the relationship between hip-hop and Christianity does not have to be as tenuous as it has been. It signals that hip-hop heads and Christian preachers and laypersons can work together to address some of the ills of the black community. In writing this with others, I had to trust my teammates; in addressing some of the problems we face as African Americans, I think it's about time hip-hoppers and Christians trust each other to get this job done.

Contributor Six

What are the consequences of male embodiment within time and space?

This question, and so many others pertaining to the shifting nature of power dynamics between men and women, has been at the forefront of my mind both in my work as a scholar and during the experiences of developing this book project. However, the posing of these questions is not merely an academic or theoretical exercise; it is an active call to a more engaged understanding of the ways in which my self-understanding as a man yields certain outcomes in the life experiences of women. The problem of gender within Christian communities is one that screams of ultimate importance—especially in black Christian communities in which the primary movers and shakers are typically women. If the black church is to remain a vital component of the spiritual and material flourishing of black communities, it is incumbent upon its *male* clergy to open themselves—to become more receptive to the insights and leadership capacities of women. I was reminded of this fact during the development, deliberation, and completion of this book.

I've had the good fortune to work with some brilliant women colleagues as a graduate student, and the coauthors of this book follow suit. In our workgroup meetings and deliberations, I found myself, more often than not, being much more open to the suggestions of my colleagues—particularly those of my female peers—in lieu of voicing my own. I was constantly aware of the inflection of my voice, my demeanor, my presentation of ideas. In part, I believe I was trying to be faithful to some of the dynamics of gender politics that the chapter discusses. On another level, however, I was also putting into practice the idea that there is value in opening oneself to the experiences of women, particularly black women. On this account, I was comfortable remaining out of the spotlight.

This is not to say that men should render themselves voiceless—no. Rather, I think I draw upon this particular element of my experience in the writing of this book as a way to suggest that perhaps black *male* clergy would do well to recover the lost art of listening—listening to the stories, perspectives, and insights of women. How might the church grow and expand by becoming a more hospitable environment for the cultivation of female leaders and religion scholars? What insights from black women's lives and thoughts can inform ministry, liturgy, and evangelism? The possibilities are endless when the fullness of all the church's gifts is utilized.

Our hip-hop sisters have given us a gift. They've shown us that black women, all women have a unique story—a critical perspective that is worth sharing and worth receiving. May the church have the wisdom to listen to that which is shared. The church's very life and vitality may depend on it.

Contributor Seven

I am hip-hop. I am Christian. These two have been engaged in a vicious war for control of my body for a good portion of my live. In my youth, I was forced to navigate two vastly different worlds that seemed to be pulling my limbs in opposite directions. On Sundays, the melodic and rhythmic sounds and tones of church choir and the preacher would invoke uncontrolled responses from by my body. Tears would form in the corner of my eyes and then roll down my face, gently kissing my cheeks, leaving a stream of salty deposits as evidence. Simultaneously, my body would begin to sway back and forth, sometimes in and other times out of syncopation with the musical tones projected by the instruments and the black church. Outside of church, a different sound called my body. Like a tuning fork, hip-hop music, especially gangsta rap, made my body sensitive to the realities I saw in everyday life. Hip-hop taught me to navigate and survive the tragic condition of my neighborhood, teaching how (and how not) to dress and avoid the imminent danger that lurked around each corner.

These two ways of thinking about my self (hip-hop and/or Christian) often were at odds with one another. Because of the conflicts, I was forced to develop a double-consciousness in order to survive in each arena. I had to learn two ways of speaking, dressing, and acting. Quickly, I noticed that the way I dressed attracted attention in both the church and my neighborhood. My clothes, the way I dressed, changed the meaning of my body and gave my body the ability to either blend in or stand out in both environments. If I walked into the church, even during the week, with super baggy pants or failed to neatly tuck my shirt into my pants or remove my hat, I would be treated awkwardly, as if I did not belong. In my neighborhood, my church clothes make me an alien—again, as if I did not belong there. The truth is that I belonged in both places. I was both a product of hip-hop and a Christian at the same time.

Since I was a part of both communities, I began to pay attention to the way I dressed in each community. However, I began to wonder what impact this costume-like dressing and performance had on my own self-understanding and awareness. As I mastered dressing up for each environment, dress revealed more about my body than I had initially recognized. Thus, the chapter in the book about embodiment has helped me explore and name what it is that I have felt for a good portion of my life. As the church and hip-hop continue to coexist and as more and more of the youth in black church communities share the same Christian/hip-hop duality that I struggled with as a youth, a question remains concerning whether or not each community will grow to accept and appreciate the other, regardless of differences.

Contributor Eight

As is true for many of my colleagues, my contribution to this project was formed out of biography. Therefore, when I lectured in our 2011 large-enrollment course, and researched and wrote my contribution here, I did so increasingly out of my social location as a member of an in-between generation—in-between the height of the civil rights movement, on the one hand, and the earliest super hits of what has become the global rise of hip-hop, on the other hand. In this space, I authentically see connecting tissue between the height of the Black Church–populated mass movement in the twentieth century and hip-hop as a movement that has transitioned from a black urban youth expression to a global phenomenon of cultural, social, economic, and political self-expression in the present age.

In the process of this writing experience, I have been challenged to take a critical, sometimes uncomfortable review of both the contemporary church and hip-hop. In part, this was driven by difficult conversations with colleagues who not only do not have a romanticized view of the relevance of the contemporary church, but also sometimes have a jaded view of the lack of moral authority the church has demonstrated to the post-civil-rights generation. Examples include the decades-long, structural cover-up of the sexual abuse of children by clergy in the Roman Catholic Church and hypocritical, sexist, homophobic abuse of power in some of the nation's megachurches and evangelical ranks. Through these conversations, I reflected on hip-hoppers as an emboldened, fearless generation who are aware and expressive of their lived experience but sometimes less so of the day-to-day actions that resulted in their generation's ability to exercise personal freedoms under fewer structural limitations than their elders from the civil rights generation. Hip-hoppers are not restricted to some of the institutional structures that members of the civil rights generation used so strategically in order to achieve some of the gains that later generations take for granted. I continue to grow to see the emergence of these critical views as personal progress that I hope our readers will also consider valuable.

My personal introduction to the possibilities of the Black Church was formed in the ideals of social justice, where there was no separation between the tenet to "love thy neighbor," a pillar of New Testament Christian living; the life-giving of the Divine who breathed on the dry bones in Ezekiel (Ezekiel 37: 1-14); and the work of Nehemiah, a Jew who had risen to a high office in the Persian court, and who took leave from the palace to help rebuild the walls of Jerusalem (Neh. 1:1—2:10). The common theme is the constancy of regeneration. The human condition has joys, pains, struggles, and triumphs. In my intergenerational location, I took to heart the words of a colleague, then twenty-five years old, who sincerely asked what could be seen as good to a generation who had always lived with the presence of AIDS. Yet, as a consequence of focused political action, federally sponsored research, and even the deaths of notable figures, today AIDS in the United States is no longer the automatic death sentence it seemed to be in the 1980s. A similar potential for hopefulness through human striving in regeneration continues to be available. But it only comes about because enough people in opposing communities are willing to listen and to learn from one another. This has been my own learning-journey, and it continues.

Furthermore, whatever expressions assuage the concerns of a generation long enough to establish a posture of dialogue are useful as a means of moving forward to enact social justice. If for one generation it is gospel music, and for another it is hip-hop beats, as a result of this experience I have come to see their relevance to intragenerational connectedness as an important first step to *inter*generational understanding and engagement.

Contributor Nine

I grew up with hip-hop in New York. Hip-hop gave voice to my childhood realities. Hip-hop said all the things I was feeling and/or thinking about growing up in America. By the time "Rappers Delight" hit the radio, we knew that racism was still alive and well, despite our parents' sacrifices and victories during the civil rights movement. As inheritors of black pride and civil rights, we were trying to tell the world what it meant to be "young, gifted, and black." As we got older, we wanted both whites and blacks to know that racism and ethnic oppression weren't over and that we were experiencing something that was real. Growing up in New York, we knew that through artistic expressions, we could create a free space in which to talk about reality, both good and bad. Yet it seems the world didn't want to hear our pleas, realities, and experiences, but just wanted us to be grateful for the opportunities we had. We were the dream of our ancestors and our parents, yet we were living a nightmare.

I remember how electrifying it was to stay up late and listen to DJ Mr. Magic on the radio, and trying to record the hip-hop songs on cassette players. We wanted to capture these empowering songs so we could play them as loud as we could on our boom boxes. We wanted the world to know that more needed to be done to end race and ethnic oppression. We were told that our songs were a fad and that it wouldn't last. We never believed it. We knew that in New York, our music, art, and dance spoke to the realities of life for young black folks, post-civil-rights. We believed it so strongly that, like our parents, we united around our common experiences, and we created a hip-hop culture. Today it is one of the greatest phenomena the world has ever seen.

Growing up in New York, we were aware that our parents had integrated social spaces, and we were often reminded of all the benefits their accomplishments afforded us. Yet we were angry that our parents thought it was enough. We knew from experience that we had to integrate social experiences. Hence, we had to make, in the words of President Barack Obama, "change we could believe in." As the first generation of African Americans to receive our civil rights, we used song, dance, and art to show that racial and ethnic oppression was not "just a black thing." Hip-hop told our stories and showed the world the injustices being done to all races in America. We convinced America through rhyme, music, dance, and art, in the words of Dr. Martin Luther King Jr., that "an injustice anywhere is a threat to justice everywhere." It wasn't long before youth from all races in the United States agreed with us, and hip-hop became mainstream at national and global levels.

I challenge those who read my words in this cipher to see the accomplishments that our generation has made to the world. Nothing in this world is perfect, and there is good and bad in all things. Yet take a closer look at hip-hop. Examine it through the lens of compassion—compassion for a generation of young people across America who were bused and forced to integrate with each other and accomplish what generations of our ancestors could never do. As a result, we have been labeled Generation X, and we have often times been misunderstood and despised. Yet as a generation, we didn't respond with terrorist attacks and mass killings. Instead, we got creative and used rhyme, music, dance, and art to change the world. Despite the drugs in the communities, teenage pregnancies, high incarceration rates, social and economic inequalities, and the exploitation of black neighborhoods, hip-hop kept the dream and hope alive among those most affected by social structures of oppression. We managed to shed light on the parts of the dream that have been deferred for so many people, from diverse racial and ethnic backgrounds. Remember, it is the hip-hop generation, not our parents, who elected our first black president.

President Obama connected with the hip-hop generation. He came into adulthood as hip-hop was being birthed, and the Black Church influenced him as he walked into manhood. The Black Church influenced him, as it has influenced so many others in positive ways. Our class on religion and hip-hop is another shining example of the positive influence and overwhelming appeal hip-hop has on the world's youth. In our class, we show how two different approaches help people make meaning out of life. By now, one must realize that black churches and hip-hop are here to stay. Let's unite black churches and hip-hop. Let's unite the Holy Spirit of black churches with the plight of men and women in a changing world. Bound together, maybe one day, one day we as a people will overcome race and ethnic oppression for all. Those with an ear, let them hear our American Dream.

Contributor Ten

I was fortunate in that much of my early experience of hip-hop took place in the location of its birth, its place of genesis: New York City. At the time, I was an undergraduate at Columbia University and spent a great deal of my free time exploring the city. Hip-hop culture, the music and aesthetic, shaped much of what I thought in terms of social critique, communal developments, organic expression, and so on. Reflecting back, I think it is safe to say I was as influenced by hip-hop as a young minister in the 1980s could be and maintain deep church sensibilities. What hip-hop represented for me involved a perspective on existence that I found compelling on a variety of levels. It spoke to much of the angst and joy I experienced exploring New York City, attending Columbia, and working at Bridge Street AME Church (Brooklyn, NY). I was content, for the most part.

As I moved from undergraduate training to Harvard Divinity School in preparation for ministry, I continued my interest in hip-hop, finding much of value in the social insights and praxis of Public Enemy. And as I moved from the master of divinity program to the PhD program, hip-hop took on a different meaning, premised on the intellectual challenge it posed. I became more sensitive to its critique of Christianity (or institutionalized religion in more general terms). This challenge involved a synergy with my evolving religious sensibilities. In response, I wanted to think about and academically explore hip-hop's challenge to traditional modalities of religiosity. My dissertation on the problem of evil in African American religious thought served as an opportunity to explore hip-hop.

This interest continued as hip-hop continued to influence and inform my thinking. Once I finished the PhD and took my first teaching job, hip-hop moved from simply influencing my thinking to shaping my teaching content and style. Without apologies, I brought it to bear on my life as an academic, and this continued as I moved from Macalester College to Rice University. The course that buttresses this book marks my ongoing commitment to the value of hip-hop. My academic connection to both religion and hip-hop made it easy and deeply important to raise questions, to analyze and interrogate the nature and meaning of churches embracing hip-hop culture. And it made perfect sense to begin this book with a few thoughts on the content and consequences of this connection between churches and hip-hop.

CERCL Writing Collective Members

Jonathan Chism is a sixth-year graduate student in African American religion. He received a BA degree from Rice University in 2004, an MDiv (summa cum laude) from Southern Methodist University, Perkins School of Theology in 2008, and a PhD in Religious Studies from Rice University in 2014. In addition, he has been awarded an African American doctoral fellowship from the Fund for Theological Education (FTE). He has presented academic papers at an American Academy of Religion Conference in Atlanta, Georgia, in October 2010; at a Society for Pentecostal Studies Conference in Memphis, Tennessee, in March 2011; and at the AIM Scholars forum in Houston, Texas, in June 2011. He has also published entries as a guest lectionary commentator with the African American Lectionary and several book reviews with the Rice *Religious Studies Review*. Recently, he has published an article with *Pneuma: The Journal for the Society of Pentecostal Studies.* His current research interests include African American Pentecostalism, theology, and movements of social justice and social transformation. His dissertation examines the involvements of Pentecostals in the Church of God in Christ in the civil rights movement in Memphis, Tennessee, 1954–1968.

Christopher Driscoll is a PhD candidate within the Religious Studies Department at Rice University, specializing in issues of race, society, culture, and religion. After receiving his bachelor's degree focused in religious studies and anthropology from Texas Christian University, Christopher continued at TCU, enrolling in Brite Divinity School, where he obtained the MTS degree with a focus in Black Church studies. His master's thesis explored black and womanist theological responses to the problem of redemptive suffering within the black Christian tradition, and he remains interested in understanding the exigencies of social suffering as they play out within and across social fields, cultural spaces, and institutions. His current research interests and teaching include theology and the social, philosophical theology, existential thought, social scientific theories of religion, race, theology, and culture, liberation theologies, and the interrelationship between religion and oppression. His dissertation seeks to theorize a cohesive white religious theological position operative within the United States historically and today. Christopher is also co-chair and founder of the American Academy of Religion's Critical Approaches to Hip Hop and Religion group.

Paul Easterling received his PhD from the Religious Studies Department of Rice University. He has been an adjunct professor of African American studies at the University of Houston and is currently an adjunct professor of history and government at Bowie State University. While attending Rice University as a PhD student, he co-designed the Hip Hop and Religion course in 2006 with Dr. Anthony Pinn. Since then, the course has blossomed into one of the most popular courses on Rice's campus and has received national notoriety. In 2010, at the University of Houston, Dr. Easterling also designed the Hip Hop History and Culture course for the African American Studies Program, which also became extremely popular and a vital part of the program's course offerings. Dr. Easterling's research interests include African American religious culture, history of African American religion, twentieth-century African American Islam, African American religion, and popular culture.

Biko Mandela Gray is a PhD candidate in the Religious Studies Department at Rice University. He earned his BA from Xavier University of Louisiana with a major in political science and a minor in theology with a concentration in Latin American liberation theology. After attending Xavier, Biko enrolled in Vanderbilt University Divinity School and earned his MTS degree, concentrating on constructive and systematic theology as well as African American religious thought. Biko's dissertation is tentatively titled "Making-Life-Matter: A Philosophical Theory of African American Religion," wherein he philosophically explores African American religious experience from within the horizon of embodiment. His research interests include continental philosophy (specifically, phenomenology and its offshoots), the philosophy of religion, embodiment, and race in the study of religion.

Margarita Simon Guillory is an assistant professor of religion in the College of Arts, Sciences and Engineering at the University of Rochester. She teaches courses in religion and popular culture, American religious history, and African Diasporic religions. Her research interests include American Spiritualism, identity construction in African American religion, and social scientific approaches to religion. She has published articles in *Culture and*

Religion and *Pastoral Psychology*. Her coedited volume (with Drs. Stephen Finley and Hugh Page), *There Is a Mystery: Esotericism, Gnosticism, and Mysticism in African American Religious Experience*, is currently under contract with Brill.

Darrius D. Hills is a PhD candidate in the Religious Studies Department at Rice University, specializing in theology, philosophy of religion, and feminist and womanist thought. After earning his bachelor's degree in religious studies (with honors) from Centenary College of Louisiana, Darrius went on to receive the MDiv from Garrett-Evangelical Theological Seminary, and the MA from Rice University. His current research interests and teaching include philosophical ethics, liberation theologies, the intersection between black masculinity and womanist criticism, and African American literary studies. His dissertation formulates a hermeneutic of relationality within black theological discourse and black male identity in which the central concept is reciprocity. In addition, Darrius has also presented several papers for the American Academy of Religion and has been awarded fellowships from the Fund for Theological Education, the General Board of Higher Education and Ministry, and a dissertation fellowship from the Louisville Institute for the Study of American Religion.

Jason O. Jeffries is a PhD candidate in African American Religion at Rice University. He earned a bachelor of business administration degree (BBA) in finance from Prairie View A&M University in 1999. He earned a master of divinity degree (MDiv) from the Samuel DeWitt Proctor School of Theology at Virginia Union University in May 2008 and a master of theology degree (ThM) at Union-Presbyterian School of Christian Education in 2009. Jason has been awarded an African American doctoral fellowship from the Fund for Theological Education (FTE). His research interests include embodiment, psychology of religion, and social scientific approaches to religion.

Terri Laws is a PhD candidate in the Department of Religious Studies at Rice University. She directs the African American Studies Program at the University of Detroit Mercy, where she is also an instructor in the Department of Religious Studies. Terri teaches courses in the social and cultural history of African American religious experience, African American studies, and health care ethics. Her interdisciplinary research focuses on interconnections between race, religion, clinical research, and health inequities. She has published in *African American Religious Cultures* and *Pastoral Psychology.* Laws has won substantial funding support and awards, including a training and research fellowship in bioethics for study at the University of Texas MD Anderson Cancer Center. Prior to graduate studies, she held administrative management positions in health care and workforce development. Her professional commitment is to underserved and underrepresented communities. She earned a bachelor of business administration from the University of Cincinnati, the master of divinity from the Interdenominational Theological Center in Atlanta, and a master of arts from Rice University.

Aundrea Matthews is a PhD candidate in African American religious studies. She received a BS and MA from Texas Christian University and an MTS from Brite Divinity School where she earned the Emerging Black Church Studies Scholar Award. Her research interests center on the connection between African American quilts and their significance to the study of African American religion. She is creator and curator of the Inaugural Quilting Exhibit titled "Hearts,

Hands, and Heritage: The Patchwork Soul of Houston at Rice University." Aundrea was selected by the President of Northeast Houston Community College (HCC) to create, curate, and manage the Northeast Art Hub Gallery, which hosts various collections that stress the importance of infusing art with education for HCC students and surrounding communities. In addition to her work in the community, Aundrea has contributed commentaries to the African American Lectionary and presented papers for the South Central Modern Language Association, the American Academy of Religion, and the Society of Christian Ethics, entitled "Weaving Ourselves: The Art of African American Quilts," "Talk to Me: Theological Discourse and the Hermeneutic of Reconciliation," and "It is an African Thing, and Now We Understand: The Legacy of Peter Paris," respectively. She is also the founding President of A.C.E.@ Rice (Academic Cultural Empowerment at Rice), a student organization providing virtual tutors to high school students.

Anthony B. Pinn is the Agnes Cullen Arnold Professor of Humanities and Professor of Religious Studies at Rice University. He is also the founding director of the Center for Engaged Research and Collaborative Learning. Pinn also founded and directs the doctoral concentration in the study of African American religion at Rice. Outside Rice, Pinn has served as the first executive director of the Society for the Study of Black Religion, and he also served on the Meadville Lombard Theological School board of trustees (2007–2012). In addition, he has served in various roles on the board of directors and the executive committee of the American Academy of Religion. He is also the Director of Research for the Institute for Humanist Studies Think Tank (Washington, DC). Pinn is the author/editor of thirty books, including *Noise and Spirit: The*

Religious and Spiritual Sensibilities of Rap Music (New York University Press, 2003).

Glossary

Agency Actions to shape or construct one's social, cultural, political and economic world.

Beat-boxing The act of transforming one's mouth and vocal abilities into sounds and beats expressed alone or with lyrics.

Beloved community An ethical ideal that implies that the church should be the primary means by which humans are reconciled to each other and restored to fellowship with God.

Black Church Congregations in seven mainline denominations in which the leadership and membership is largely African American.

Black feminist hip-hop aesthetic An approach on the part of female rappers that is focused upon creating music that offers a direct assault upon sexism and gender inequalities within black communities.

Black freedom struggle African Americans' activity in search of dignity and full citizenship rights throughout their history in the American colonies. The term acknowledges that this activity was not restricted to the 1960s civil rights movement and that on this soil, Africans and persons of African descent have used a variety of approaches at the individual and institutional levels, including black nationalist, integrationist, armed, nonviolent, and economic protest, to name a few.

Black liberation theology A theological approach that interprets Scriptures and Christian faith in light of African Americans' experience of oppression.

Black megachurches Churches that have 10,000 to 25,000 members, that have large buildings on large campuses, and whose membership and leadership is predominantly African American.

Black Power A call for blacks to build communities based on cultural recognition and self-run organizational development.

Black religion The responses to the horrors of separation, torture, enslavement, and the good and bad circumstances that shape people's desire to ask the big questions of life—the who, what, when, where, and why of theirs and their community's existence.

Black supremacy The idea, especially as used by Reverend Albert Cleage, that the history of Christianity has African and non-white origins.

Bling Flashy, materialistic possessions that are worn by hip-hop artists to signify individual economic prosperity.

Body (a) A biochemical reality; a physical, material substance that navigates the world and thinks and engages with others. (b) The image or idea of bodies that people hold in their heads; a social or discursive body.

Break dance *See* Breaking.

Breaking A unique form of dance developed in New York City and emerging within what we now know as hip-hop culture; characterized by bodily movements corresponding to breaks in songs; often based on highly acrobatic and athletic movement. The physical, bodily expression of hip-hop's creative impulse.

Capitalism An economic system that promotes ownership of private property and seeks to maximize profits through controlling the means of production and maximizing the sale of goods and services within a free market.

Deep symbols Words and/or ideas that constrain and guide individuals as they navigate through the social world.

DJ An artist who makes use of a sound system and turntables during a party or concert.

DJing The act of playing two records, side by side, moving between the two to create breaks, which increase the enthusiasm of crowds and offer dancers a unique embodied form of expression. The central feature of hip-hop culture historically. The musical expression of hip-hop's creative impulse. *See also* Scratching; Emceeing.

Economic double consciousness Artists' jointly held desires to ostensibly accommodate to capitalism through promoting bling in their music, many of these same artists have indicated a desire to participate in the struggle to combat poverty.

Emcee An artist who raps over the beats provided by a DJ or at times without a beat. The emcee is responsible for the lyrical expression of the creative impulse.

Emceeing Applying spoken words and lyrics over the sounds provided by DJs, meant to excite and motivate a crowd. Emceeing is rapping, which often includes bragging, elevating the excitement of a crowd and reflecting on a variety of social and cultural situations to present a portrait that creates a mood experienced by the emcee and her or his listeners.

Ethic of doubt A nontraditional ethical framework that calls into question those things inherited from the social and cultural institutions of the larger society without completely refuting that inheritance.

Ethic of embodiment and style An ethical framework derived from and created by an emphasis on personal style and artistic creativity.

Ethic of formation An ethical framework that begins with the moral and ethical guidelines from the Bible—including aspects of both the Hebrew Bible and the New Testament Jesus—and seeks to bring about the kingdom of God on earth.

Ethic of impossibility An ethical framework derived from the impossibility of escaping sin and the impossibility of ever fully arriving at the kingdom of God.

Ethic of liberation An ethical framework based on an awareness that God is on the side of the oppressed and dispossessed and that ethics should involve a commitment to the liberation of the oppressed from bondage in all forms.

Ethic of rebellion An ethical framework derived from a push against any sort of constricting understanding of right action or right thought as offered by social institutions.

Ethical framework The sum total of factors influencing an ethical system. These include social context (the social experiences a person or group faces), norm clarification (the definitions of and concerns for a community based on these social experiences), and criteria of evaluation (the religious or philosophical beliefs and objects used to make sense of those experiences within and across communities).

Ethics Right thought and action; an effort to make sense of behaviors, moods, and motivations that are guided by any combination or amount of a variety of life experiences, religious beliefs, and/or community concerns.

Gangsta rap A form of rap that provides a critique of society by highlighting the damage that has been done by humans because of capitalist greed and oppression.

Gender A social construct highlighted as standards and norms for appropriate (read: "acceptable") male and female behaviors and attitudes.

Globalization A process of accelerated flows or intensified connections—across national and other boundaries—of commodities, people, symbols, technology, images, information, and capital, as well as disconnections, exclusions, marginalization, and disposition.

Glocalization The process of incorporating global and local elements in order to form a new creative product.

Graffiti art The art of employing spray paint to mark one's signature, or "tag," on public buildings, trains, or anywhere else. An artistic cultural expression that makes use of spray paint to fashion names and images onto artifacts of postindustrial urban life such as building walls, trains, and subways. The visual expression of hip-hop's creative impulse. *See* Tagging.

Great Migration Population movements, in two waves between 1910–1940 and 1940–1970, of African Americans from the rural South to cities in northern, mid-western, and to a lesser degree, western states. Black rural Southerners also moved to urban areas in southern states.

Hard-core rap A vehicle to popularize and vent the anger and the frustrations of many disadvantaged or sometimes mistreated individuals and to defend the cause of the poorest and least socially integrated segments of French society.

Health-and-wealth gospel *See* Prosperity gospel.

Hermeneutic A modified interpretative approach that views and confronts the more deformed and deforming aspects of Black Church politics and practice.

Heteronormativity The privileging of heterosexuality as the normal and therefore most—if not only—appropriate sexual orientation.

Hip-hop A multivocal, multiethnic cultural phenomenon and movement framed and emerging from African American musical expression and characterized by certain key features, including the DJ, breaking/break dance, the emcee, graffiti art, human beat-boxing, and individualistic expressions of clothing. These features are built from creative appropriation of the cultural materials and social resources.

Hiplife A syncretic mix of highlife (a hybrid musical form composed of jazz and Christian hymns) and hip-hop.

History A story of a people; a story of ideas, of events concerning an individual or a group of people's ways of thinking and being in the world, and of who a person or a people think they are, or their sense of identity.

Holy hip-hop A brand of hip-hop created specifically to glorify Jesus Christ and bring the good news of Jesus Christ to those who are living in and influenced by hip-hop culture.

Homophobia The fear or hatred of same-sex loving persons.

Ideology A systematic body of concepts, especially about human life and culture, that integrates assertions, theories, and aims that constitute a sociopolitical program.

Liberation ethics *See* Ethic of liberation.

Materialistic Preoccupied with acquiring material property and goods.

Megachurches Churches that have memberships of at least two thousand and are housed in spectacular buildings on large campuses.

Mutual aid society Persons who voluntarily organize themselves for the purpose of meeting each other's material, financial, and other needs as determined by the members. In African American history, mutual aid societies were sometimes the forerunners to forming a faith community. Such was the case of the Free African Society that led to the assembly of Bethel African Methodist Episcopal Church, the first congregation of the African Methodist Episcopal denomination, now known as Mother Bethel.

New Thought metaphysics A philosophy that assures believers that they will experience social and economic prosperity by learning to recognize God in ordinary life situations and to apply positive thought principles.

Ontological blackness The idea that race, even if not biologically grounded, is real in a different sense. Its realness is based on a shared experience of dealing with the social construction of race.

Parachurch organizations Faith-based organizations, including businesses and nonprofits, that are unconnected to specific denominational governance and often grounded in Christian principles to achieve specified social aims. In the twenty-first century, these organizations are often linked to evangelicalism.

Patriarchy The privileging of men over women in virtually every aspect of interpersonal and social existence.

Pharaohism A religious sensibility coined by Andre Prevos that is premised on mythological images of Egyptian pharaohs and systems of numerology.

Postindustrial Describing an economic environment that has a dramatically shrunken manufacturing industry, shows signs of faltering social institutions, and is experiencing growing urban poverty.

Postmodern Describing an awareness that the motivations and methods used to make sense of the world come unraveled when tested.

Poverty An economic condition in which a person or group of people lack essential material goods and resources and are incapable of meeting their basic human needs for items such as food, clothing, and shelter.

Praiseco A West African musical form that incorporates Christian elements with indigenous African music.

Progressive rap The lyrical form of hip-hop that interprets the cycle of poverty and dehumanization producing limited life options and despair.

Prosperity gospel The theological position that Christians can experience spiritual and material blessings or healing and prosperity through having faith in Jesus Christ and through properly interpreting and applying Scripture.

Race A personal characteristic that, according to Rashawn Ray, can be defined in several ways: ethnoracially, historically, or by social construction. This book views race as a social construction that occurs through human interaction, and through relationships between people and institutions which then prescribe hierarchical power structures.

Racism The belief that certain races are inferior or superior to others.

Real The idea of upholding one's personal convictions without succumbing to the demanding dictates of society.

Relational blackness A moral attitude toward the world and human life beyond one's preoccupation with his or her own group.

Scratching A feature of DJing; including the sound of a vinyl record being scratched by the needle of the player as though it were another part of the rhythmic composition. *See also* DJing.

Sex The many ways we use our bodies to give and receive physical pleasure.

Sexuality The process of making sense of what is the proper way to handle the body's ability to give and receive physical—and primarily genital—pleasure.

Social Gospel Movement A liberal theological Christian movement that originated in the early twentieth century in the United States and sought to improve oppressive social conditions by emphasizing salvation of social groups and working to advance the kingdom of God on earth.

Socially conscious Having an awareness and emphasis on social structures and systems.

Status rap A form of rap music concerned with status and social standing within the hip-hop world and the larger society.

Tagging Making graffiti by painting one's name or an image or mural on a public location; spray-painting an artifact to create graffiti art. *See* Graffiti art.

Transnationalism A localized phenomenon or product that develop under multi-national or multi-cultural (ethnic) influence.

Womanism Based on a term described by Alice Walker in the 1980s and appropriated by black female religious studies scholars that encompasses theological, ethical, and literary methods that make the experiences of black women in North America central to its intellectual process.

References

Discography

Selected songs/artists for each chapter. These songs were chosen by the authors because they best capture the theme of each chapter, but they are in no way exhaustive of the subject matter. They are listed in this manner in order to provide a makeshift soundtrack for the book. Enjoy!

Chapter 1

Kweli, Talib, featuring John Legend. "Around My Way." Recorded on *Beautiful Struggle*. Rawkus Entertainment, 2004.

Chic. "Good Times." Recorded on *Pure Funk*. UMG, 1979.

Sugar Hill Gang. "Rapper's Delight." Recorded on *Rapper's Delight*. Sugar Hill, 1979.

Grand Master Flash and the Furious Five. "The Message." Recorded on *The Message*. Sugar Hill, 1982.

Afrika Bambaataa and the Sonic Soul Force. "Looking for the Perfect Beat." Recorded on *Planet Rock*. Tommy Boy, 1983.

N.W.A. "Fuck Tha Police." Recorded on *Straight Outta Compton*. Priority/Ruthless, 1988.

Ice-T. "Cop Killer." Recorded on *Body Count*. Warner Bros., 1992.

Boogie Down Productions. "Self Destruction." Recorded on *Live Hardcore Worldwide*. Power Play Studios, 1990.

Run-D.M.C. featuring Pete Rock and CL Smooth. "Down with the King." Recorded on *Down with the King*. Profile, 1993.

God's Property. "Stomp." Recorded on *God's Property and Kirk Franklin's Nu Nation*. Gospelcentric, 1997.

Chapter 2

Run-D.M.C. "My Adidas." Recorded on *Raising Hell*. Profile, 1986.

Crime Mob. "My White Tee." Recorded on *Crime Mob*. Crunk, 2004.

Jay-Z featuring Jermaine Dupri. "Money Ain't a Thang." Recorded on *Vol. 2 . . . Hard Knock Life*. Def Jam, 1998.

X-Clan. "Verbs of Power." Recorded on *To the East Blackwards*. 4th * B'way, 1990.

Public Enemy. "Fight the Power." Recorded on *Fear of a Black Planet*. Spectrum City, 1989.

Lecrae. "Church Clothes." Recorded on *Church Clothes*. Reach, 2012.

Chapter 3

Dead Prez. "I'm an African." Recorded on *Let's Get Free*. Columbia, 2000.

DMX. "My Niggas." Recorded on *Flesh of My Flesh, Blood of My Blood*. Def Jam/Ruff Rydas, 1998.

Outkast. "Rosa Parks." Recorded on *Aquemini*. LaFace, 1998.

Run-D.M.C. "King of Rock." Recorded on *King of Rock*. Profile, 1985.

Run-D.M.C. featuring Aerosmith. "Walk This Way." Recorded on *Raising Hell*. Profile, 1986.

Beastie Boys. "Fight for Your Right to Party." Recorded on *License to Ill.* Def Jam, 1986.

Vanilla Ice. "Ice Ice Baby." Recorded on *To the Extreme.* SBK, 1990.

Eminem. "Rock Bottom." Recorded on *The Slim Shady LP.* Interscope/Aftermath, 1999.

3rd Base. "Pop Goes the Weasel." Recorded on *Derelicts.* Def Jam/Columbia, 1991.

Chapter 4

Linne, Shai. "False Teachers." Recorded on *Lyrical Theology.* Lamp, 2013.

UGK. "Hi Life." Recorded on *Ridin' Dirty.* Jive, 1996.

B.G. "Bling-Bling." Recorded on *Chopper City in the Ghetto.* Cash Money, 1999.

50 Cent. "Poor Lil Rich." Recorded on *Get Rich or Die Trying.* Aftermath/Interscope, 2002.

Mos Def. "Mathematics." Recorded on *Black on Both Sides.* Rawkus/Priority, 1999.

Chapter 5

Nelly. "Tip Drill." Recorded on *Da Derrty Versions: The Reinventions.* Derrty Entertainment, 2003.

MC Lyte. "Lyte as a Rock." Recorded on *Lyte as a Rock.* Atlantic, 1988.

Queen Latifah. "Ladies First." Recorded on *All Hail the Queen.* Tommy Boy, 1991.

Chapter 6

Sir Mix-a-Lot. "Baby Got Back." Recorded on *Mack Daddy*. Def American, 1992.

Lil Wayne. "Love Me." Recorded on *I'm Not a Human Being II*. Cash Money, 2013.

Salt-n-Pepa. "Push It." Recorded on *Hot, Cool and Vicious*. Next Plateau, 1986.

Lil' Kim. "How Many Licks?" Recorded on *Notorious KIM*. Atlantic, 2000.

Lil' Kim featuring 50 Cent. "Magic Stick." Recorded on *La Bella Mafia*. Atlantic, 2003.

Ocean, Frank. "Thinking bout U." Recorded on *Channel Orange*. Def Jam, 2012.

Ocean, Frank. "Bad Religion." Recorded on *Channel Orange*. Def Jam, 2012.

Nas. "Ether." Recorded on *Stillmatic*. Columbia, 2001.

Lord Jamar. "Lift Up Your Skirt." Recorded on *Known Associates*. Babygrande, 2013.

D/DC. *BourgieBohoPostPomoAfroHomo*. Sugartruck, 2001.

Chapter 7

Shakur, Tupac. "Brenda's Got a Baby." Recorded on *2Pacalypse Now*. Interscope, 1991.

Shakur, Tupac. "Violent." Recorded on *2Pacalypse Now*. Interscope, 1991.

Common. "Heat." Recorded on *Like Water for Chocolate*. MCA/ Universal, 2000.

Chapter 8: Artists

The following hip-hop artists highlight the international scope of this work. While the artists above may be familiar to the reader, as they are a part of American pop culture, it is hoped that the reader will review the catalogs of the artists listed below and not just one or two songs.

- La Fouine
- Canardo
- Diam
- Abd Al Malik
- André Prévos
- IAM (Imperial Asiatic Men)
- LSD
- Drick–C
- Dernier Rempart (Last Stand)
- Princess Aniès
- Lord Kossity
- Red One
- MC Solaar
- Manou Bolomik
- Leader Vocal

Selected Bibliography

Angell, Stephen Ward. *Bishop Henry McNeal Turner and African-American Religion in the South.* Knoxville: University of Tennessee Press, 1992.

Arthur, Linda B. *Religion, Dress and the Body.* Berg, NY: Oxford, 1999.

Baker-Fletcher, Karen, and Garth Kasimu Baker-Fletcher. *My Sister, My Brother: Womanist and Xodus God-talk.* Eugene, OR: Wipf & Stock, 2002.

Basu, Dipannita, and Sidney J. Lemmelle. *The Vinyl Ain't Final: Hip Hop and the Globalization of Black Popular Culture.* London: Pluto, 2006.

Billingsley, Scott. *It's a New Day: Race and Gender in the Modern Charismatic Movement.* Tuscaloosa: University of Alabama Press, 2008.

Bonhoeffer, Dietrich. *Ethics.* New York: Macmillan, 1955.

Brewster, Bill, and Frank Broughton. *The Record Players: DJ Revolutionaries.* New York: Grove/Atlantic, 2011.

Butler, Anthea D. *Women in the Church of God in Christ: Making a Sanctified World.* Durham: University of North Carolina Press, 2012.

Cockerham, Geoffery B., and William C. Cockerham. *Health and Globalization.* Cambridge: Polity, 2010.

Common. *One Day It'll All Make Sense.* New York: Simon and Schuster, 2012.

Cone, James H. *Black Theology and Black Power.* Maryknoll, NY: Orbis, 1997.

———. *A Black Theology of Liberation.* Maryknoll, NY: Orbis, 2010.

———. *God of the Oppressed.* Maryknoll, NY: Orbis, 1977.

Cone, James H., and Gayraud S. Wilmore. *Black Theology: A Documentary History.* Maryknoll, NY: Orbis, 1993.

Cunningham, Patricia Anne, and Susan Voso Lab. *Dress and Popular Culture.* Bowling Green, OH: Popular, 1991.

Darby, Derrick, Tommie Shelby, and William Irwin. *Hip-Hop and Philosophy: Rhyme 2 Reason.* Chicago: Open Court, 2013.

Davis, Angela Y. *Blues Legacies and Black Feminism: Gertrude Ma Rainey, Bessie Smith, and Billie Holiday.* New York: Random House, 2011.

Du Bois, W. E. B. *The Souls of Black Folk.* New York: Bantam Classics, 1989.

Dyson, Michael Eric. "Ecstasy, Excess, and Eschatology." In *Open Mike: Reflections on Philosophy, Race, Sex, Culture and Religion.* New York: Basic Civitas, 2003.

———. *Holler if You Hear Me: Searching for Tupac Shakur.* New York: Basic Civitas, 2001.

Fehrenbacher, Don Edward. *The Dred Scott Case: Its Significance in American Law and Politics.* New York: Oxford University Press on Demand, 1978.

Floyd-Thomas, Juan, and Carol B. Duncan. *Black Church Studies: An Introduction.* Nashville: Abingdon, 2007.

Forman, Murray, and Mark Anthony Neal. *That's the Joint! The Hip-Hop Studies Reader.* New York: Routledge, 2004.

Gilkes, Cheryl. *If It Wasn't for the Women: Black Women's Experience and Womanist Culture in Church and Community.* Maryknoll, NY: Orbis, 2001.

Glaude, Eddie. *In a Shade of Blue.* Chicago: University of Chicago Press, 2007.

Hamilton, Charles, and Kwame Ture. *Black Power: Politics of Liberation in America.* New York: Random House, 2011.

Harrison, Milmon F. *Righteous Riches: The Word of Faith Movement in Contemporary African American Religion.* New York: Oxford University Press, 2005.

Heilbut, Anthony. *The Gospel Sound: Good News and Bad Times.* Hal Leonard Corp., 1975.

Hoban, Phoebe. *Basquiat: A Quick Killing in Art.* New York: Penguin, 1998.

Jordan, Don, and Michael Walsh. *White Cargo: The Forgotten History of Britain's White Slaves in America.* Washington Square, NY: NYU Press, 2008.

Lincoln, C. Eric and Lawrence H. Mamiya. *The Black Church in the African American Experience.* Durham, NC: Duke University Press, 1990.

Majors, Richard. *Cool Pose: The Dilemma of Black Manhood in America.* New York: Simon and Schuster, 1993.

Mitchell, Tony. *Global Noise: Rap and Hip Hop outside the USA.* Indianapolis: Wesleyan, 2002.

Morgan, Joan. *When Chickenheads Come Home to Roost: A Hip-Hop Feminist Breaks It Down.* New York: Simon and Schuster, 2000.

Niebuhr, Reinhold. *An Interpretation of Christian Ethics.* New York: Harper & Row, 1987.

Nietzsche, Friedrich. *The Gay Science: With a Prelude in Rhymes and an Appendix of Songs.* New York: Random House, 2010.

Ntarangwi, Mwneda. *East African Hip Hop: Youth, Culture, and Globalization.* Champaign: University of Illinois Press, 2009.

Osumare, Halifu. *The Hiplife in Ghana: West African Indigenization of Hip-Hop.* New York: Palgrave Macmillan, 2012.

Paris, Peter. *The Social Teaching of the Black Churches.* Minneapolis: Fortress Press, 1985.

Parker, Paul Plenge, ed. *Standing with the Poor: Theological Reflections on Economic Reality.* Cleveland: Pilgrim, 1992.

Perry, Imani. *Prophets of the Hood: Politics and Poetics in Hip Hop.* Durham, NC: Duke University Press, 2004.

Pinn, Anthony B. *Noise and Spirit: The Religious and Spiritual Sensibilities of Rap Music.* New York: NYU Press, 2003.

———. *Terror and Triumph: The Nature of Black Religion.* Minneapolis: Fortress Press, 2003.

———. *Why, Lord? Suffering and Evil in Black Theology.* New York: Continuum, 1999.

Powell, Richard J. *Black Art and Culture in the 20th Century.* New York: Thames and Hudson, 1997.

Price, Emmett G. III. *The Black Church and Hip Hop Culture: Toward Bridging the Generational Divide.* Lanham, MD: Scarecrow, 2011.

Raboteau, Albert J. *Slave Religion: The "Invisible Institution" in the Antebellum South.* New York: Oxford University Press, 2004.

Reeves, Marcus. *Somebody Scream! Rap Music's Rise to Prominence in the Aftershock of Black Power.* New York: Faber and Faber, 2009.

Rose, Tricia. *Black Noise: Rap Music and Black Culture in Contemporary America.* Middletown, CT: Wesleyan University Press, 1994.

Ross, Rosetta E. *Witnessing and Testifying: Black Women, Religion, and Civil Rights.* Minneapolis: Fortress Press, 2003.

Salley, Columbus, and Ronald Behm. *What Color Is Your God? Black Consciousness and the Christian Faith.* New York: Citadel, 1988.

Schwartz, Seth J., Koen Luyckx, and Vivian L. Vignoles. *Handbook of Identity Theory and Research.* New York: Springer, 2011.

Seale, Bobby. *A Lonely Rage: The Autobiography of Bobby Seale.* New York: Times Books, 1978.

Simmons, Russell. *Life and Def: Sex, Drugs, Money, and God.* New York: Random House, 2002.

Smith, Efrem, and Phil Jackson. *The Hip-Hop Church: Connecting with the Movement Shaping Our Culture.* Downers Grove, IL: InterVarsity, 2012.

Stampp, Kenneth Milton. *The Peculiar Institution: Slavery in the Ante-Bellum South.* Norwalk, CT: Easton, 1995.

Toop, David. *The Rap Attack: African Jive to New York Hip-Hop.* Boston: South End, 1992.

Tshimanga, Charles, Didier Gondola, and Peter J. Bloom. *Identity and Uprising in Contemporary France.* Bloomington: Indiana University Press, 2009.

West, Cornel, and Eddie S. Glaude. *African American Religious Thought: An Anthology.* Louisville: Westminster John Knox, 2003.

White, Calvin Jr. *The Rise to Respectability: Race, Religion, and the Church of God in Christ.* Fayetteville: University of Arkansas Press, 2012.

Williams, Delores S. *Sisters in the Wilderness: The Challenge of Womanist God-Talk.* Maryknoll, NY: Orbis, 1993.

Wilmore, Gayraud S. *Black Religion and Black Radicalism: An Interpretation of the Religious History of African Americans.* Maryknoll, NY: Orbis, 1998.

Yancy, George, and Janine Jones. *Pursuing Trayvon Martin: Historical Contexts and Contemporary Manifestations of Racial Dynamics.* Lanham, MD: Rowman & Littlefield, 2012.

Young, Amos, and Estrelda Y. Alexander, eds. *Afro-Pentecostalism: Black Pentecostal and Charismatic Christianity in History and Culture.* New York: New York University Press, 2011.

Young, Amos, and Katherine Attanasi. *Pentecostalism and Prosperity: The Socio-Economics of the Global Charismatic Movement.* New York: Palgrave Macmillan, 2012.

Index